Islam, globalization and postmodernity

Events in the last decade have transformed the Muslim world: the Iranian Revolution, the Rushdie affair, the Gulf War. Other influences on Muslim society have perhaps been more penetrating but less obvious. The outside world now reaches into even the most closeted Muslim home through the various channels of the mass media. Processes of globalization have hit traditional cultures so hard and in such a way that they have raised issues for Muslims which can no longer be ignored; Muslims are now forced to engage these issues and to formulate responses to them so that matters which in the past might have been considered by the well-informed few are now debated throughout society by people at every level of social organization.

This book examines how Muslims across the globe have responded to these changes and contradictions. It tries to capture and explore some of the debate, uncertainty and conflict which they have generated as Islam moves towards the twenty-first century. The case studies presented – of Turkish, Trinidadian, Malaysian, Pakistani, Egyptian, North American, Middle Eastern and British Islam – describe both the general global processes now affecting Muslims everywhere, and the way in which these processes are moulded by particular local cultural, political and economic configurations.

This volume will interest anyone concerned with understanding the dynamics of contemporary Muslim society or seeking insight into the direction in which the Muslim world is moving.

Akbar S. Ahmed is Visiting Scholar, Cambridge University; **Hastings Donnan** is Reader in Social Anthropology, Queen's University, Belfast

Contributors; Richard Antoun; Abubaker Bagader; Ernest Gellner; Tomas Gerholm; Fred Halliday; Judith Nagata; Martin Stokes; Gustav Thaiss; Helen Watson; Anita Weiss; Pnina Werbner.

Islam, globalization and postmodernity

Edited by
Akbar S. Ahmed and Hastings Donnan

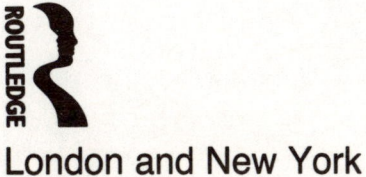

London and New York

First published 1994
by Routledge
11 New Fetter Lane, London EC4P 4EE

Simultaneously published in the USA and Canada
by Routledge
29 West 35th Street, New York, NY 100001

Typeset in Times by Florencetype Ltd, Stoodleigh, Devon
Printed and bound in Great Britain
by Mackays of Chatham PLC, Chatham, Kent.

British Library Cataloguing in Publication Data
A catalogue record for this book is available from the British Library

Library of Congress Cataloging in Publication Data
A catalogue record for this book has been requested

ISBN 0–415–09366–X
ISBN 0–415–09367–8 (pbk)

Contents

List of contributors

Akbar S. Ahmed is a Fellow of Selwyn College, Cambridge and was until recently Iqbal Fellow at the same university. He is the author of many books on Pakistan and Islam, including *Discovering Islam: Making Sense of Muslim History and Society* (Routledge & Kegan Paul, 1988) and *Postmodernism and Islam: Predicament and Promise* (Routledge, 1992). The former was made into a television series by the BBC and forms the basis of his latest book, *Living Islam* (BBC, 1993).

Richard T. Antoun has written three books on the basis of his several research trips to Jordan: *Arab Village: A Social Structural Study of a Transjordanian Peasant Community* (Indiana University Press, 1972); *Low-Key Politics: Local-Level Leadership and Change in the Middle East* (State University of New York Press, 1979); and *Muslim Preacher in the Modern World: A Jordanian Case Study in Comparative Perspective* (Princeton University Press, 1989). He is currently working on a fourth book, describing and analysing the implications of international migration for higher education and work from Jordan to Europe, Asia, North America and the Arabian Peninsula.

Abubaker A. Bagader was born in Makkah, Saudi Arabia in 1950. He graduated from the University of Wisconsin-Madison and currently teaches at King Abdel Aziz University in Jeddah. His areas of interest include the anthropology of Islam, social theory, and the sociology of knowledge. He has published several articles and books in Arabic and a number of articles in English. His publications include 'Islamic and contemporary anthropological discourse', 'Islamization of the social sciences', 'The "kutab": An ethnography of a Qur'anic school in Makkah', 'Marriage contracts in Jeddah, Saudi Arabia', 'Assassination of light: A collection of short stories from Saudi Arabia', and 'The ulema and the modern nation-state'.

Hastings Donnan is Reader in Social Anthropology at the Queen's University of Belfast. He is the author of *Marriage among Muslims:*

Preference and Choice in Northern Pakistan (E J Brill, 1988) and co-editor of *Economy and Culture in Pakistan: Migrants and Cities in a Muslim Society* (Macmillan, 1991), *Border Approaches: An Anthropology of Frontiers* (University Press of America, 1994) and *Inside the Household: Family and Gender in Pakistan* (forthcoming), as well as of several books on Ireland. Since 1993 he has been the editor of *Man: The Journal of the Royal Anthropological Institute*.

Ernest Gellner was formerly Professor of Social Anthropology at the University of Cambridge. He is the author of many books and articles including *Muslim Society* (Cambridge University Press, 1981), and *Postmodernism, Reason and Religion* (Routledge, 1992). He is currently Director of Research at the Centre for the Study of Nationalism at the Central European University, Prague.

Tomas Gerholm is Associate Professor of Social Anthropology at Stockholm University, Sweden. His main regional interest is the Middle East and he is the author of *Market, Mosque and Mafraj* (1977), a study of social inequality in what was North Yemen. He is also interested in Islam in the West and is co-editor of *The New Islamic Presence in Western Europe* (1988). He has also published more generally (mainly in Swedish) on the anthropology of intellectual life and is co-author (with Lena Gerholm) of *Doktorshatten* (1992). For many years he was on the editorial board of *Ethnos*. At present he is engaged on research on the rise and fall of cosmopolitanism in Alexandria, Egypt.

Fred Halliday studied Politics, Philosophy and Economics at Oxford and later took an MSc at the School of Oriental and African Studies, London and a PhD at the London School of Economics. He was from 1974 to 1982 a Fellow of the Transnational Institute, Amsterdam and Washington, and has since 1983 been teaching at the International Relations Department of the London School of Economics. Since October 1985 he has held a Chair in International Relations at the London School of Economics. His books include *Arabia without Sultans* (1974), *Iran: Dictatorship and Development* (1978), *Threat from the East?* (1982) with Maxine Molyneux, *The Ethiopian Revolution* (1982), *The Making of the Second Cold War* (1983), and *Cold War, Third World* (1989), *Revolution and Foreign Policy: The Case of South Yemen, 1967–1987* (1990), *Arabs in Exile: Yemeni Communities in Urban Britain* (1992), *Rethinking International Relations* (1994). Several of his books have been translated into Persian and Arabic.

Judith Nagata is a professor in the Department of Anthropology at York University, Toronto, Canada. Over the past twenty years, her research has revolved around problems of ethnic identity and has focused on religious movements. Recently, her focus has been on the variable forms and expressions of world religions in different areas, including international

Islam, Buddhism and Christianity, principally in Southeast Asia and Canada. Through studies of migrants and other cosmopolitan communities, she attempts to link these strands in a more global framework. Her work on ethnicity in Malaysia is recorded in two volumes, *Malaysian Mosaic: Perspectives from a Poly-ethnic Society*, (UBC Press, 1980) and *Pluralism in Malaysia: Myth or Reality?* (Leiden, E J Brill, 1976), while her work on religious change, particularly in Malaysian Islam, has resulted in *The Reflowering of Malaysian Islam*, (UBC Press, 1984), and a volume, edited with Bruce Matthews, *Religion, Values and Development in Southeast Asia* (Institute of Asian Studies, Singapore, 1986), as well as numerous chapters and articles in scholarly books and journals.

Martin Stokes received a BA (Hons) in Music from Oxford University in 1984, and the MSt in Social Anthropology (also at Oxford) in 1985. He received a DPhil in Social Anthropology in 1989, after conducting fieldwork in Istanbul and the Black Sea region of Turkey. He has travelled and worked extensively in Turkey since 1980. He is currently Lecturer in Social Anthropology and Ethnomusicology at the Queen's University of Belfast, and is the author of *The Arabesk Debate: Music and Musicians in Modern Turkey* (Clarendon, 1992), and of a number of articles on music and popular culture in Turkey. His ongoing research is focused on issues of transnationalism, place, identity, and the politics of culture in the Middle East.

Gustav Thaiss is Chair of the Department of Anthropology at York University, Toronto. He has conducted a study of the bazaar of Tehran focusing on the interrelationship between religion and trade, as well as studying the organisation and rhetoric of religious opposition to the Shah. His interest in the cross-cultural study of Islam led to research on the Shi'a community in Trinidad. Among his recent publications are articles for the soon to be published *Encyclopaedia of the Modern Islamic World* (Oxford University Press).

Helen Watson is a Fellow of St John's College and lecturer in social anthropology at the University of Cambridge. She studied social anthropology at Queen's University Belfast and in Cambridge. Her research interests include gender, conflict, and change. She has worked in North Africa, primarily in Egypt, on urbanization, migration, and gender relations. She has published on women and Islam, fundamentalism, sexual harassment in Europe, and institutionalized violence. Her book on Cairo is entitled *Women in the City of the Dead* (Hurst, 1992). She is interested in the politics of representation and culture. Current research interests include sectarianism and ethnonationalism in Ireland, and perceptions of exile among the Irish in London.

Anita M. Weiss is Associate Professor of International Studies at the University of Oregon. Her doctorate is in Sociology from the University of California at Berkeley. She has published extensively on socioeconomic development and women's issues in Pakistan and is the author of *Walls Within Walls: Life Histories of Working Women in the Old City of Lahore* (Westview Press, 1992) and *Culture, Class and Development in Pakistan: The Emergence of an Industrial Bourgeoisie in Punjab* (Westview Press, 1991). She has been a member of the Executive Board of the American Pakistan Research Organization and a member of the National Democratic Institute for International Affairs' delegation monitoring the October 1993 elections in Pakistan. Her current research compares and analyses the social implications of rising female literacy rates in Pakistan, Egypt, Jordan and Malaysia.

Pnina Werbner is a senior lecturer in social anthropology at Keele University and Research Administrator of the International Centre for Contemporary Cultural Research at the universities of Manchester and Keele. Her publications include *The Migration Process: Capital, Gifts and Offerings among British Pakistanis* (Berg, 1990), *Black and Ethnic Leaderships in Britain: The Cultural Dimensions of Political Action*, co-edited with Muhammad Anwar (Routledge, 1991) and *Economy and Culture in Pakistan: Migrants and Cities in a Muslim Society*, co-edited with Hastings Donnan (Macmillan, 1991). She is currently completing two books, one on Islam and politics in Britain, and the second on a trans-national Sufi cult. She is the director of a major research project funded by the Economic and Social Research Council, UK, on 'South Asian popular culture: gender, generation and identity'.

Foreword

Ernest Gellner

One of the best known and most widely held ideas in the social sciences is the secularization thesis: in industrial and industrializing societies, the influence of religion diminishes. There is a number of versions of this theory: the scientific basis of the new technology undermines faith, or the erosion of social units deprives religion of its organizational base, or doctrinally centralized, unitarian, rationalized religion eventually cuts its own throat. No doubt there are other forms still.

One thing, however, is clear: the secularization thesis does not apply to Islam. In the course of the last one hundred years, the hold of Islam over the minds and hearts of believers has not diminished and, by some criteria, has probably increased. Moreover, this hold is not limited to some restricted zones of social life: it is not backward or socially underprivileged strata which are specially prone to the preservation of faith, or rustics, or women, or those linked to traditional regimes. The retention of a religious orientation marks the populations of socially radical countries as much as traditionalist ones. Christianity has its Bible belt: Islam *is* a Qur'an belt.

My own suspicion is that this is somehow linked to the old internal division of Islam into a High and a Low variant, and the manner in which this old tension has played itself out under conditions of modernization. In the past, there had been the unitarian, scripturalist, puritanical, rule-oriented, sober, literalist and anti-esoteric religious style of the urban scholars and their bourgeois clientele, and there had been the ritualistic, ecstatic, mediation-prone, esoteric path of both the rural populations and the lower strata of the towns, visible in the commitment to saint cults and the adherence to the *turuq*, the organizations appearing in the literature as Orders or Brotherhoods. These two versions of the faith were only intermittently in conflict: at most times, they interpenetrated each other and tolerated each other in peaceful *detente*. All the same, the 'High' form remained normative, recognized as valid even if not implemented, and periodic attempts to impose it, in periods of zeal, did occur. However, these never were nor could be permanently successful: the spirit is willing but the social flesh is weak. Society simply did not possess the resources to impose an individualist faith which dispenses with mediation and presupposes literacy. So Islam became a kind of permanent or cyclical reformation.

Under the impact of industrial modernity, all this has changed, and changed for good. In most places, the colonial and post-colonial state was strong enough to destroy those rural self-help associations known as tribes, thereby eliminating the social need for the services of saints who mediate between groups in the name of mediating between man and God. Even in the towns, people turned to fundamentalist rather than saint-sectarian forms of religion.

There are various reasons why this should be so. The availability of a High Culture, or Great Tradition, which has many features making it compatible with the requirements of modern life – individualism, a rule ethic, a low loading of magic, scripturalism – saved Muslims from the dilemma so characteristic of the situation of other regions facing 'underdevelopment' – the painful choice between Westernizing and populism, between the recovery of dignity through emulation of the technologically superior outsider, or through the idealization of the local folk tradition (given the failure of the local *ancien regime*). Muslims could turn to a genuinely local High Tradition which in many places was not sufficiently identified with the old political regime to be compromised by its failure; so the self-reformation could be carried out in its name. It provided the idiom for the new reactive nationalism: the nation tended to be the sum total of Muslims of a given area (where previously there had only been local communities and a town-based dynasty, but no 'nation').

So, underlying the conspicuous fundamentalist trend in Islam, there is that same shift to a literate, codified, shared culture of an anonymous and mobile society, which is at the root of nationalism in Europe. Of course, nationalism is not unknown in the House of Islam, just as religious revivalism is not unknown in Europe: but, intertwined though the religious and national currents are, it seems clear that the religious one is predominant in Islam, whilst it is the other way round north of the Mediterranean.

The puzzle remains – *why* should it be so? Why should the *general* switch from diversified Little Traditions to a shared, codified, anonymous Great Tradition take the form of nationalism in one area and of fundamentalism in another? In Europe, there had been links between Protestantism and nationalism: Bernard Shaw commented on this eloquently when he causes St. Joan to be burnt as a Protestant by the Church and as a nationalist by the English. She herself considered supporting a crusade against the Hussites who also seemed to combine both elements. But in Europe, in the end the victory of a literate shared High Culture became predominantly nationalist: the literate culture shed the links it once had to Revealed Doctrine, and revered itself without the interposed medium of religion. Nationalism in a way refutes the Durkheimian view that society worships itself through the medium of religion, for it allows society to worship itself with brazen directness. But in Islam, in the main this did not occur. The one attempt to bring this about, in Turkey, by imposing a secular and Westernizing nationalism, has not carried the masses with it and lives under a perpetual threat of electoral reverse. Presumably it was tried in Turkey because there, thanks to the links between the scholars and the old political order, religion was more heavily compromised by the failure of the old system *vis-à-vis* the West, than it was elsewhere. There is also the extraordinary phenomenon of the latest and ultra-radical wave of fundamentalists, who reject the old scholars as unduly willing to compromise with an imperfectly Muslim state.

The vigour and imperviousness to secularization of Islam also stands in fascinating contrast to Marxism. For a long time, Marxism was plausibly seen as a formally secular version of religion. In the end, however, it turned out to possess none of that tenacious hold over the hearts of believers which characterizes religion proper. When it collapsed, there were precious few who were willing to take any kind of stand on its behalf. There are many who regret the previous stability and national power, or who mourn their own positions under the old system, and who would restore it if they could, and may struggle to do so: no one is eager to do it in the name of the doctrine which seemed for quite a time to be held with conviction. That too is a mystery.

My own guess is that, on this point, Durkheim was right: societies and men need both religion and profanity. It is quite often said that man cannot do without religion, but it may be even more pertinent that men cannot do without profanity. Marxism had attempted to abolish it. Marx's deep moral intuition was that the dualistic vision of the world was but an echo of a pathologically bifurcated society, and the overcoming of the division would be mirrored in a similarly unitary ontology. No further need for pie in the sky, whether in religious or philosophical idiom. He inherited the pantheism of Spinoza, mediated by Hegel. The sacred was now to be with us, here and now, pervasively. All life and work was to be equally sacred, no need to seek a consoling Other. But if that is so, routinization during periods of diminished zeal becomes impossible. There simply is no humdrum profane bolthole into which to retire, for the time being.

So the strength of Islam, which is to explain its brilliant success in contrast with the dismal failure of Marxism, lies not merely in its unambiguous, unbowdlerized commitment to a firmly delineated divine message, providing through its rules for social life a sustained handrail in the conduct of life, but also in the fact that, though it firmly regulates daily life, it does not sacralize it. Marxist societies, committed to a soteriology promising that *this* life will now be noble, could not cope with the squalid reality of 'real socialism'. Islam may be socially demanding but it does not abolish the dualism, which saves the sacred from being compromised by the profane.

These would seem to me to be the kinds of general issues which need to be faced in studying Islam. General issues can inspire questions, they cannot answer them. That can only be done by concrete and thorough research and analysis, such as is in fact provided by the studies assembled in this volume. They have a remarkable range and penetration, and unquestionably make a significant contribution to this most important aspect of our social world. If they stimulate further work of comparable quality, we shall be very fortunate.

Chapter 1

Islam in the age of postmodernity

Akbar S. Ahmed and Hastings Donnan

Islamic studies – or the study of Muslim groups and their religion Islam – has been changing dramatically in the last decades. Until recently, Islamic studies was largely the exotic focus of a relatively small group of academics who wrote books about it mainly for one another's consumption. Many of these intellectuals were based in the West, and few of these were Muslims. The Muslim voice itself was seldom heard outside the Muslim world. This has been changing, partly in response to the fact that the lives of many ordinary Muslims have been changing, and partly as a reflection of the equally dramatic changes taking place in the world more generally. Many factors can explain this, and this book sets out to trace both their impact on Muslims and the latter's responses to them.

GLOBALIZATION

Firstly, we consider the phenomenon sometimes referred to as globalization. Since it is not always clear that people mean the same thing when they talk about globalization – some talk about globalization theory, others about a global process defined with varying degrees of precision (see Robertson 1987; 1990: 19–20) – it is as well to be clear at the outset about how the term is used here. By globalization we principally refer to the rapid developments in communications technology, transport and information which bring the remotest parts of the world within easy reach (cf. Giddens 1990: 64). For instance, today if a development takes place in New York it can be relayed instantly across the world to Cairo or Karachi. A good example of this process of globalization is the controversy surrounding Salman Rushdie which began in the late 1980s in the United Kingdom with the publication of *The Satanic Verses*. Within hours, developments in the United Kingdom – in Bradford and London – provoked responses in Islamabad and Bombay. Indeed, people died as they protested against the book. Government pronouncements, media chat shows, editorials, vigils and protests reflected the heated debate. Never before in history had such developments taken place in this manner and at such speed.

One consequence of the globalization process is the necessity to look at Islamic studies not as an esoteric or marginal exercise but as something that concerns the global community. We are thus forced to look at Muslims in different parts of the world not as the preserve of specialist scholars but as an ever-present and ubiquitous reality that relates to non-Muslims in the street. And let us not forget the truly global nature of Muslim society which totals something like one billion people living in about 50 countries with significantly some ten to fifteen million living in the USA and Europe. Issues of migration arise from this reality. Here Muslims face major problems as immigrants, including racism.

Owing to the developments in and around Islam, words such as *fatwa* (a sermon), *jihad* (struggle, including armed effort), *ayatollah* (highly learned scholar and cleric) are now common in the West. The tabloids have popularized these words and they have entered the English language. This again is a consequence of the Western media using or misusing words and adopting and adapting them to the local usage. It also reflects the interplay and interchange of ideas between Islam and the West. An earlier example of borrowing is the word *mughal*, which signified the great Mughal emperors and dynasty of India and is now used for any powerful person, and particularly to refer to business tycoons ('moguls'). Another earlier example is harem, which in Arabic designates a female sanctuary to which only close male relatives have access but which in English often suggests only the voluptuous and licentious exploitation of women. It is clear, then, that borrowing of this kind has been going on for some time. Indeed, the process of globalization itself might be said to have a long history, even if the term is of fairly recent currency.

Like much of the rest of the world, Muslims and the West have long been interconnected through international trade and economic exchange (or exploitation), locked together in what has been referred to as the 'economic world-system' (Wallerstein 1974; 1984). An embryonic form of late twentieth century globalization might thus be discerned in the collaborations between the representatives of colonial power and the indigenous élites who helped them to rule. Indeed, there are those who consider this period of human history to be one stage – and not necessarily the first stage – in the development of what we now call globalization. For example, it has been suggested that the historical path to current global complexity has passed through five phases, beginning in the early fifteenth century (Robertson 1990: 26–7). Globalization is thus not necessarily the wholly novel phenomenon, unique to the latter half of this century, that some commentators appear to imply. As a process it is of considerable historical depth, and as a theory it exhibits all the notions of 'system' and 'stages of growth' which distinguish its forerunner, world-systems theory.

Nevertheless, and most commentators appear to agree, late twentieth-century globalization does seem different from earlier forms in certain important respects (see Appadurai 1990: 1–5).

For one thing, the historical connections between nations have generally been previously understood largely in terms of an *economic* world-system. The economic content of international contact has thus been emphasized at the expense of the *cultural* flows which were obviously also taking place alongside the material exchanges; indeed, the place of 'culture' in analyses of global interconnections such as world-systems theory is a matter of some disagreement, with some alleging that it has mostly been left out (see Hannerz 1989a: 204; Wallerstein 1990; Boyne 1990; Worsley 1990). But there are obviously many examples of collaborations between colonials and locals which involved much more than just political and economic co-operation; thus when the values of gentlemanly behaviour and fair play arrived in India as a cultural export from Victorian and Edwardian England, they were quickly adopted by those – such as the Parsis (see Luhrmann 1994) – who wished to please their then colonial masters. But while these cultural flows clearly existed in the past, they never seem to have been an end in themselves, and they have usually been of less interest to scholars than the material realities which underpinned them.

Today the emphasis has shifted and it is the cultural flows between nations which above all else seem to typify the contemporary globalization process (or its current phase) (cf. Robertson 1987: 24). These cultural flows are not, of course, detached from economic and political realities. Because of their origins, some flows – mainly those in 'the West' – have more force than others and so reach a wider audience. Accordingly, there has been much discussion about the possible homogenization of culture – the move towards a 'global culture' in which everyone will drink the same soft drinks, smoke Marlboro cigarettes, and emulate JR. Such an homogenization of culture has been questioned from a number of perspectives, and the situation is certainly more complex than is sometimes supposed. Firstly, the notion of a hegemonic global cultural centre dispensing its products to the world's peripheries is more often assumed than described; and even if there is such a thing, it is not clear that its exports have any more significance to those they reach than its exports of a generation or two ago (Parkin 1993: 85–6). Secondly, even though the same cultural 'message' may be received in different places, it is domesticated by being interpreted and incorporated according to local values (see Featherstone 1990: 10). And finally, cultural flows do not necessarily map directly on to economic and political relationships, which means that the flow of cultural traffic can often be in many different directions simultaneously. We shall return to these points later.[1]

The globalization process today is also marked by the accelerated pace at which informational and cultural exchanges take place, and by the scale and complexity of these exchanges (on the latter, see Appadurai 1990: 6). Facilitated by the new technologies, it is the sheer speed, extent and volume of these exchanges that have engaged popular imagination, and that seem to have led to globalization being so often represented, if perhaps a little glibly, by the VCR. Cheater (1993: 3–4) lists an impressive array of such technologies from electronic mail to the satellite dish, and although these are clearly not accessible to all, they have obviously been directly or indirectly responsible for exposing many different sorts of people to new influences. Such technologies are able to uncouple culture from its territorial base so that, detached and unanchored, it pulsates through the airwaves to all those with the means to receive it.

Whatever the ultimate outcome might be – greater homogeneity or heterogeneity of culture – and this is hotly disputed, the contemporary phase of globalization has thus resulted in more people than ever before becoming involved with more than one culture (cf. Featherstone 1990: 8). It is perhaps this which above all else captures the sense in which the term is used here.

DIASPORA

Of course, it is not just technologies which carry culture across national boundaries; people clearly do as well, and the twentieth century has witnessed dramatic developments in the ease with which people cross from one state to another. Moreover, unlike the population movements of the past, these post-industrial diasporas occur in a world where even the old 'geographical and territorial certainties seem increasingly fragile'; thus today's diasporas seem much less likely to have 'stable points of origin, clear and final destinations and coherent group identities' (Breckenridge and Appadurai 1989: i; see also Malkki 1992: 24).

These changes have resulted in diasporas of various kinds: that of the cosmopolitan academic parodied by Lodge (1985) in a book whose very title – *Small World* – plays on the sense of compressed global space characteristic of globalization, that of the international business/management/design consultant, and that of the migrant labourer and refugee. The former – who are always on the move – have given rise to the so-called 'third cultures', while the latter – often in search of a new home – have resulted in the linguistically, culturally and socially heterogeneous communities now typical of many parts of the globe.[2] Muslims are represented in all these groups, and this volume tries to deal with each: peripatetic intellectuals as well as labour migrants. Several of the contributors thus address directly the question of how people manage the cultural uncertainties typical of such poly-ethnic situations and of how Islam is moulded to 'foreign' settings (Gerholm, Antoun, Werbner, this volume).[3]

It has often been noted that Islam explicitly encourages and even enjoins certain forms of travel, and that the movement of Muslims from one part of the world to another, whatever the purpose, resonates with the historical foundations of their religion (Eickelman and Piscatori 1990: 5; Donnan and Werbner 1991: 9–10). But here too globalization seems to have greatly encouraged this willingness to move, and has added a dimension to it. Transformations of the world economy brought about by the globalization of markets and labour under late capitalism – or 'disorganized capitalism' as it has been called by Lash and Urry (1987) – have resulted in enormous numbers of people moving round the globe in search of work. Muslims constitute a large proportion of this population movement. It is in this manner that Muslim societies have today become part and parcel of Western countries. Muslim doctors and engineers live as American or British citizens. Their children have no intention of going back to their place of origin. The study of this Muslim diaspora raises both empirical and conceptual issues.[4]

Since the bulk of Muslim migrant labour has settled abroad on a permanent basis, it is important to now look at these societies as local, as indigenous not as the other, the exotic or the Oriental, pace Edward Said (1978). Thus Said's Orientalism is dated in this new theoretical frame and we need to move beyond its position. Although pointing to something important – that is, the imbalance or asymmetry between Islam and the West and the continuing prejudice, stereotypes and caricatures created of Islam by the West – Said's position has created serious intellectual problems, principally because of the manner in which it has been received and applied. It has led to a cul-de-sac. 'Orientalism' itself has become a cliché, and third world literature is now replete with accusations and labels of Orientalism being hurled at critics and at one author by another at the slightest excuse. This has had a stultifying affect on the dispassionate evaluation of scholarship. Thus, for example, in the passion generated by the debate what has been missed out is the great contribution of many Orientalist scholars. The writings of Ibn Khaldun, Ibn Battuta, or the Mughal emperor Babar come to us only through the painstaking scholarship of Orientalists who spent a life-time deciphering notes in Asian languages and sitting in remote libraries. For them it was a labour of love. To dismiss their work as simply Orientalism or as an attempt to suppress or subjugate Muslim peoples denies an important truth. Unfortunately, after Edward Said, that is how many Muslim writers do see the work of the Orientalists. If research on contemporary Muslim societies is not to be similarly dismissed as the most recent manifestation of Orientalism, it is clearly imperative to introduce conceptual innovations which both surmount the limitations of Islamic studies as identified by Said, and transcend the shortcomings of his own analysis. This would seem to be possible only by contextualizing local versions of Islam within global structures.

Sensitive and innovative research seems particularly critical for understanding the Muslim diaspora. The diaspora has led to the oft-remarked quest for identity and authenticity, particularly for those who find themselves abroad but also, to some extent, for those who remain behind and who now find that their culture, transported to new settings, is being defined and practised in novel and sometimes disturbing ways. The empirical issues raised by diaspora thus chiefly revolve around questions of identity and the vulnerability of having to redefine the self in a world which seems constantly on the move. The hyphen of hyphenated identities like that of British-Muslim or American-Muslim, for example, both reflects and obscures the necessary conjunction of disparate cultural traces brought together in the act of 're-membering' and 're-creating', to borrow Fischer and Abedi's terms (1990: 253).

In the liminal zone of the culturally displaced, Muslims in the diaspora experience a range of practical, psychological and pragmatic difficulties, some of which are examined in this volume. These include the problems of establishing enduring relationships with the opposite sex, of contracting acceptable marriages, and of adapting religion to a new life (Antoun, Gerholm, Werbner). But they also include the problems of negotiating with other Muslims and agreeing with them on the meaning of Islam on foreign soil (Werbner). After all, Muslims who migrate are not only often in a minority in their place of destination, where they must encounter the cultures of the majority, but they also come from different sectarian and cultural traditions themselves. In some cases, as with Turkish Alevis in Germany for example, residence abroad may permit a greater freedom of religious expression. Thus the diaspora has released these Alevis from what they see as Sunni hegemony in Turkey, as well as enabling them to substantially reverse their hierarchically subordinate position to Sunni Turks based in Germany (Mandel 1990: 163, 166).

But the diaspora raises issues of identity and direction at 'home' too, among those faced with the fantasy if not the reality of moving (cf. Gardner 1993), and among those who now find their 'local cultures less pervasive, less to be taken for granted, less clearly bounded toward the outside' than they perhaps once were (Hannerz 1990: 249). Migrants return to their place of origin not only with novel versions of the world which challenge the views of those who never left (see Antoun, this volume), but also on occasion with fossilized and outmoded versions of what they left behind: ways of dressing, behaving, believing and so forth which have been developed and reshaped in their absence but which they have lovingly and carefully preserved intact while abroad. Either way, old certainties are challenged. To draw again on Fischer and Abedi writing about Iran, but to slightly modify their focus, the Muslim world and the Muslim habitations abroad 'mirror each other at acute or oblique angles, mutually affecting each other's representations, setting off mutating variations' (1990: 255). The very elasticity of the diasporic tie thus ensures the reciprocal redefinition of identity at both ends of the migratory chain as elements of culture rebound first this way and then that. Renewed attempts to define proper behaviour for Muslim women in Cairo and Lahore (Watson and Weiss respectively, this volume), and to establish an Islamic basis for the state in Malaysia (Nagata, this volume) might thus be interpreted as a search for identity which is at least partially stimulated by the Muslim diaspora.

The detachment of culture from territory which is entailed by diaspora, with its generation of cultures with no clear anchorage in any one space (Hannerz 1990: 237), has unleashed powerful forces which affect us all and not just those most directly involved. According to Appadurai (1990: 11), for example, it is this deterritorialization which is 'now at the core of a variety of global fundamentalisms, including Islamic and Hindu fundamentalism'. The 'problems of cultural reproduction for Hindus abroad' Appadurai suggests, have become 'tied to the politics of Hindu fundamentalism at home' (1990: 11). The same could easily and realistically be said of the Muslim diaspora, with the added complication that, unlike the Hindus, Muslims abroad do not even share a common homeland. It is in this sense that the new Islamic movements in the Arab world described by Bagader (this volume) must be seen in the context of the Muslim diaspora. Indeed, the politics of all Muslim countries in this postmodern age must similarly be seen within a global frame.

GLOBAL POLITICS

New political developments have increased this awareness of the need to study Muslim societies in a global context. The recent events in Bosnia have created a sharp awareness of Muslims as a world community, both in the West and among Muslims themselves. Bosnia has become a rallying point for Muslims throughout the Muslim world, much in the manner of the Palestinians. The case of Bosnia is even used in *khutbas* (sermons) in a closed society like Saudi Arabia to attack the monarchy for not doing enough. The sub-text is that the élite are far too much under the sway of the West. In the West itself, Bosnia has driven home the point that Muslims tend to see the world through Islamic spectacles and interpret the suffering of the Bosnian Muslims as brought about by a West indifferent to the plight of ordinary Muslims: the feeling is that had they been Jews or Christians, the Western response would have been very different.

This in itself colours and affects how Muslim scholarship is seen or is to be seen in the current time. It tends to polarize tensions between Muslims and non-Muslims. For instance, many Muslims now argue that although the Bosnians were Europeanized – they drank alcohol, ate pork, married non-Muslims and so on – nontheless, when the killings began, these secularized Muslims were the first victims of the Serbs. In short, there is no compromise and sooner or later the enemies of Islam will victimize Muslims whatever they do. It is thus best to rally round Islam. Bosnia has created and sharpened the sense of polarization and radicalization in Muslim societies, while at the same time increasing the sense of being a Muslim.

This too was the effect of the publication of Rushdie's *Satanic Verses*, and of the Gulf War, when the political symbolism of Islam readily mobilized the ordinary Muslim in the street. But if, in the case of the Gulf War, Muslims almost everywhere seemed to rally round Saddam Hussein, they did so in complex ways and not in some monolithic stance of Islam against the West. Muslim responses to the war certainly reflected suspicion of the West's motives, but they also drew on local political circumstances and on the long-standing unpopularity of the Gulf monarchies among Muslims living outside the Arabian Peninsula (cf. Piscatori 1991: 12–13). Furthermore, the response in one Muslim nation depended in important ways on the reaction in others, with sometimes surprising outcomes. Thus, for example, the Jamaat-i-Islami in Pakistan, who were long-time supporters of the Saudi Arabian government and who before the war had described Saddam Hussein as 'an enemy of Islam', took an aggressively anti-Saudi stance during the war itself. What seems to have contributed to this apparent volte-face were the Jamaat's growing contacts and identifications with Islamic movements elsewhere, and particularly with 'the anti-American and anti-Saudi orientations of the movements in Jordan . . . and in the Gaza strip' (Ahmad 1991: 174). Such connections again underline the significance of the web of global linkages.

Similar interactions between the local and the global can be discerned in the responses to *Satanic Verses* which again, while superficially uniform, were composed of a diverse range of motivations and objectives. These too, like responses to the Gulf War, were played out according to the parameters and concerns of localized and often very different national political arenas (see Fischer and Abedi 1990: 389–400). Thus the response in Britain, for example, differed in important and significant ways from that elsewhere, because of the particular configuration of relationships there, both between Muslims and non-Muslims, and among Muslims themselves (see Modood 1990; Asad 1990: 257–60; Samad 1992). If wider political events have led to a greater sense of polarization in the Muslim world, the resiliency and intensity of this feeling can therefore only be understood by examining the play between these global developments and the circumstances of each local setting.

To some extent this tension between the local and the global was reflected in the Western media who, while exacerbating and facilitating the sense of polarization among Muslims by apparently being intent on delivering a message of a monolithic East versus West (during the Gulf War and Rushdie affair, simultaneously broadcast evidence of the diversity of the

Muslim response which belied that interpretation of events. Thus while many news headlines tended to cast these confrontations in fairly stark terms, a number of television panel discussions and broadsheet leaders were informed by more moderate Muslim voices. This raises the whole question of the powerful Western media and their relationship to Islam.

THE MEDIA

The Western media are largely seen by Muslims as a negative influence. This view is perhaps not without foundation. The traditional Orientalist stereotypes of Muslims as political anarchists and as tyrants at home subjugating their women have been disseminated in the media as caricatures and stereotypes. Very often the news that is shown about Muslims centres around negative stories.

It is this negative collage of images that allows the idea of Islam as the new enemy after Communism to circulate and take hold in the popular imagination. Popular surveys in the West indicate that the majority of people feel that Islam will be the main villain in the coming time. In turn, Muslims feel that the suffering of their community – in Bosnia, in Palestine, in Kashmir – is ignored by the world, although it has the law and UN resolutions on its side, simply because of hostility to Islam. Many Muslims talk of a new crusade against them; of the need for *jihad*.

However, there is an element of simplification in this. The media by their nature tend to select stories that are sensationalist. They do not pick only on Muslims. Jews in Israel or Hindus in India often complain of bias against them. Besides, the iconoclastic nature of the media encourages them to focus on celebrities and then spoil their image. Examples of Princess Diana or John Major in England support this. Nonetheless, the perception of hostile Western media affects the way Islamic studies are perceived both by Muslims and non-Muslims.

The role of the media is crucial in understanding and appreciating Muslims today. Although Muslims are highly critical of the media and see them as inimical, there are examples when the media have worked in their favour. But first an example in which the media developed a climate of hostility towards Muslims: this is provided by the destruction of the mosque in Ayodhya and the subsequent communal killings in India. In December 1992, a well-planned campaign to destroy the Ayodhya mosque culminated when the structure was razed to the ground. This was the result of a cultural milieu that was spear-headed by the media in the 1990s. In particular, the popular television series *Mahabharata* and the *Ramayana*, although themselves not directed against Muslims, nevertheless created a highly charged religious atmosphere in India.[5] The series was watched by six to seven hundred million people and ran for years. The revivalist, communal political party, the BJP, was the direct beneficiary of the cultural revivalism. From only two seats in Parliament it secured over one hundred and twenty seats in a couple of years. Many of its candidates were the actors and actresses from these two television series. The BJP's demand to destroy the Ayodhya mosque and then many other mosques built by Indian Muslims – because, they argued, these mosques had been built on Hindu sites – struck a chord. The government of India had little political will to resist. Indeed, we saw on television and in other Western media how the Indian police stood aside while individual policemen went up to pay their homage to the Hindu deities.

In contrast, we have the example of Bosnia. It has been the courageous reporting of Western media people, many of whom have been injured and lost their lives, which has brought to the notice of the world the horrors of the Serb rape, death and torture camps. This in turn has helped to create a climate in the West of acknowledging the horrors perpetrated against Muslims. It is not the failure of the media in this case which has prevented the West from taking action against the Serbs to prevent the killing of Muslims. There are many other factors. One of them, no doubt, is the reluctance to see a fully fledged Muslim state emerge in Europe. That is, at least, how some Muslims interpret events.

This apparent ambivalence towards Muslims in the Western media, and their apparent willingness to credit Muslims with the moral high ground in one case but not in another, has raised suspicions and doubts about the media's overall credibility in the minds of many Muslims (cf. Said 1981). Some Muslims seem to be supported, others not. Such ambivalent and even contradictory messages, while obviously reflecting the realpolitik of geo-political relations, sometimes seem to be the very stuff of the post-modern age in which we live, as we shall see in a moment.

First, however, we should emphasize that once again studies of specific Muslims in particular locales are required to fully grasp how media products – television programmes, advertisements, rock concerts – are received and interpreted. As we mentioned earlier, the very fact that media images reach a range of cultural contexts means that audiences are unlikely to respond in identical ways. Instead, like other cultural imports, these images are 'indigenized' (Appadurai 1990: 5), and fitted around local concerns. Yet while there is much talk in general terms about the likely impact which television programmes such as *Dallas* and *Dynasty* might have in the African bush or in Middle Eastern shanty towns like Cairo's City of the Dead, there is not the corresponding empirical evidence which would allow us to comment confidently on how these Western-generated media images are actually integrated into and influence people's everyday practices (cf. Hannerz 1989b: 72). The evidence which does exist, especially that on Muslims, is often anecdotal (though see Stauth and Zubaida 1987). But even this suggests that we should exercise some caution. If television programmes, for example, are viewed not in domestic isolation as they tend to be in much of the West, but as the focus for neighbourhood sociability as in many parts of rural Pakistan, might this not have an influence on how broadcasts are understood? The evidence on divergent viewing practices in the West itself (which vary with class, age and gender; see Featherstone 1991: 57–8) should lead us to be particularly wary when discussing television viewing in contexts where cultural under-standings vary widely. In such situations meanings seem almost to multiply and fracture faster than we can accommodate them.

POSTMODERNISM

Finally, elements of postmodernism – although a vague and even slippery concept to define – may prove important in helping us to focus on Islamic studies. Like globalization, not everyone is agreed on precisely what is meant by postmodernism. Indeed, that is part of its allure. Postmodernism encompasses a variety of forms and definitions and this in itself seems to some to be 'postmodern'. While a number of good guides exist to lead us through the dense foliage which has now sprung up around this notion (see, for example, Harvey 1989; Turner 1990b), even these can provide no single understanding; any attempt to 'fix' the meaning of postmodernism seems necessarily self-contradictory, with those who have tried being accused of constructing the very kind of grand narrative that post-modernism sets out to attack (see the summary of Kellner's [1988] critique of Lyotard in Featherstone 1991: 9). If there is agreement, then, it is that the term is impossible to pin down definitively (Featherstone 1991: 1; Boyne and Rattansi 1990: 1).

Some sense of the breadth and 'breathlessness' of what is included under the heading of postmodernism is given by Fardon, who cites the following lengthy (though given the task in hand, succinct) quotation:

> the inventory of features assigned to post-modernism includes: self-referential discourse, heterodoxy, eclecticism, marginality, death of utopia (read: communism), death of the author, deformation, disfunc-tion, deconstruction, disintegration, displacement, discontinuity, non-lineal view of history, dispersion, fragmentation, dissemination, rupture, otherness, decentering of the subject, chaos, rhizoma, rebellion, the subject as power, gender/difference/power (probably the most positive as a revision of patriarchy), dissolution of semiotics into energetics, auto-proliferation of signifiers, infinite semiosis, cybernetics, pluralism (read: freedom versus 'totalitarianism'), critique of reason, procession of simulacra and representations, dissolution of legitimizing 'narratives' (hermeneutics, emancipation of the proletariat, epic of progress, dialec-tics of the spirit), a new episteme or sign system.
>
> (Zavala [1988] cited in Fardon 1992: 25)

Since many of these elements are also typical of modernism, 'postmodernism' can be understood only as one of a relational pair. 'Both terms feed off each other and often seem propelled by a binary logic of opposition which sharpens the differentiation' between them and between the family of terms to which they belong – post(modern), post(modernity), post-(modernization) (Featherstone 1991: 144; see also Harvey 1989: 43). So though, as its prefix indicates, the postmodern comes after the modern, their boundary is blurred and each is mutually implicated in the other (on the difficulty of arriving at an adequate periodization, see Turner 1990a). This makes it rather difficult to determine just how 'new' the changes allegedly typical of postmodernity are and whether they must be subjected to a new (postmodernist) form of analysis.

It was sometime during the 1980s that postmodernist developments in sociology, literature and the arts most visibly began to create an intellectual milieu in counterdistinction to the modern. In addition to those mentioned above, its characteristics were: the juxtaposition of the high and the low, the serious and the frivolous, the historical and the contemporary; the deliberate breaking down of traditional ideas and thought patterns; the notion of 'magical realism'; a cynicism regarding religion and a conscious abandonment to the consumerist society of our times. All these have helped to challenge the traditional method of looking at Islamic studies.

While postmodernism – seen as a term that characterizes a 'series of broadly aesthetic projects' (Boyne and Rattansi 1990: 9) – is probably unknown to all but a small band of artists and intellectuals, postmodernity – as a 'social, political and cultural configuration' (Boyne and Rattansi 1990: 9) – affects everybody to varying degrees, Muslims included. This raises a number of quite different questions. How would a postmodernist perspective affect Islamic studies? Does it herald a new manner of studying Islam? Are these developments making an impact upon Muslims themselves? How have Muslims responded to postmodernity? Although the preoccupation with Euro-American analysis has so far largely precluded asking what postmodernity might mean to Muslims, or what it might mean elsewhere in the globe (cf. Fardon 1992: 37), such questions will need to be asked in the coming time. This book and its contributors do not pretend to answer all of these questions, but we do hope that it will give some sense of how Muslims have been inescapably touched by postmodernity, as well as an insight into how and why they have responded as they have.

ISLAM, GLOBALIZATION AND POSTMODERNITY

Of course, as social scientists we accept that there are serious problems in traditional societies – not only Muslim, but also Hindu or Buddhist or indeed, even Christian – confronting and coping with the postmodern age. It promotes a culture based on youth, change and consumerism. It emphasizes noise, movement and speed. Traditional religions emphasize quiet, balance and discourage change. There are thus intrinsic points of conflict. This particular area of conflict is causing concern and anxiety among traditional people throughout the world. In Muslim societies one aspect of this is the so-called Islamic fundamentalist response: people concerned about the pace of change and what this will do to the next generation, people genuinely worried that their culture and traditions which have held for a thousand years will now be changed and even be in danger of being wiped out.

All the contributors to this volume focus to some extent on how Muslims have formulated and responded to these anxieties. However, only some of them dwell particularly on fundamentalism as a response. Fred Halliday in Chapter 5, for example, examines at length contemporary fundamentalisms in Iran and Tunisia, arguing that these can be understood only within their historical context and by using the traditional tools of social and political analysis. He thus questions whether there is, or need be, a distinctively postmodernist approach at all to Islamic studies, and seriously wonders about its applicability and appropriateness in this case. Nevertheless, he recognises that the 1990s are a particularly critical and potentially instructive vantage from which to examine what he calls 'Islamism', with more than a decade of successful Iranian revolution now completed, and the melange of emotions and passions whipped up by the Rushdie affair and the Gulf War leading the way to new Muslim definitions of the self.

This search for identity and distinctiveness in a shifting world has, in some Muslim countries, taken the form of demands for a Muslim state. For an existing regime, these demands raise all kinds of questions and difficulties, especially if the country concerned is both polyethnic and multi-faith. The course pursued by the Malaysian state in the face of such demands, as Judith Nagata demonstrates in Chapter 4, has been one of trying to achieve a workable 'balance' between as many of the interests involved as possible: the various Malaysian Islamic parties, other local political interest groups, and investors from abroad. As Nagata indicates, the task is fraught with contradictions, and the outcome in Malaysia has been a fragile compromise – characterized by the pursuit of modernity under what Nagata calls the 'cloak of Islamic correctness' – which juxtaposes the 'modern' Islam espoused by the state to more fundamentalist versions. Moreover, it is a compromise always susceptible to the perturbations of both the global and local arenas.

Abubaker Bagader's contribution (Chapter 6) provides an interesting counterpoint and complement to Halliday's and Nagata's analyses by offering a glimpse of the new Islamic movements from a Muslim point of view. Bagader both extends the historical and geographical scope of Halliday's discussion of fundamentalist Islam, and identifies the dependence of the new Islamic movements in the Arab world on reciprocal cultural flows between different Muslim nations (cf. Roff 1987). In the world media fundamentalism has become a shorthand for fanaticism and intolerance. It is a word taken from Christian Europe and applied to Muslim revivalist movements. It tells us little and does not clarify. On the contrary, it obfuscates and confuses. Certainly there have been Islamic movements in the modern era before the word became fashionable. But although we know of those in the last century – the great movements among the Sanusi in North Africa and of the Mahdi in Sudan and the Akhund in Swat in northern Pakistan – in the context of current Western media (mis)representations of revivalist Islam, it is particularly important that we also hear the voice of a Muslim academic who has studied them.

Muslim women in particular seem to be squeezed between Islamic fundamentalism and modernity, and between modernity and postmodernity (see Baykan 1990). The chapters by Weiss and by Watson (Chapters 7 and 8 respectively) suggest that, partly as a consequence of the special place which women occupy in Islam, and partly because of the ways in which religion is embedded in local social values (cf. Delaney 1991), Muslim women are frequently perceived as the most vulnerable to radical change and outside influence, the more so since the front door and compound wall are no longer effective barriers to such forces. Indeed, it is now often *behind* such barriers that these influences are strongest through television and the VCR. But, as Weiss reminds us, we should be careful of over-generalizing the impact which such influences can have. Thus class, for example, filters the female response to global processes. In contrast to the women of the Pakistani élite, many of whom lead lives like those of wealthy and professional women everywhere, it is the poor women studied by Weiss in Lahore's walled city who experience most acutely the contradictions thrown up by contemporary demands. Among these women modern demands for educated brides sit uneasily with conservative notions of respectability which require a woman to stay at home. But this is true only for the moment. These very same women predict that in a decade none of them will be wearing the full body veil (*burqa*) typical of Pakistan.

This prediction is particularly interesting in the light of Watson's account of how the veil has recently been 'revived' by Muslim women living in Britain, France and Egypt as a way of coping with the challenges of contemporary life in these countries, and of emphasizing an Islamic identity.[6] This difference between the women described by Weiss and Watson both underlines the polyvalency of the veil and – at least in the case of the Asian women in Britain and perhaps also the Algerian women in France – recalls the point made earlier about the potentiality for cultural disjuncture between diasporic Muslims and those they leave behind. Above all, though, Watson emphasizes how the practice of veiling has become a politicized act whose meaning shifts depending on the articulation of the local with the global in any particular setting. In short, the perpetuation of the practice of veiling is no unreflective continuation of 'tradition', but is a considered response to the way the world is changing (cf. Baykan 1990: 136). Only by looking at veiling in these terms, Watson argues, can we transcend the polarized views of those Western feminist writers who see all veiling as oppression and those Muslim apologists who claim that it is liberating.

The richness and diversity of forms evoked by the notion of postmodernity is a central concern of the chapters by Martin Stokes and Gustav Thaiss. Drawing on his analyis of 'arabesk', Stokes (Chapter 2) sets out to trace how wider national and global cultural and political forces have been inscribed on this particular form of popular culture among Turkey's displaced urban migrants. He suggests that this has resulted in the use of 'global' metaphors, such as East–West, as a form of social and spatial practice. This is best seen in relation to belly dancing and social dancing, two practices which Stokes argues reveal with special clarity the conflation of global, urban, bodily and moral spaces. Though not discussed in these terms, Gustav Thaiss (in Chapter 3) is similarly concerned with the marking out of global, urban and moral spaces through performative behaviours of a different kind – in his case by analysing how the central Shiʿa ritual commemorating Husain's martyrdom is enacted in Trinidad.

This ritual centres on a major tragedy – the death of the grandson of the Holy Prophet, Husain, at the battle of Karbala in 680 AD. It is one of the most important events in Muslim history. For Muslims it signifies the need to stand up to tyranny and injustice. For the Shiʿa sect it could be described as an umbilical ritual which both links them to their past and defines who they are. They perform it annually wherever they live, especially in Iran, India and Pakistan. In Trinidad it is transported across the world to a different cultural and political setting, where it is influenced by local colour and rhetoric – now called 'Hosay' rather than 'Husain'. Non-Muslims participate in the Hosay ritual alongside the Shiʿa, bringing to it a set of meanings that transform it (for them if not for the Shiʿa themselves) from a solemn ritual reminding participants of the terrible events at Karbala into a carnival of fun. For these non-Muslim participants, the Hosay is merely another event in the carnival calendar, and the sorrow is converted into celebration. The symbolism of death (the colour black dominates among the Shiʿa because of memories of Karbala) is overwhelmed by the exotic colours of the Caribbean. Drums and dancing characterize the Hosay festival. Competing and antithetical messages thus co-exist. Trinidadian Shiʿa are aware that they now have little control over the Hosay and that, because of its wider popularity, its original meaning and structure have been transformed and extended.

If the aims of postmodernism are to seek and celebrate the rich variety of local styles and practices, and to grasp the development of cultural hybridity, then some might see these two chapters by Stokes and Thaiss as suggesting what a postmodernist version of Islamic studies can offer. Both Stokes and Thaiss raise questions about the globalization of culture and its 'creolization' (Hannerz 1987). These themes are amplified in the contribution by Pnina Werbner (Chapter 11), whose finely detailed account shows how Western media representations of the Gulf War were reworked as a locally meaningful narrative among British (mainly Pakistani) Muslims. This is no recently arrived community having to work through the first difficulties of contact with another culture. British Muslims are well-established, with a complex and elaborate culture which draws from the area in which they now live, as well as from their place of origin. Many of them have been formed from birth by 'creole systems of meaning' (Hannerz 1992: 264). Only an account which constructs global events like the Gulf War in terms of local experiences speaks persuasively to such people, and is likely to contribute towards a resolution of the predicaments which persist even among this long-established diaspora. The term 'fabulation' which Werbner uses to capture the manner in which local Muslim preachers interpreted events in the Gulf (and their media imaging) to their congregations thus seems very apt, with its implications of telling a tale of legendary and mythological proportions.

Similar processes can be discerned at work in different ways among other elements of the Muslim diaspora who must also negotiate identity and define Islam in different cultural contexts. In a contribution which usefully focuses on the lives and views of a type of Muslim traveller largely ignored in the literature, Richard Antoun (in Chapter 9) documents the experiences and perceptions of three Jordanian Muslims who left the Middle East to pursue higher education in Britain, Germany and the USA. Antoun argues that, surprisingly perhaps, the desire for secular education continues to have important religious dimensions, even when this education is sought in a non-Muslim country, and even when these religious dimensions are confronted by ways of living which directly contradict them. Such contradictions generate different responses and Antoun evaluates the usefulness of a range of concepts, such as 'compartmentalization' and 'exclusionary closure', for understanding the solutions which these Muslims have arrived at for the predicament of living abroad, as well as for understanding the less frequently remarked predicament of returning home.

Antoun's account of how ordinary Muslims manage their identity and religion while pursuing a university education overseas provides a useful backdrop to Tomas Gerholm's chapter (Chapter 10) on how Muslim intellectuals, through their written texts, elaborate (or fabulate?) their personal visions of Islam. In some respects, Gerholm's intellectuals might be Antoun's students ten or twenty years further on. Similar problems remain of how to follow an Islamic life-style when, in a predominantly

Christian country, the institutions and the ethos are not there to meet the particular and often pragmatic needs of the practising Muslim. However, the difficulties of maintaining an Islamic identity are perhaps especially acute, Gerholm suggests, for the Muslim academic or intellectual who must deal with and engage the scientific arguments of their Western and often Christian counterparts. Whereas the traditional Islamic scholars like Allama Iqbal and Maulana Maududi wrote in Persian, Urdu and Arabic, contemporary Muslim scholars like Hossein Nasr, Ismail Faruqi and Ali Ashraf, as well as those discussed by Gerholm, write primarily in English. This lays their work open to a wider, critical and even antagonistic audience. Gerholm focuses mainly on two Muslim intellectuals, and since one of them is Akbar Ahmed, Gerholm's concerns might in some sense be said to encompass the present collection in a reflexive loop that incorporates his own contribution.

Gerholm's chapter, and the volume as a whole we feel, thus suggest that it is a critical moment in Islamic studies. We are at a cusp. It is time to point out the different features on the landscape – to point out where we were in the past and where we are heading for in the future. In the spirit of the age, although we are writing for a traditional scholastic and academic audience, we also wish to address a far wider audience of those interested in Islam and Islamic studies – journalists, writers, media commentators, indeed the average person who now has to grapple with words like *fatwa*, *jihad* and *ayatollah*.

Events in the last decade or so have transformed and shaken the Muslim world: the Iranian Revolution, the Rushdie affair, the Gulf War. Other influences on Muslim society have been more insidious but have resulted in no less significant transformations. The outside world now reaches into even the most guarded Muslim home, most obviously through television and the VCR. The processes of globalization have influenced traditional cultures and in such a dramatic way that they have raised issues for Muslims which can no longer be ignored. Muslims are forced to engage with these issues and to formulate a response to them. The response has not been slow in coming, but so far it has been a response more based in anger and passion as we saw in the Rushdie affair. Matters which in the past were considered only by the well-informed few are now debated in markets, at village wells and in tea houses – in short, at all those meeting places frequented by ordinary Muslim men and women of whatever level of society. One result seems to have been a more pronounced polarization in the Muslim world, one which creates a disjunction between radical Islam and the West.

This has also resulted in the populist response of Muslims to the world. It is a response formed and fed by the emotions of the bazaar. It reduces the Muslim response to the anger and passion of the spokesmen at the level of the bazaar. And through television this particular response dominates the response of the more reflective, more sophisticated Muslim scholar and statesman or stateswoman. This again is a legacy of the postmodernist era.

We are therefore suggesting that the challenge of understanding Islam in an age of postmodernity will demand all our powers of analysis, old and new. Neither the Orientalism that Said so passionately denounced, nor indeed the anti-Orientalism that Said himself has set in motion, are of much help. We point to a much more complex and more diverse situation, one that requires looking ahead and the forging of more nuanced ways of thinking about Muslim society. We hope that this volume will offer an introduction to that path.

NOTES

1 This is not to deny that there is a 'world culture', but it is a 'world culture' marked 'by an organization of diversity rather than by a replication of uniformity' as Hannerz has suggested (1990: 237; see also Hannerz 1989a: 208).

2 Not everyone is agreed on the kinds of people who might properly be considered agents of globalization. Thus, for example, while both Appadurai (1990: 7) and Cheater (1993: 10) regard tourists as such, Hannerz (1990: 241) does not. Hannerz argues that since tourists – like exiles and most ordinary labour migrants – encapsulate themselves in a circle of compatriots, this usually precludes any sustained engagement with alien systems of meaning (1990: 241–3).

3 Although there is not space to dwell on them here, it is nevertheless worth pointing out that the displacement of culture from its territorial base has given rise to a number of conceptual and methodological problems for anthropologists. The (post)modern age seems to have rendered the notion of the bounded society obsolete (compare Kuper 1992 *passim*), and Paine wonders whether or not participant observation will be able to handle the new 'polycultural kaleidoscope' of the 'compressed world' of the twenty-first century (1992: 201–3).

4 Unfortunately, however, we do not deal, except in passing, with the global dispersal of religious scholars. Many religious groups, such as the Jamaat-i-Islami, the Tabligh, the Deobandis, and the Barelwis, have long-standing networks both in the West and throughout the Muslim world. Nor are we able to discuss those pan-Islamic, globalizing movements, such as the World Muslim League and the Islamic Conference, which have sought to organize the *umma* on a formal basis.

5 And to a lesser extent elsewhere, since these series were also screened outside India. It is sometimes forgotten that the global media flow is not always in the same direction, even if it does have recognizable asymmetries. As Hannerz points out, there is not only the question of to what extent the 'peripheries' talk back, but also the question of the extent to which they influence one another. The Indian film industry, which offers entertainment for many parts of the third world, is a good example of the latter (Hannerz 1989b: 68, 69). Thus Stokes (this volume) remarks on its influence on the development of popular culture in Turkey.

6 This, of course, is not the only time that Muslim dress has come into conflict with westernization. One of the 'less well-known crises of modernisation' was that of the Tunisian soldiers' trousers (see Gellner 1981: 177).

REFERENCES

Ahmad, M. (1991) 'The politics of war: Islamic fundamentalisms in Pakistan', in J. Piscatori (ed.) *Islamic fundamentalisms and the Gulf Crisis*, Chicago: The Fundamentalism Project, American Academy of Arts and Sciences.

Appadurai, A. (1990) 'Disjuncture and difference in the global cultural economy', *Public Culture* 2 (2): 1–24.

Asad, T. (1990) 'Ethnography, literature, and politics: Some readings and uses of Salman Rushdie's *The Satanic Verses*', *Cultural Anthropology* 5 (3): 239–69.

Baykan, A. (1990) 'Women between fundamentalism and modernity', in B. S. Turner (ed.) *Theories of modernity and postmodernity*, London: Sage.

Boyne, R. (1990) 'Culture and the world system', in M. Featherstone (ed.) *Global culture: nationalism, globalization and modernity*, London: Sage.

Boyne, R. and Rattansi, A. (1990) 'The theory and politics of postmodernism: By way of an introduction', in R. Boyne and A. Rattansi (eds) *Postmodernism and society*, London: Macmillan.

Breckenridge, C. and Appadurai, A. (1989) 'On moving targets', *Public Culture* 2 (1): i–iv.

Cheater, A. (1993) 'Globalisation and the new technologies of knowing: Anthropological calculus or chaos?' Paper presented to the Association of Social Anthropologists' Decennial Conference, St Catherine's College, Oxford, July 1993. Cited with the permission of the author.

Delaney, C. (1991) *The seed and the soil: Gender and cosmology in Turkish village society*, Berkeley: University of California Press.

Donnan, H. and Werbner, P. (eds) (1991) 'Introduction', in H. Donnan and P. Werbner (eds) *Economy and culture in Pakistan: Migrants and cities in a Muslim society*, London: Macmillan.

Eickelman, D. F. and Piscatori, J., (1990) 'Social theory in the study of Muslim societies', in D. F. Eickelman and J. Piscatori (eds) *Muslim travellers: Pilgrimage, migration, and the religious imagination*, London: Routledge.

Fardon, R. (1992) 'Postmodern anthropology? Or, an anthropology of postmodernity?', in J. Doherty, E. Graham and M. Malek (eds) *Postmodernism and the social sciences*, London: Macmillan.

Featherstone, M. (1990) 'Global culture: An introduction', in M. Featherstone (ed.) *Global culture: Nationalism, globalization and modernity*, London: Sage.

—— (1991) *Consumer culture and postmodernism*, London: Sage.

Fischer, M. J. and Abedi, M. (1990) *Debating Muslims: Cultural dialogues in postmodernity and tradition*, Madison: University of Wisconsin Press.

Gardner, K. (1993) 'Desh-bidesh: Sylheti images of home and away', *Man* 28: 1–15.

Gellner, E. (1981) *Muslim society*, Cambridge: Cambridge University Press.

Giddens, A. (1990) *The consequences of modernity*, Cambridge: Polity Press.

Hannerz, U. (1987) 'The world in creolisation', *Africa* 57: 546–59.

—— (1989a) 'Culture between center and periphery: Toward a macroanthropology', *Ethnos* 54: 200–16.

—— (1989b) 'Notes on the global ecumene', *Public Culture* 1 (2): 66–75.

—— (1990) 'Cosmopolitans and locals in world culture', in M. Featherstone (ed.) *Global culture: nationalism, globalization and modernity*, London: Sage.

—— (1992) *Cultural complexity: Studies in the social organization of meaning*, New York: Columbia University Press.

Harvey, D. (1989) *The condition of postmodernity: An enquiry into the origins of cultural change*, Oxford: Basil Blackwell.

Kellner, D. (1988) 'Postmodernism as social theory: Some challenges and problems', *Theory, Culture and Society* 5: 2–3.

Kuper, A. (ed.) (1992) *Conceptualizing society*, London: Routledge.

Lash, S. and Urry, J. (1987) *The end of organized capitalism*, Oxford: Polity Press.

Lodge, D. (1985) *Small world*, Harmondsworth: Penguin Books.

Luhrmann, T. M. (1994) 'The good Parsi: The postcolonial "feminization" of a colonial elite', *Man* 29(2).

Malkki, L. (1992) 'National geographic: The rooting of peoples and the territorialization of national identity among scholars and refugees', *Cultural Anthropology* 7 (1): 24–44.

Mandel, R. (1990) 'Shifting centres and emergent identities: Turkey and Germany in the lives of Turkish gastarbeiter', in D. F. Eickelman and J. Piscatori (eds) *Muslim travellers: Pilgrimage, migration, and the religious imagination*, London: Routledge.

Modood, T. (1990) 'British Asian Muslims and the Rushdie Affair', *Political Quarterly* 61(2): 143–60.

Paine, R. (1992) 'The Marabar Caves, 1920–2020', in S. Wallman (ed.) *Contemporary futures: Perspectives from social anthropology*, London: Routledge.

Parkin, D. (1993) 'Nemi in the modern world: Return of the exotic', *Man* 28: 79–99.

Piscatori, J. (1991) 'Religion and realpolitik: Islamic responses to the Gulf War', in J. Piscatori (ed.) *Islamic fundamentalisms and the Gulf Crisis*, Chicago: The Fundamentalism Project, American Academy of Arts and Sciences.

Robertson, R. (1987) 'Globalization theory and civilizational analysis', *Comparative Civilizations Review* 17: 20–30.

—— (1990) 'Mapping the global condition: Globalization as the central concept', in M. Featherstone (ed.) *Global culture: nationalism, globalization and modernity*. London: Sage.

Roff, W. R. (1987) 'Islamic movements: One or many?', in W. R. Roff (ed.) *Islam and the political economy of meaning*, London: Croom Helm.

Said, E. (1978) *Orientalism*, Harmondsworth: Penguin Books.

—— (1981) *Covering Islam: How the media and the experts determine how we see the rest of the world*, London: Routledge and Kegan Paul.

Samad, Y. (1992) 'Book burning and race relations: Political mobilisation of Bradford Muslims', *New Community* 18(4): 507–19.

Stauth, G. and Zubaida, S. (eds) (1987) *Mass culture, popular culture and social life in the Middle East*, Boulder, CO: Westview Press.

Turner, B. S. (1990a) 'Periodization and politics in the postmodern', in B. S. Turner (ed.) *Theories of modernity and postmodernity*, London: Sage.

—— (ed.) (1990b) *Theories of modernity and postmodernity*, London: Sage.

Wallerstein, I. (1974) *The modern world-system*, New York: Academic Press.

—— (1984) *The politics of the world-economy*, Cambridge: Cambridge University Press.

—— (1990) 'Culture is the world-system: A reply to Boyne', in M. Featherstone (ed.) *Global culture: nationalism, globalization and modernity*, London: Sage.

Worsley, P. (1990) 'Models of the modern world-system', in M. Featherstone (ed.) *Global culture: nationalism, globalization and modernity*, London: Sage.

Chapter 2

Turkish arabesk and the city
Urban popular culture as spatial practice[1]

Martin Stokes

For Christians and Muslims, Istanbul has long been an icon of the meeting of East and West, and the place of Turkey in the world. For Europeans, this image of the city is familiar from a substantial travel literature, and a media treatment which has justified the Western promotion of the state in a 'troubled neighbourhood'. In Turkish historiography, the conquest of the city in 1453 opened up the 'Age of Conquest'. Istanbul became a complex and often contradictory image of the significance and power of a European Islam, and at the same time, an image of the modernizing role championed by the Ottoman Turks in the Middle East. For the Ottoman Sultans, Istanbul was not just a capital but a theatre in which imported ideas of progress and development were played out in utopian planning schemes (Çelik 1986). Today, contrary to the claims of many theorists of modernity, in which cultural experience has become fundamentally 'delocalised' (Berland 1988), this is a place which has lost none of its power to signify, although the global order of today has wrought fundamental changes in the ways Istanbul is experienced. Istanbul continues to emblemize modern Turkey more than anywhere or anything else, and although it has lost its status as the capital city to Ankara, it has lost none of its contradictory force as an image of the East in the West, and the West in the East. This image is of vital significance to a state which is currently so concerned with the projection of a European and secular image. It also asserts the vital political claims: that it is capable of dealing with the fundamentalist 'threat', maintaining its civilizing role in the Middle East, and assuming the natural responsibilities, conferred by its geographical and cultural position, for the economic development of former Soviet Central Asia. As Keyder has recently pointed out, the city's business élites have not been slow to develop new ways of 'selling Istanbul' (Keyder 1992).

However, this is not just an élite myth. Istanbul has a population of over ten million. To live in Istanbul, a city straddling Europe and Asia, is to be exposed to the full force of Turkish myths of East and West. It is to live with constant reminders of the global histories of two worlds which those Turks with no stake in the dominant mythologies often consider themselves to be awkwardly, and sometimes powerlessly, 'between'. However, I am not concerned with the extremely significant cultural dynamics of this perceived failure to 'be', to reconcile the East–West divide in contemporary Turkey. My general intention in this chapter is to look at how ideas about East and West are 'managed' in the routine events of daily lives in this city, and to illustrate the ways in which the language of space and place is used in everyday life. A city is not a static or passive symbol: it is lived in, used and appropriated. In terms of De Certeau's useful distinction (1987: 115), it is vital that we understand the social and cultural experience of cities in terms not of place, but of space, by which he means the social practices that occupy, use, and make social 'sense' of places. What constitutes the social and cultural life of a place is then a set of 'spatial practices' or 'proxemics'. The practices operate at a number of different levels, from the construction and ordering of urban, architectural, 'planned' spaces to the small scale events of daily itineraries and socializing, embodied in the practice of 'walking'. For De Certeau 'walking' is a metaphor for a range of urban social practices which can underscore or undermine the received spatial order. 'Walking' takes place in, and in terms of, spaces which are simultaneously global, national, urban, domestic and, ultimately, bodily. If we are to understand the significance of globalization for Turks, we need to understand the nature of these spatial practices.

A form of popular culture in Turkey known as arabesk, associated primarily with music, but also with film, novels and 'foto-roman' (photo dramas in newspapers with speech bubbles), focuses these spatial practices in a particularly sharp way. The dominant metaphors of arabesk are explicitly constructed around a series of essentially spatial binary oppositions. A 'Western' (i.e. modern) Turkey is opposed to a subversively 'Oriental' (backward) Turkey; planned and ordered urban space is opposed to the disordered and unplanned spaces of Istanbul's squatter town districts (*gecekondu*); control of the body is opposed to ecstatic lack of control; 'outsides' (*iç*) are opposed to 'insides' (*dış*); that which is 'covered' (*kapalı*) is opposed to that which is 'open' or 'exposed' (*açık*). All of these dualisms are closely connected to ideas of moral order ('The West', ordered urban space, and controlled, 'covered' bodies) and disorder ('The East', disordered urban space and 'exposed' bodies). The protagonists of arabesk musical films are invariably from the south east of Turkey (a barbarized, internal 'Orient'), they live lives of misery and despair in the gecekondu districts, their weakness and sexual powerlessness is exposed by the machinations of wicked employers and beautiful women: with tears in their eyes, they sing, in a vocabulary laden with emotion and masochistic eroticism, of the futility of their lives. Arabesk can be seen not only as a Geertzian cognitive map of the spatial schemas of this dramatic conception of urban life, but is also a set of practices with which these schemas are manipulated and used. For this reason, this chapter looks at arabesk in relation to two practices which are often ignored by recent commentators: belly dancing (*raks şarki*, or 'Eastern dance') and social dancing. In these practices one can see with particular clarity the conflation of global, urban, bodily and moral spaces.

ARABESK AND THE ISLAMIZED CITY

Firstly, what is arabesk? As a term, arabesk has a fairly long history. Öztuna (1987: 48–9) points out the currency of the term in describing film music, in particular those imitations of Egyptian and later Indian musicals popular in the 1930s and 1940s. As a musical genre, Orhan Gencebay applied the term to his first hit single, *Bir Teselli Ver* in 1969. Gencebay simply used the term for his own particular synthesis of Turkish classical music, rural folk genres, Western popular music and *'Oryental'* (dance styles modelled on Egyptian music). This synthesis had been developed previously by a number of musicians, such as his mentor Ahmet Sezgin, Suat Sayın and Abdullah Nail Baysuğ to cater for a thriving *gazino* culture which had emerged in the late forties and fifties. The gazino was, and is, a kind of club, where one can drink, eat, and watch some kind of floor show. They range from the cheap and respectable *aile gazinosu* to the 'Büyük Maksim' in Taksim square, and to the run down *pavyon* of Beyoğlu and Tarlabaşı. As Güngör has pointed out (1990), these developed as versions of the urban *meyhane* (bars where Christian minorities in Istanbul were licensed to sell alcohol) which catered for the tastes of a new migrant bourgeoisie which had profited from the aid-driven rural modernization programmes of the Menderes era (1950–60). Whilst the classical *fasıl* (suite) thrived in this atmosphere, it was also a hothouse for the development of the new genres. Musicians were not slow to realise that a music which spoke of 'the rural', 'the city', modernity and tradition would have a great appeal. Musical entrepreneurs such as Gencebay were quickly able to create and then occupy a niche in this lucrative market. Though the clientele has diversified, the music continues to change rapidly in the wake of technological changes, and the gazino environment itself continues to spawn new genres, arabesk is still very much music of the urban gazino. Nilüfer Göle aptly summarised the significance of the gazino as 'a place where men and women belly dance to a piyanist-şantör under disco lights in order to work out their urbanite fantasies and Alaturka proclivities . . .' (Göle 1992: 38).

Arabesk is difficult to define, and in Turkey, definitions of arabesk are inseparable from critique. These definitions have, over the last ten years, been mobilized frequently in public arenas in the context of a debate concerning the nature and place of civil society in the modern Turkish state. Modern Turkey, in common with many of the polities which emerged from the disintegration of the Ottoman empire, inherited a strong tradition of bureaucratic reformism. This reformism and the institutions of state legitimated by it dominated Turkish life with a particular intensity in the three decades following the establishment of the modern Republic. In 1950, however, this changed. The emerging cold war balance of power and the increasing absorption of the state into global patterns of debt and economic dependence resulted in the intensification of pressures by the state's creditors to 'liberalize'. A vital symbol of this, which mobilized an entire electorate in 1950, was the public face of Islam. Turkish nationalism had emerged in relation to ideas of modernity (citizenship, statehood, industrial development) which were vigorously secular. This secularism had been sharpened by the need that was perceived by the reformist bureaucratic élites to develop a national culture which was diametrically opposed to the Islamic multiculturalism of the Ottoman state. Islam was relegated to the domain of private morality – every aspect of the public practice of the faith was to be dismantled and swept away on the road to modern nation-statehood. An antagonism between the bureaucracy and the industrial bourgeoisie, which Keyder (1988) traces back at least to the reforms of the Tanzimat era, became overlaid in the new Republic with an antagonism between secularism and Islam: the industrial bourgeoisie were thus able to present Islam as the voice of a periphery which had been unjustly excluded by the state's reformist zeal. In this context every aspect of reformism, which touched people's day to day lives in powerful and intimate ways, became areas of struggle – often in complicated ways – in which the state's power continues to be contested. The victory of Adnan Menderes in the 1950 elections was widely understood as a victory for Islam. The situation was complicated by the military coup of 12 September 1980, which marked a rapprochement between the military (the traditional guardians of Ataturkian secularism) and the industrial bourgeoisie: the result was a smooth transition in 1983 from military rule to the Anavatan (ANAP) government of Turgut Özal. The acquiescence of the military to the programme of intense 'Islamization' promoted by Özal (again, often at a level of apparent trivia: the language of speeches and media policy in relation to language, the reluctance to intervene in the headwear dispute), in direct contravention of the secular heritage which the military were supposed to protect became a matter of outrage for the Turkish left and of great satisfaction to the Turkish right.

This rapprochement was accompanied by a number of significant trans-formations of Istanbul's urban space in the late 1980s, carried out in the name of Anavatan mayor Bedrettin Dalan's highly publicized programme of urban restoration. The Haliç (the Golden Horn) was to be cleaned, leaving its highly polluted waters as blue as Dalan's famously blue eyes (at least, they became famous after he made that statement). The decaying market area just behind the Galata bridge, and the low grade housing around the waterside were cleared to make way for parks and a huge inner city one way system. This, together with the second Bosphorous Bridge was in the first instance a response to the unprecedented pressure of traffic, noise and pollution at the very heart of the city that had accompanied the laissez-faire politics of the Özal years. It was also an explicit attempt to reconstruct Istanbul as the Islamic and Ottoman capital of the Age of Conquest – a statement that carried a great deal of weight as the Özal government sought to present Turkey as a European Muslim power, as the Ottoman empire had once been, to its trade partners in the Middle East and the European Economic Community. Monuments in public space, once exclusively and conspicuously reserved for Ataturk, now focused upon the conqueror of Istanbul, Mehmet the II, as an image of an outwardly oriented and very different kind of Turkey.[2]

These transformations of the city backfired in a number of ways, chief amongst which was the fact that many areas designated and cleared as new parks were rapidly sold to private speculators and turned into multi-storey car parks. Whatever the extent or truth of such claims, the charge of corruption and cynicism stuck. Dalan was quickly voted out of office and replaced by Nurettin Sözen of the left-of-centre Sosyal Halkçı Partisi. For critics, what was happening to urban space represented not only a crucial back-pedalling on issues of Ataturkian, secularist reformism, but cynicism and corruption, and a failure to attend to the ongoing problems of the city's fringes, in particular, its peripheral squatter towns (gecekondu), which no amount of cosmetic change to its centre was going to improve. In numerous interviews shortly after being elected, Sözen's statements that the gecekondu problem was going to be one of his top priorities signalled a very different notion of urban administration (sober, socially conscious) from Dalan's flamboyant vision. Dalan's policies thus focused, for his critics, multiple notions of disorder, all deeply embedded in political and historical mythology: the first, the perception that this was an attempt to return Istanbul to its status of Ottoman capital (echoing other rejections of Ataturkian reformism), the second, the perception of the cynical mismanagement of this project, and the third, the perception that the gecekondu problem (the periphery) was growing and out of control.

If urban order and disorder in Istanbul became a vital symbol of the nation in the late 1980s, it was closely tied to perceptions of arabesk and Turkish music. For the right (for example, Yılmaz Öztuna), Turkish classical music had been irreversibly debilitated by the music reforms, which sought to banish every trace of 'Islamic/Arab' music by closing the 'Eastern music' sections of the conservatories (in 1924) and attempting to ban it from the state radio airwaves (1934–6). The attempt by the state to install in its place a pure Turkish musical culture through the Turkish Radio and Television (TRT) and the new state conservatories, based on Anatolian rural melodies, only alienated the people to whom it was supposed to appeal. Driven underground, it withered, assuming the degenerate forms of arabesk. Öztuna therefore understands arabesk very much in terms of a bastardization of the classical genre, and draws a direct line from the popularized art music forms of the late nineteenth century, through art-music-educated composers of film music in the 1930s (such as Sadettin Kaynak) to the arabesk of the seventies (1987: 50–1).

For the left, the reforms had been justified, but mismanaged. When eastern music was banned, and no attempt was made to replace it, radio sets were tuned into Arab (particularly Egyptian) stations in the 1930s, opening the floodgates to an oppositional musical culture which defined itself in terms of all things Arab. Writers such as Eğribel (1984) are less inclined to stress the internal dynamics of the art music tradition, and emphasize instead the new social context of rural–urban migration and the 'folk' arabesk of İbrahim Tatlises and Ferdi Tayfur. Finally, for critics on the left, the rapprochement of the industrial bourgeoisie with the institutions of the state in 1983 is considered to have lead inexorably to the unopposed use of arabesk by the Özal government for its own hegemonic purposes (by, for example, enlisting the aid of arabesk stars at elections, using arabesk tunes as electoral jingles, and working towards reversing the state media's ban on arabesk). For critics of the left, arabesk celebrates the inherently 'Islamic' values of fatalism and passivity, which flourish in the culture of *'alternatifsizlik'* ('lack-of-alternatives') created by the state's heavy handed reformism (Eğribel 1984: 38), and, it is argued, this fatalism has been cynically manipulated in the populist strategies of the rightist parties. The reluctance of arabesk musicians to become politically committed (and their tendency to support ANAP when they do) has been a matter for concern on the part of otherwise sympathetic commentators such as Belge (1990) and Özbek (1991). What both critical discourses have in common is the idea that arabesk induces a masochistic sense of powerlessness. This idea derives from constructions of emotion, gender and urban space in films, lyrics and promotional iconography.

EMOTION, GENDER AND URBAN SPACE

Arabesk – in the opinion of its urban practitioners – is undoubtedly about emotion, by which they understand the workings of the inner self – the *gönül*. Musically this operates as a series of structural oppositions between solo voice or instrument against the chorus of violins, ornament against melodic structure, free time against strict time, and so on.[3] It is, for musicians and producers, a language designed for the communication of emotion (*duygu*). In the opinion of its critics on the other hand, it is about emotion out of control, 'uncovered' or 'revealed'. From the élitist perspective of art music, in which emotion and structure should exist in a certain balance, arabesk is unbridled emotion.

This perceived emotional imbalance relates closely to the idea that this is the music of the city's outsiders – its pariah and migrant communities living lives of social imbalance on the fringes of the city. One hears it constantly stated as absolute fact that arabesk is the music of the gecekondu squatter town and the *dolmuş* drivers who provide the unofficial transport system between the gecekondu and the city proper. Films are situated with great frequency in an unambiguous gecekondu environment, and many of the protagonists play the role of star-crossed migrants working as lorry or dolmuş drivers. A number of the dramas themselves take place in the environs of the Topkapı garage – perceived as a liminal area of the city situated by the city walls between the city and the gecekondu areas to the west of the city which, in the 1980s, was seen as the epicentre of not just the arabesk drama but of the informal transport system and the entire informal urban economy.

The idea that the gecekondu is disordered urban space has two principal components. Whilst the history of the gecekondu is conventionally traced back to the modernization programmes of the Menderes government, representations of urban order and disorder, through which the present day gecekondu continues to be seen, has a longer history. The association of urban order with an architectural language of straight streets, facades, viewpoints and parks arose explicitly in the urban planning of the Tanzimat era (1839–1976). As Mitchell points out (1991: 162), Saadatlı Kutlu Bey's new European quarter in Pera, built in the 1860s, was intended as a model of urban planning for the entire empire. The Tanzimat marked an orientation of the entire Levant towards the emerging domination of north west European capital from the 1860s onwards. As Mitchell argues, the new language of rationality and order, with its hierarchical relationships of structure and content, representation and reality, gradually colonized not just urban space but political, domestic and bodily space (Mitchell 1991: 149). This colonization was, he suggests, an essential part of the political and economic practices of capitalism.

The squatter towns which emerged in Turkey's industrializing cities in the late 1940s were not, of course, 'disordered'. In the first instance they were organized in relation to the demand for labour in industrial zones (Rami, Kocamustafapasa, Ümraniye, Kartal). They also brought a mass market for industrial goods right to the doorstep of the factories (Keyder 1987: 159). Successive governments have attempted to control (1963, 1968 and 1973), but never to enforce a ban on squatter development outright (Keleş 1990: 375–6). Gecekondu construction is a tightly controlled business, operating through gecekondu *aghas* (bosses), and large networks of brokers (see Duben 1991). Even the earliest sociologists working on the 'gecekondu problem' remarked at the extent of tidiness and organization of these areas (see Karpat 1976), and today, as each gecekondu area gains its title deeds in return for votes at elections, roads and refuse collection are quickly brought in, and small apartment blocks replace the single storey gecekondu buildings. In spite of this, the gecekondu as an image of disorder remains deeply entrenched in the language of political and cultural critique.

Secondly, a substantial sociological literature has focused on the gecekondu in some detail in Turkey since the early 1960s, its pervasive theme the role of the gecekondu in mediating between rural and urban, tradition and modernity, *gemeinschaft* and *gesellschaft*, the periphery and the centre (see for example Saran 1976; Kongar 1976; Karpat 1976). Underpinning this is the Lerneresque assumption that the two poles of development are known, stable social states; the gecekondu is thus seen in the sociological literature as potentially beneficial, according to then current paradigms of modernization theory (following Lerner 1958). They were nonetheless considered to be inherently unstable, a passage between two known states, capable of going, as it were, both ways. In this context it becomes easy to think of arabesk as the product of rural musicians struggling to appropriate an urban musical culture. It is easily identifiable with this image of the gecekondu, on the way from being one thing to becoming another, 'outsiders' trying to get 'in'. This construction of urban outsidership is emphasized by the recurrent statement that arabesk singers are all 'from the south east', referring to those underdeveloped provinces on the borders of Syria, Iraq and Iran. These constructions of an ideal-typical arabesk singer stress their liminality and their partial or rather unsuccessful integration into the city and the Turkish state. Once again, a number of arabesk films and songs deal explicitly with the theme of the south east and the south eastern migrant in Istanbul.

This spatial liminality is linked by its critics with the gender ambiguities of the singers. Here, undoubtedly, they have plenty to work on. Arabesk stars divide into 'machos' and effetes. The machos are associated particularly with the south eastern singers (Ferdi Tayfur, İbrahim Tatlises, Burhan Çaçan, Mahmut Tunçer). For the northern metropolitan, the south east is associated with a male gender 'style' considered utterly inappropriate in a modern urban environment. The Kurdish term 'kırro' has found its way into Turkish slang to describe precisely this kind of overstated machismo in dress and behaviour, behaviour associated with arabesk singers (particularly İbrahim Tatlıses) and 'arabesk types' in popular 'high-brow' journalism and spoken language alike. What is particularly striking, therefore, is their dramatic emasculation in arabesk films. This emasculation is effected through the exposure of weakness and sentiment, through the machinations of unscrupulous employers, the attractions of drink and women, and their inability to abandon the only code of morality and honour that they know. Masculinity is presented as being crucially compromised by the economic powers and the moral choices that the protagonist faces.[4]

The foregrounding of a problematic manhood amongst the arabesk 'effetes' is equally striking. Zeki Müren moved from art music to mainstream arabesk with *Helal Olsun* in 1987. Bülent Ersoy is perhaps one of the most enduring icons of arabesk: he underwent a sex change operation in London in 1981, and was subsequently banned from stage performance in Turkey on account of a law requiring women to request police permission to perform. This was always refused, and the result was that she was obliged to live in exile (extremely lucrative exile) in Germany. In 1987 she became a liberal 'cause' for reasons that I have mentioned above. Debate raged over whether a transsexual was a woman or a man – if considered the latter, then the law preventing her performing on the basis of the fact that she was a woman had been incorrectly applied. The 'Bülent Ersoy ban' was repealed in 1988, spawning a wave of transsexual and transvestite singers (or, rather, a wave of singers associated with the hitherto 'invisible' transsexual and transvestite subculture of Elmadağ in Istanbul), many of whom have followed Bülent's example by getting engaged to men.

Female singers are also constructed in ways which foreground a 'lost' femininity. A classic case is that of Bergen. She made her name as an arabesk singer in Mersin and Adana. She never married but lived under the protection of a lover/business-manager who was subject to fits of violent jealousy. Her face was permanently scarred after, in one assault, he emptied a car-battery over her face. Only two years ago she was killed – shot to death by the same man. With crashing predictability, every tabloid headline proclaimed 'A real arabesk story', and 'She died just as in her films'. What made this horrific event 'arabesk' was not simply the fact that it is an ugly tale of domestic violence, but that her tragedy relates to the fact that her gendered personhood had been taken away from her as a result of somebody else's actions. The extent to which one is considered to have, or to lack 'face' as a determinant of one's social standing is a commonplace of Mediterranean ethnography. The deprivation of a gendered 'face' is a deprivation of personhood in a fundamental sense – and this a constant theme of arabesk lyrics: a fated inability to 'be'.

I am conflating a number of critical discourses here to make my point: that arabesk is constructed in terms of a play on emotion, peripheral urban space and gender ambiguity. Even for the fan, this is what arabesk 'is': a decaying city, tragedy, alienation, the disrupted state of the *gönül* (the inner self), acts of defiant and despairing non-conformity. Having attempted to understand the situation from the perspective of professional musicians in Istanbul, my initial response has been to point out that this representation has very little to do with their rather humdrum business lives (Stokes 1992b). There is not, for example, the split which some people assume exists between the personnel of the official and the unofficial media: musicians working during the day at the TRT often work in the evenings singing arabesk in the *gazinos* around Istanbul, or work as arabesk producers and composers. Arabesk musicians do not, on the whole, live in gecekondus. One of the most famous, Orhan Gencebay, is not from the south east of Turkey. Few (at the kind of level at which I was working) would associate themselves with the more famous gender stereotypes. As far as fanship is concerned, the research which I conducted in music clubs whose clientele were from gecekondu and ex-gecekondu suburbs, but also central city clubs (which I attempted to back up with facts and figures; see Stokes 1992a:44–7) demonstrated that no simple conclusions could be drawn about gecekondu identification with arabesk. If anything, the more peripheral the musician might be deemed to be in terms of jobs (or lack of them), education, and place of birth, the more they identified themselves with the officially sanctioned genres, in these clubs at least. And finally, arabesk's appeal was in no way limited to urban marginal populations. Even the people who criticized it would listen to it and enjoy it, sometimes justifying themselves by recourse to a certain intellectual antiquarianism: 'Orhan's first cassettes were superb – it's never been the same since', my bağlama (long-necked lute) teacher, and otherwise implacable foe of arabesk, once lamented.

Arabesk is not 'the music of the gecekondu' in any sociologically useful sense – that is, if one is trying to identify musicians and audiences. One has to understand, however, the force of these ideas, their discursive manipulation and the ideological positions that they maintain. For those people whose positions and institutions are legitimated by the idea that Turkish culture needs to be 'protected' in this way (in the first instance those associated with the TRT and the state conservatories) this critical language demonstrates the classic strategies of control: identifying in it an excess of emotion (which of course feminizes the thing which is to be controlled), identifying it with urban disorder, and assuming that as music its effects are going to be to unhinge people's emotional capacities and contribute towards further urban disorder. In this language of control, representation of the body and the representation of the city are linked through arabesk. This homology is one which suggests itself to the Turkish observer and is in need of minimal 'construction': it is simply what arabesk 'is' and what it 'does'. Secondly, to adapt Mitchell's point mentioned above, both bodies and cities (along with everything else) had been reorganized in the late nineteenth century in ways which constructed sharp dualities between order and disorder, bounded space and content, structure and substance, leisure and work, representation and reality – dualities which were part of a colonial process which made domination inevitable, inescapable and self-policed.

In modern Turkey, urban planning continues to be a vehicle for bringing expanding urban populations into a relationship of subordination to capitalist industrial production, to the state and ultimately to an international economic and political order. In architecture and urban planning, the state has a powerful tool. Social groups construct ways of managing around this given environment. The anthropological literature on urban networks of kin, friendship, religion and ethnicity always seems to stress the act of managing – correctly implying the problems of exclusion and inadequate and unequal access to resources which so many people face in cities such as Istanbul. Architecture and urban planning are difficult things to argue with. You can try. In a widely publicized case (see front page of *Cumhuriyet*, 27 July 1987), a certain Abdülhadi Güneş, a migrant from Kars living in a gecekondu threatened by a demolition order in Izmir, took his daughter onto the roof of his house in July 1987 and threatened to throw her into the path of the oncoming municipality bulldozers. But you fail. The French colonial planner, Marshall Lyautey once famously remarked that in French North Africa, 'a construction site is worth a battalion' (Rabinow 1989: 290). Under these circumstances one cannot sustain arguments for plurality, or construct coherent strategies for resisting the orders of the state, and its particular notion of urban order, which are not simultaneously self-destructive. How can you argue with a bulldozer?

Since arabesk invites us to construct homologies between the city, music and the body, are the techniques of power that are so successful in the context of urban planning operable in music? Or, to put the question in another way, does arabesk, a music of and about the city, constitute in any way a method of subverting, or at least commenting upon the operations of power manifested in urban planning?

POWER, VISIBILITY AND AUDIBILITY

There are certainly few obvious grounds for a romantic celebration of the politics of resistance or subversion in arabesk. The state appears to have scored a number of successes in its attempt to define, control and intervene in musical pleasures. Its own constructed TRT 'folk music' has a great deal of support (particularly since it began to be televised, and a new generation of young and good-looking singers were recruited). This is not what one is led to expect from critics of the TRT style, such as Eğribel, Güngör, and Özbek, but is a fact nonetheless. When the popular journalistic debates about reform, development and civil society began to be focused on arabesk, the state moved quickly to co-opt it. Many arabesk stars rushed to support Özal at elections in 1987. TRT notions of musical order (involving exactly the same notions of discipline, regularity and systematicity mobilized in the debates about modernization and urban planning) are precisely those of arabesk singers, composers and producers: the large, hierarchically organized string section, tightly disciplined so that the bows are moving in the same direction at the same time, that they are wearing the same clothes, the importance of structurally separate yet interdependent '*alt yapı*' (substructure) and '*üst yapı*' (superstructure), the concept of '*partisiyon*' making for neat alternations between instrumental soloists and the group, the importance of mastering and putting to use every bit of new technology. The overlap is to be explained by the fact that there is so much connecting official and unofficial music-making circles (Stokes 1992b).

The state has not, however, been able to control in the same way the countless everyday practices in which arabesk is embedded: the domestic reproduction of popular music, talk about music, turning over a tune whilst waiting for a bus or train, and, most specifically, dance. Whilst metaphors of power transfer easily into brick and stone, and the visions of urban planners, sound is more difficult stuff to handle. If planners are concerned with ideas of order which are tactile and visual, sound rarely enters the equation. Are cities planned with what they sound like in mind? Notions of control relating to sound: noise, noise control, noise pollution enter later, as an afterthought – and, as Atalli has pointed out, a somewhat obsessive afterthought (1985:122–4). Sound cannot be controlled with precision. Sources and boundaries can be ambiguous. The environments created by sound can be radically at odds with the architectural environment: a ghetto-blaster, the walkman or the car sound system create an alternative aural environment, or rather, alternative relations of the aural to the visual and tactile environment. These practices not only construct their own aural spaces, but also bring the people within them into specific relationships. The ghetto-blaster in the pedestrian space outside a shopping arcade, for example, defines the group around the music in antagonistic opposition to those outside it. And rather than channelling them in space (for music does not have the hard unambiguous edges of architectural space), sound brings people into a relationship with one another which is of a different order – the 'tuning in', to use Schutz's celebrated phrase (1977), of internal simultaneities of beat, accent and bodily movement. Music does not create an empty space, as it were, waiting to be filled in with a design or a structure. There is, of course, a more obviously 'culturally constructed' element, which ethnomusicologists have pointed out with regularity in such diverse societies: sound in Turkey, and music in particular, is considered to mediate between the inner and outer self. It brings the '*iç*' into the realm of the '*dış*', coming from the former and going out into the latter – like breath. It brings the concealed interior into the revealing exterior. It mixes things which order requires keeping separate.

The connection of these ideas of concealed interiors and revealing exteriors relates the practices of music and social dance directly to the processes through which the Middle Eastern city has been imagined and organized. The city came to be considered not only by colonial but by indigenous planners in terms of revealing order organized around exteriors, facades, external, 'revealing' viewpoints (revealing in terms of allowing one to see where one is in relation to the rest of the city), in opposition to the closed, 'interior' world of the *medina*, the bidonvilles, shanty towns or the gecekondu of the city. So too is bodily order seen in terms of a relationship between the revealed and the concealed self, things which should be concealed (emotions, genitalia) and things which should be revealed (who one 'is' in the world), a set of relationships which achieved a new clarity in the context of Turkey's emerging relations with north west European capital. In these processes of domination, the revealed should 'englobe' and control the concealed, as clothes cover the body, as the 'popular quarters' of the city are controlled by the state, and – the most fundamental of all, as the male is believed to inevitably and inexorably englobe the female (Delaney 1991: 211). These ideas imply a hierarchy, a structure of domination which music and dance (as conceived by the actors involved) are always capable of upsetting. My argument is that the play on bodily space in music and dance comments upon the organization of social urban space in a powerfully critical way. The question is, how? To answer this question in relation to arabesk, we must look in some detail at the organization of social dance.

THE BELLY DANCE

The bodily language of social dance in Turkey – the *çifte telli* – is essentially the language of the belly dance.[5] Its social context is the engagement, the wedding, the circumcision festivity, or the family evening out in the *aile gazino* located at nodal points in the suburban and gecekondu transport networks and at beauty spots at the fringes of the city. Social dance is remarkably gender unspecific in Turkey. It plays with bodily gestures of domination and submission. One can play at both. But at the same time, the fact that the performance is considered to be about ecstatic abandonment, 'other worldly states', enables these enactions of domination and submission to be put into inverted commas, in a world of play. It is nonetheless an intense and erotically charged performance – drawing attention to precisely those parts of the body which have to be kept so carefully covered (for both men and women). As an awkward social dancer whose erotic charge seldom manifests itself on the dance floor, these were, for me, always moments of intense self-consciousness and embarrassment.

On reflection, I should not have been too hasty in dismissing my own reactions (as my friends and informants assured me I should) as those of a repressed European outsider. Embarrassment is never far from the surface in a slightly different context: the belly dance as danced by the professional belly dancer in the *pavyon* for an audience of men: a single man is chosen, danced in front of, and confronted by the female dancer. All attention at this moment is upon the male – total humiliation is possible if one creases up in embarrassment and fails to 'play one's part'. If one stands up, dances a bit with an idiotic smile on one's face, and then, with a flourish, puts a large bank note into the dancer's clothing (which of course means physical contact with breasts, buttocks or stomach), the tables in this ritual psycho drama have been turned – the dancer once more becomes the object of the male controlling gaze – and 'is danced' (to use the Turkish causative expression) by the observer. Of course, this invariably happens because the 'game' has been rigged, and professional belly-dancers in Istanbul live lives of manipulated misery on the fringe of organized prostitution. But there is also in the performance a perception that there is a moment of critical balance in which things could go either way. The male observer is put on the spot: he must dominate or be dominated, and whilst there is humour (of a kind) involved, and play with the conventions recognized, there is no halfway house. Although the game is loaded in the favour of the observing male, manhood and the order that this implies is nonetheless at stake.

This moment of critical balance in belly dancing is reproduced in social dancing. On the one hand, social dance is undoubtedly performance which lies under the control of the male gaze. Young girls are taught the erotically charged movements of the çifte telli almost as soon as they can stand up: the adulation that they receive from parents and relatives as they dance – particularly at weddings – teaches them to regard themselves as objects: valuable objects whose value necessitates control and discipline. If this process of socialization is an exercise in control, it is only partially successful. The fact that the music to which people are dancing is arabesk – with its images of defiant gender non-conformity, and its spatial implication of an uncontrollable periphery – is far from insignificant. Precisely because arabesk lies on the edge of permissibility, and on the fringes of order, it is an area full of ambiguities. What is going on in arabesk, and consequently in dance, can never be totally controlled. Playful flirtation and the meaningful exchange take place through momentary eye movements and facial expressions, and are matters of immensely subtle readings and counter readings. There are certainly conventions and even rules, but no 'plan' to which the social dance must conform. So much can, but at the same time cannot be controlled. It lies, as Cowan has pointed out (1990), on the fringes of hegemonic practice, in a domain of negotiation and contest.

To conclude that the spatial practices of arabesk and social dance maintain a kind of question mark over the strategies and practices of domination does not perhaps say very much, except that we should not be too surprised at the fact that people are capable of mobilizing, through music, an implicitly critical commentary on urban space. The organization of ideas of domination, gender ambiguity, pain and abandonment in arabesk provide, according to interpretation, a resource through and in which other performances are structured. These performances cut across urban life, from the domestic to the public. For example, to take a brief fieldwork anecdote, I returned to my bağlama-teacher's flat in Üsküdar one day with an old Orhan Gencebay cassette, after a shopping expedition. Seeing the cassette, he began a tirade; as a TRT employee he maintains a strong line against arabesk. His sister Jasemin had come to join him from their natal village. Their father had died, and her brother, my teacher, was looking after her whilst she took the opportunity, through much intrigue and quiet deceit, to explore the city. His authority over her movements in the city, and his demands on her domestic help evidently exasperated her (she frequently told me as much). Her brother's high handed dismissals of arabesk were therefore a perfect opportunity for her to assert her right to some kind or degree of autonomy. On this occasion, she had me there as a captive audience. Taking the cassette from me, she looked at the picture of the singer on the cover and murmured *'ama ne güzel pozları var!'* ('but don't you just love the way he stands!'). This was a beautifully weighted *non sequitur*. Her brother's criticisms were evoking the cultural health of the nation and the evils of the then ruling political party. Her own comment, evoking the erotic and subversive semiotics of the poses and the 'glance' (*bakış*) cultivated by arabesk stars (precisely those re-enacted in social dance), instantly deflated her brother's pompous commentary. There was no possible reply which did not acknowledge that her apparently absurd remark did not contain a subtle understanding of just why arabesk stars are so significant and successful. Jasemin thereby scored a valuable point.

To take a radically different case, politics is often much more directly and explicitly involved in the performance of arabesk. In 1989, Bülent Ersoy was shot on stage by a right wing extremist for refusing to sing a nationalist song upon request. This extremely violent assault was as much as anything an assault on a convenient symbol of a Turkey that had slid out of control, whose centre had been claimed and appropriated by its periphery. Conversely, arabesk has also had a role to play in the resistance movement often referred to as the Kurdish intifada. Kurdish writers have recently mobilized a strong argument that arabesk and much of the TRT repertoire is a Kurdish music appropriated for the purposes of assimilation and control by the Turkish state (Bayrak 1991).

Arabesk lives and breathes at a level of minor urban social pleasures, dramas and frustrations. Through arabesk, the practices of the state and the agencies which shape the physical urban environment are momentarily arrested and queried. For young men, and particularly women who get up and engage in the playful erotic exchange of çifte telli dancing, for a group of lads listening to a cassette or playing over a tune on the bağlama, these are moments in which the apparent inevitabilities of global and urban order, and the domestic and bodily orders which resonate with it, are seen with some clarity as a state of affairs which could be otherwise.

NOTES

1 This chapter is based on fieldwork in Turkey between 1985 and 1988 funded by the ESRC. It has been presented in various forms at seminars at the School of Geography at Oxford University, the Department of Anthropology at the University of California, Berkeley and the Department of Social Anthropology at the Queen's University of Belfast. I am particularly indebted to Ayfer Bartu at Berkeley for her comments on drafts of this chapter.
2 Conspicuous examples include the statue of Fatih Sultan Mehmet in the park in the Fatih district of the old city, and the naming of the second, Japanese-built Bosphorous bridge, opened in 1990, as the Fatih Sultan Mehmet Köprüsü.
3 For a more detailed musicological elaboration of this approach, see Stokes 1992a: chapter 6.
4 For a discussion of the films see Stokes 1992a: 138–42 and Özbek's interview with Gencebay on the subject of the film *Batsın Bu Dünyayı* (Özbek 1991: 219–36).
5 Belly dancing is a highly significant but little researched topic. I am grateful to Reinhard Schultze for pointing out that a recent seminar on the subject of belly dancing lead by Oleg Grabar has begun to examine the history of this art form. Amongst other things, belly dancing was reputedly the late nineteenth century 'invention' of a nightclub owner in Berlin seeking touristic erotica to rival the French Can-Can. There is clearly evidence of a complex interplay between local social dance forms in Turkey and these imported orientalist fantasies in contemporary Turkish belly dancing.

REFERENCES

Atalli, J. (1985) *Noise: The Political Economy of Music*, Manchester: Manchester University Press.
Bayrak, M. (1991) *Kürt Halk Türküleri (Kilam U Stranên Kurd)*, Ankara: ABC.
Belge, M. (1990) 'Toplumsal Değişme ve Arabesk', *Birikim*, 17: 16–23.
Berland, J. (1988) 'Locating Listening: Technological Space, Popular Music, Canadian Meditations', *Cultural Studies*, 2. (3): 343–58.
Çelik, Z. (1986) *The Remaking of Istanbul: Portrait of An Ottoman City in the Nineteenth Century*, Seattle: University of Washington Press.
Cowan, J. (1990) *Dance and the Body Politic in Northern Greece*, Princeton: Princeton University Press.
De Certeau, M. (1987) *The Practice of Everyday Life*, Berkeley: University of California Press.
Delaney, C. (1991) *The Seed and the Soil: Gender and Cosmology in Turkish Village Society*, Berkeley: University of California Press.
Duben, A. (1991) 'The Rationality of an Informal Economy: The Provision of Housing in Southern Turkey', in M. Kıray (ed.) *Structural Change in Turkish Society*, Bloomington: Indiana University Turkish Studies.
Eğribel, E. (1984) *Niçin Arabesk Degil?*, Istanbul: Sureç.
Göle, N. (1992) 'Istanbulıun Intikamı', *Istanbul* 3: 36–9.
Güngör, N. (1990) *Arabesk: Sosyo-Kültürel Açıdan Arabesk Müziği*, Ankara: Bilgi.
Karpat, K. (1976) *The Gecekondu: Rural Migration and Urbanisation*, Cambridge: Cambridge University Press.
Keleş, R. (1990) *Kentleşme Politikası*, Ankara: Imge.
Keyder, Ç. (1987) *State and Class in Turkey: A Study in Capitalist Development*, London: Verso.

—— (1988) 'Class and State in the Transformation of Modern Turkey', in F. Halliday and H. Alavi (eds) *State and Ideology in the Middle East and Pakistan*, London: Macmillan.

—— (1992) 'Istanbulıu Nasıl Satmalı?', *Istanbul* 3:80–5.

Kongar, E. (1976) 'A Survey of Familial Change in Two Turkish Gecekondu Areas', in J. Peristiany (ed.) *Mediterranean Family Structures*, Cambridge: Cambridge University Press.

Lerner, D. (1958) *The Passing of Traditional Society: Modernising the Middle East*, New York: The Free Press.

Mitchell, T. (1991) *Colonising Egypt*, Berkeley: University of California Press.

Özbek, M. (1991) *Popüler Kültür ve Orhan Gencebay Arabeski*, Istanbul: Iletisim.

Öztuna, Y. (1987) *Türk Musikisi: Teknik ve Tarihi*, Istanbul: Türk Petrol Vakfi, Lale Mecmuası Neşriyatı.

Rabinow, P. (1989) *French Modern: Norm and Form in the Social Environment*, Cambridge MA: MIT Press.

Saran, N. (1976) 'Squatter Settlement (Gecekondu) problems in Istanbul', in P. Benedict, E. Tümertekin and F. Mansur (eds) *Turkey: Social and Geographic Perspectives*, Leiden: E. J. Brill.

Schutz, A. (1977) 'Making Music Together: A Study in Social Relationship', in J. Dolgin, D. Kemnitzer and D. Schneider (eds) *Symbolic Anthropology*, New York: Columbia University Press.

Stokes, M. (1992a) *The Arabesk Debate: Music and Musicians in Modern Turkey*, Oxford: The Clarendon Press.

—— (1992b) 'Islam, The Turkish State and Arabesk', *Popular Music*, 11 (2): 213–27.

Chapter 3

Contested meanings and the politics of authenticity
The 'Hosay' in Trinidad

Gustav Thaiss

A number of years ago, the Brooklyn Academy of Music, in association with Mel Howard Productions, (and the cooperation of the Turkish Ministry of Tourism and Information) presented 'The Whirling Dervishes of Turkey'. The printed programme accompanying the performance noted 'The program is a religious ceremony. You are kindly requested to refrain from applause' (Schechner 1976: 85).

A few years later another Sufi group, the Halveti-Jerrahi dervishes of Istanbul engaged in a ritual *dhikr*, also in New York, causing one reviewer to comment: 'it was not a concert, a dance ritual or a program of therapeutic exercise, although it was something like all of them . . . it was a religious ritual . . . and one was able to choose whether to enjoy it as a more or less conventional concert spectacle or to participate' (Palmer 1979). The review later went on to note that when the audience was invited to participate in the circling, head-tossing and rhythmic breathing, many people 'thought they were taking part in an evening of folk dancing . . . while some of the participants continued to treat the whole thing as a lark'.

Clearly, members of the audience who paid to see these two events found themselves in an ambiguous situation where the norms regarding theatrical performances and those governing religious ritual were confused.

An event that seems to be a paradigmatic example of such an interplay between ritual and theatre and the ambiguity of the situation is the so-called 'Hosay' festival in Trinidad.[1] Over the last century or so, what has been the major tragic event in the Shi'a Muslim ritual calendar has been increasingly transformed into a 'fête' or a festival with a carnival-like ambience second only to the main carnival in popularity in the festival schedule of Trinidad.[2]

The main actors in the Hosay are three social groups, broadly defined, namely the Shi'a Muslim organizers, the Sunni Muslims, and the non-Muslim populace of which the Creole or Afro-Trinidadian is the largest segment. Each year the Shi'a Muslim organizers of the Hosay in Trinidad wish to commemorate this ritual of tragedy. They deeply believe in the spiritual significance of this event and carry out the ceremonial practices handed down to them from their forefathers. However, the thousands of non-Muslim spectators who come to watch the symbolic funeral processions have only a vague general knowledge of the religious significance of the occasion. For various reasons, as we shall see, they treat it as a fête, as a joyous occasion and use terms borrowed from carnival such as 'bacchanal', 'jump-up', 'shake-up', 'mas' which are appropriate to their definition of the situation but which, to more orthodox believers, especially the Sunni Muslims, 'makes a mockery' of the Muharram commemorations.

This chapter, then, will look at the Hosay as a case study of a number of social processes occurring in Trinidad, particularly that of creolization. I will argue that there is an attempt by these social groups, each of which has its own view of what is really true about the occasion, to make their definition of the situation prevail. What is presently occurring in Trinidad with regard to the Hosay is a 'cultural struggle' between different ethnic and religious groups which is newly defining the reality of Hosay, and by extension an authentic, national cultural heritage for Trinidad.

Theoretically, a postmodernist issue arises here, an issue concerned with ambiguity, uncertainty, incompleteness; of concerns with a world made up of different discourses of heritage and for which there are no simple answers. Questions arise from these discourses on how to define a social or ritual situation, which in turn gives rise to problems of 'ownership'.[3] To whom does the Hosay 'belong'? Does it 'belong' to the Shi'a? To Muslims? To Trinidadians regardless of religious persuasion? Have the Muharram ritual observances become a national treasure which now extends beyond the control of the Shi'a Muslim organizers and believers? Even the question of 'ownership' is perhaps more a modernist assumption than a postmodernist one which fosters not exclusiveness but 'the importance of diversity, the need for tolerance, the necessity for understanding the other' (Ahmed 1992: 27).

THE DRAMA OF HUSAIN

To better understand the significance of the Hosay it is useful to place it in a wider historical context. Upon the death of the Prophet Muhammad in 632 AD the Muslim community found itself in great disorder and uncertainty. The Prophet had no sons to succeed him, nor did he name a successor (caliph), although the partisans (Shi'a) of 'Ali believed that he did indeed name 'Ali, his cousin and son-in-law, as his successor. Others, however, wished to follow traditional custom and elect a leader who was felt to be the most capable in guiding the community (known today as the Sunni). After much bitter debate, the party of Abu Bakr won, but he died after two years and was succeeded by two other caliphs, so it was not until more than two decades after the death of the Prophet that

'Ali, the husband of the Prophet's daughter Fatima and father of Hasan and Husain, became caliph.

After five years of rule, 'Ali was assassinated. His eldest son, Hasan, temporarily succeeded him but almost immediately resigned in favour of the rule of Mu'awiya, the governor of Syria, who had earlier challenged 'Ali's right to govern. Mu'awiya instigated the poisoning of Hasan and thereby seized firm control of the caliphate.

It was not until 680, some twenty years after the death of 'Ali, that his younger son, Husain, undertook to avenge his father's death and to champion the cause of the 'Alids, who sought sanctuary in Kufa in southern Iraq. The Shi'a of Kufa invited Husain to lead a revolt against the Ummayad caliphs of Damascus. Husain accepted this role and set out with his family and an escort of about seventy followers to join them. However, in the desert plain at Karbala, near the present-day city of Baghdad, Husain's group was surrounded by the sizeable army of Yazid, Mu'awiya's son and successor, and deprived of access to water. Husain refused to give in to the demand of the enemy that he acknowledge Yazid as caliph and renounce his opposition, though defeat was certain. The grandson of the Prophet and his followers managed to survive the burning desert heat and the onslaught of the enemy for ten days, from the first of Muharram to the tenth (known as 'Ashura), the day of Husain's martyrdom. His body was pierced with arrows, decapitated and trampled by the enemy horses. The body was left in the desert sun, while his head and those of his followers were placed on spears and carried in triumph, eventually to Yazid in Damascus.

Quite soon after his death the battlefield became a place of veneration and pilgrimage to the Shi'a and over time this lamentable enterprise was transformed in the imagination of the Shi'a into an event of incalculable importance. Husain's refusal to capitulate to overwhelming odds was interpreted as a voluntary self-sacrifice, and through his suffering and obedience to the will of God it is believed that he was given the exclusive privilege of making intercession for believers to enter Paradise.

Each year, commemorative ceremonies are held by the Shi'a throughout the world, beginning on the first of Muharram and culminating on the tenth, when a symbolic funeral procession is held designed to offer Husain the funeral and burial he was denied on the battlefield. Throughout the first nine days the commemoration consists of religious gatherings where narrators recite stories, in graphic detail, of the events at Karbala. These stories elicit much profuse weeping, cries of lamentation and, not uncommonly, ecstatically induced rhythmic chest beating. In some extreme groups there is self-flagellation with barbed metal chains. Believers fast and refrain from various personal indulgences. Participation in the Muharram ceremonies and showing one's support for and sympathy with Husain's actions by weeping, mourning and other acts of condolence are believed to be an aid to salvation (see Thaiss 1972; Chelkowski 1986; Neubauer 1972). Indeed, 'his martyrdom on the tenth of Muharram marks to this day the height of the religious calendar and his tragic death symbolizes fully the ethos of Shi'ism' (Nasr 1966: 164).

The 'ethos of Shi'ism', however, finds different expressions in different cultures. In Iran there is an additional practice which is unique to the Muharram ceremonies and that is the *ta'ziyah*. In Iran this term refers specifically to a ritual theatrical performance or passion play in which spectators and performers re-enact the drama of Husain and his suffering (see Chelkowski 1979). In India the commemoration centres about street processions in which the focal point is the *ta'ziyah*, which here has a totally different meaning and refers to elaborately decorated, colourful facsimiles of the tombs of Hasan and Husain.

The Muharram ceremonies were apparently introduced into India by Timur (Sharif 1972: 164) and were encouraged by various independent Shi'a states as well as by the Moghul dynasty which had strong ties with the Shi'a Safavid dynasty of Iran (Momen 1985: 122). The ritual processions became popular throughout India with all segments of the population – Shi'a, Sunni and Hindu – participating in the processions and the construction of the *ta'ziyahs*. Indeed, Shakeel Hossain argues that 'the ritual ceremony of *Ta'zia* owes its beginning to Hindu festivals of carrying flamboyant shrines and idols' (1990: 12), while M. L. Nigam, for instance, suggests that 'Bhakti devotionalism and ritual practices such as the *rathyatra* or public procession of idols helped incline Hindus to the acceptance of Shiite Muharram practices and the veneration of Husain' (cited by Pinault 1992: 194, fn. 27). Despite strong antagonism between Muslims and Hindus over the centuries (see Gaborieau 1985 for an overview of this confrontation), there is the interesting reality of religious tolerance and cooperation between Muslims and Hindus in India. This is not the place to discuss this in any detail, suffice it to say that Sunnis and Hindus are active participants in the Muharram rituals even to the point of themselves erecting *ta'ziyahs* and taking part in the processions (Hjortshoj 1987; Pinault 1992; Cole 1988; Saiyid *et al*. 1981; Sharif 1972; Hossain 1990). In her study of a West Bengal Hindu community, of which Muslims make up some 5–6 per cent of the total population, Fruzzetti notes that 'Although the Muslims of the town are Sunnis, they celebrate the festival of Muharram with a mixed feeling of gaiety and mourning. Newly bought dresses, a festive atmosphere, men drinking or performing *mataam* (beating one's breast), are all part of the Muharram celebration in this town' (1981: 104). Saiyid, who also studied Sunni Muslim communities in India, expresses some surprise that a ritual which is a 'grim reminder of a dastardly tragedy [should] become a curious amalgam in which the festive and recreational aspects stand out' (1981: 114–15).

ISLAM IN THE CARIBBEAN

The history of Islam in the Caribbean can be traced back to two events. The first is the enslavement of Africans, some of whom were from predominantly Muslim tribal groups such as the Mandingo and the Fulani of West Africa, among others, and their subsequent transport to the New World and the Caribbean (Mintz and Price 1976: 29). Forced conversions to Christianity on the plantations led to the eventual demise of Islam among Blacks in the Caribbean.[4]

The second event was the importation of indentured workers from India to the Caribbean beginning in the mid-nineteenth century. These East Indians were brought by the British Colonial authorities to Trinidad beginning in 1845 to work the plantations which had been abandoned by the former slaves who had been freed by the abolition of slavery in 1838.

By 1917, the year the British government ended the indentureship of foreign labour to the colonies, almost 144,000 Indian indentured labourers had been brought to Trinidad, while nearly 239,000 were brought to British Guiana (van der Veer and Vertovec 1991: 150). The largest number of emigrants came from North India. Jha notes that up to the year 1870, almost 42 per cent of the total number of Indian immigrants to Trinidad came from Agra and Oudh; 29 per cent from Bihar and approximately 22 per cent from Bengal (1973: 28–30). The vast majority of these were Hindu, but there were also a number of Muslims, a minority of whom were Shiʿa. Indeed, the proportion of Hindus to Muslims at the latter part of the nineteenth century was essentially the same in North India as it was in Trinidad. For example, at the turn of the century, the census of India shows 85 per cent of the population in Uttar Pradesh were Hindus and 14 per cent Muslims while in Shahabad (in Bihar) 92 per cent were Hindus and 7 per cent Muslims; while the figures for Trinidad, just ten years earlier, show that almost 86 per cent of the Indians were Hindus and 13 per cent Muslims (Jha 1974: 5).

The province of Oudh (Awadh) was at the time of the initial recruitment of the indentured workers in 1845 ruled by a Shiʿa lineage of Persian descent and its capital, Lucknow, is still considered to be the centre of Indian Shiʿite culture (Hjortshoj 1987; Cole 1988; Pinault 1992). These rulers

> financed the construction of many mosques, funded madrasas, pilgrimages, and studies abroad for Shiʿi scholars and turned the commemoration of Muharram into an elaborate occasion of state in which Sunnis and Hindus participated in large numbers.
>
> (Hjortshoj 1987: 293)

The Muslims brought their sectarian practices with them to the Caribbean and the Shiʿa among them continued to commemorate, during the month of Muharram, the tragic martyrdom of Husain. The first celebration of the drama of Husain in Trinidad occurred in the 1850s when the first ta'ziyah was built at the Philippine Estate near Couva (Wood 1968: 152). Other estates (or plantations) followed, with friendly (and sometimes, not so friendly) competition developing between the estates in the construction of the ta'ziyahs and in the processions which followed. Workers on the estates, including Muslims, Hindus, Creoles and Chinese, donated funds for the construction of the ta'ziyahs. Intense competition between the estates developed focusing on the size and splendour of the ta'ziyahs, the number of people in the processions and the stamina, duration and 'sweetness' of the drumming. Precedence in the processions was, and still is, based on which group was historically first in constructing the ta'ziyah in that locale. Since the Philippine Estate at Couva is acknowledged to have been the first to build the ta'ziyah in the San Fernando region (the district of Naparima), it took precedence and led the procession. Despite the apparent general acceptance of this rule of precedence, conflicts often arose when others tried to ensure that their group should be first. This occurred, for example, in 1881 when an Indian overseer and supervisor at the Palmyra Estate, who interestingly is reported to have been a Hindu convert to Christianity rather than a Muslim, felt his ta'ziyah group should go first in the procession. A fight broke out and the supervisor was killed by members of the rival Philippine Estate (Singh 1988: 44–5, 122).

Processions were always potentially explosive situations since they involved mobility through a community and the domains or 'sacred space' of other religious groups (Yang 1980). Colonial government authorities, whether in India or the Caribbean, also retained for themselves the right to demarcate boundaries between 'us' and 'them' and the Muharram Massacre of 1884 in San Fernando was a prime example of this purported invasion of governmental 'sacred space'.[5] Trinidadian newspapers of the nineteenth century show the great alarm expressed by plantation owners, the British authorities and other colonists about the threat to public order of the Muharram rituals, as well as the carnival celebrations; fears no doubt exacerbated by what the latter referred to as the 'Indian mutiny' of 1857 (Singh 1988: 16). The Canadian Presbyterian Missionaries in particular found the practices of both carnival and Hosay quite reprehensible, and did all they could to have them banned as savage and barbaric affairs (Brereton 1979: 184–5; Singh 1988: 1–36). The Hosay, however, very quickly became the main symbol of Indian nationalism in the face of British colonialism and of a sense of identity vis-à-vis Indian minority status in the Black Caribbean. The Indians, or 'Coolies', as they were called, were generally disliked by the British, and resented by the Creoles who felt they were being pushed aside, economically, by the new wave of indentured workers, and such views were also encouraged by the dominant

Whites (Singh 1988: 3–8). Despite this ethnic exclusiveness, the Creoles and Indians joined together in the Hosay processions to protest various injustices, including the reduction of wages on the plantations and the concomitant increase in the workload (Brereton 1979: 183). And, indeed, one author has suggested that the Hosay gave symbolic form to a growing working-class consciousness throughout the Caribbean (Rodney 1981: 178).

THE HOSAY IN TRINIDAD TODAY

The Hosay is performed annually throughout Trinidad, albeit in certain traditionally specific locations. It is performed in Port of Spain, Couva, Tunapuna, Cedros, San Fernando, Arima and Tacarigua and a number of other even smaller towns and villages, such as Edinburgh Village, in the Chaguanas district. Until the Muharram Massacre of 1884, San Fernando, located in the heartland of the sugar estates, had been the major site of the Muharram celebrations. After that event the focus shifted to the St. James area north of the capital, Port of Spain, which was known, in the latter part of the nineteenth century, as 'Coolie Town' because of the concentration of Indians there (most of whom were, and are, Muslims; see Crowley 1954) in contrast to the predominantly Afro-Trinidadians in the rest of Port of Spain and the surrounding areas to the south (Singh 1988: 31).

The St. James Hosay is the best organized, the most elaborate and colourful as well as the most well-attended ceremony drawing thousands of people who come not only from the city and its suburbs but also from other areas of Trinidad. It is organized by six Shi'a Muslim extended families comprising, perhaps, some 200 individuals.[6] Of the six families, four are involved in the construction of the *ta'ziyah* while the other two families specialize in the construction of the so-called 'Moon'. One family builds the 'Moon of Husain' while another the 'Moon of Hasan'.[7]

Three of the *ta'ziyahs* are privately financed solely by the individual families that are responsible for their construction (the cost in the summer of 1990 was estimated by builders at about TT$15,000 or $6,200 US each). One, however, is known as the Village *Ta'ziyah* or Panchayati *Ta'ziyah* which is sponsored by the community and which must be built each year. The family responsible for its actual construction is the only one entitled, by community agreement, to collect public contributions in order to build the *ta'ziyah*. The Village *Ta'ziyah* also has the place of honour at the head of the Hosay procession when the *ta'ziyahs* are paraded on the streets. The other *ta'ziyahs* follow each other in order of seniority based on the year in which the family first began to construct *ta'ziyahs*, with the most recently built coming last. Thus, the Village *Ta'ziyah* is first, the Gholam Husain *Ta'ziyah* second, the Cocorite *Ta'ziyah* third and the Ali family *Ta'ziyah* last.[8] The Village *Ta'ziyah* is based on the historical precedent set on the sugar estates in the nineteenth century when all workers on the estates contributed a portion of their meagre earnings to finance the ta'ziyah. In India, Fruzzetti has noted a similar pattern of precedence: 'the tazziya from the para [i.e., neighbourhood] of the mosque will be at the front of the procession and the rest will follow accordingly'; she also points out that people of that neighbourhood contribute money for the construction of the ta'ziyah (1981: 104).

The ta'ziyah is constructed largely of bamboo sticks, some wood, cardboard, styrotex, tin foil and other types of decorations.[9] It varies in height, but averages ten to fifteen feet with the entire structure covered in many colours of bright tin foil, with added variations depending on the design in a given year with strings of coloured lights, flowers, mirrors, or coloured cloth (Bettelheim and Nunley 1988 have excellent colour photographs of the Hosay). Foil decorations and styrofoam balls (bought as Christmas decorations) are used as well to create a dazzling display. The upper section is decorated with domes of varying shapes and sizes, turrets – some round, some square – and finials attached to the domes and turrets. Set into the walls – both upper and lower – are recessed ojivals, large rosettes, floral motifs and other geometric patterns which are intricately cut out of styrotex, covered in foil and glued to the tin-foiled, cardboard surfaces (Bettelheim and Nunley 1988: 133). The whole structure is delicately worked by members of the families who have developed specialized skills and artistic talent, combined with an intense devotion to their cause.

These skills are handed down from one generation to the next, although not always in a direct line of descent. Collateral kin often take over responsibility for maintaining the ta'ziyah traditions. Even then, there are differential skills involved. Some are more artistically inclined than others and will take over the design and overseeing functions, while others assume responsibility for making and maintaining the drums. Still others contribute by finding sources for their needed raw materials both within Trinidad and abroad, while still others act as family representatives to the panchayat association[10] and through that group to the police and municipal authorities. Young boys take great pleasure in making the coloured flags while older and stronger boys take an active part in the drumming which requires a great deal of stamina.

The ta'ziyah is constructed with some degree of secrecy in the imambarah, a large enclosure dedicated to the Imam. It is built by an all male team of workers, many of whom are family members, who abstain from meat and sexual relations for the first ten days of Muharram. Women are not permitted inside the imambarah (i.e., while it is sanctified) and do not participate in the building of the ta'ziyah. Apparently this gender restriction does not apply to the building of ta'ziyahs in India (see Fruzzetti 1981: 105–6). Women do participate, however, in the ta'ziyah processions with young girls carrying flags, throwing rice and flower petals and, at least in the recent past, singing mournful laments (*marseeha*). Afro-Trinidadian males also take part in the building of the *ta'ziyah* and especially in the preparation of the drums. Although not Muslim, they are trusted to observe the rules of purity for entering the *imambarah*. Young, Afro-Trinidadian boys (roughly aged 8 to 17) also take an active part in drumming and form a large segment of the drummers in the procession. The Afro-Trinidadians, as team members, have important and skilled tasks to perform and their work is an integral part of the success of the Hosay. In fact, one builder of the *ta'ziyah* noted 'The Blacks – the Negroes – in our yard [and] in our *imambarah* especially – you get more negroes than Indians'. He noted further:

> we live in a cosmopolitan country; we are not living in the Middle East – Saudi Arabia, Iran or Iraq and these places. We are living in Trinidad . . . where 45% of the population is Negro and 42% is Indian. We must integrate. If you keep them out, you get lost. You can't be that selfish. . . . I've always maintained that the *ta'ziyah* in itself is a form of togetherness. It keeps us together.

When the *ta'ziyahs* and the moons come out for the daylight processions they glisten in the bright, intense tropical sunlight while at night, they radiantly reflect the street lights and neon signs and create a dazzling display of colour, light and design. Combined with the loud, intense rhythm of the drums, the dancing of the moons, the wailing and shouts of 'Hosay', 'Hosay', 'Hosay' and the tens of thousands of spectators who actively take part by shouting and dancing as well, the procession becomes an intense emotional experience for all participants.[11]

When the Hosay makes its appearance in the streets, what is a tragic ritual of religious significance to the East Indian Shi'a becomes redefined and transformed into public entertainment, into street theatre. As the procession gains momentum on the streets, it is met by more and more Afro-Trinidadians and other participants who join in as the emotional tension is heightened. 'The battle drums, with their deep and powerful sounds that seem to reverberate within one's insides, give a feeling of great excitement' (Ahye 1978: 63). A young, Afro-Trinidadian woman whom I interviewed among a gathering of Trinidadians of various racial, ethnic and religious groups had this to say about the drumming: 'there is the Gholam Husain [group] they're known for the sweetest drums. There is the Clarence Street – real *bacchanal* drum. (Another interjects, 'yes, yes, the hot drums'.) I would tap my toes because the drums are really sweet'. Many of the *tassa* drums have identifying 'names' painted on them as do the pan or steel-drums in carnival.[12] Some are traditional such as 'Husain', 'Karbala', 'Hasan', while others have such 'names' as 'Conan', 'Rock and Roll', or 'Poison'. This last 'name' is an interesting double-entendre in the best tradition of calypso in that it represents both a significant word in the Muharram tradition, namely the poison associated with the death of Hasan, as well as being the name of a currently popular hard rock group. The dancing of the moons is especially inviting, and gives an impetus and legitimacy to people to dance themselves, the bodily movements of which sometimes border on the erotic. As the Shi'a shout the chants, 'Hosay', 'Hosay', 'Hosay', spectators join in with slight, quickly spoken, modifications such as 'Hosay, I Say', 'Hosay, I say' the rhyming patterns of which are borrowed from the Calypso tradition in Trinidad.

People attend the Hosay not only for the music and dancing, but also to meet people, to flirt and have fun. One Afro-Trinidadian said: 'most of the young fellas [come to] look at the girls cause they jumpin' and dancin' '. Another commented, 'It has very nice people, nice people – nice women [laughing]. They usually come out – the youth usually come out – in their numbers and, I suppose, for – you know – having a good time.' Other young men (and women) confirmed that it is a good place to meet people and to follow up on whatever that may lead to. Sunni informants to whom I spoke even noted that because some of the parents are very strict, girls have secret boyfriends, 'and they're glad also for the night time to come to get a break, to come meet their boyfriends . . .'. Popular Indian foods, such as roti and various sweets, are available from street vendors along with the standard soft drinks. And a fête, which is what the Hosay is considered to be by most of the non-Muslim participants, would not be complete without the drinking of rum and beer.[13] It has been reported that in the rural areas, the Hosay is often associated with rum shops (Crowley 1954: 208), a statement partially confirmed by my informants, although only in reference to the so-called 'forty-day ta'ziyah'.[14] Several studies in India also note the drinking of alcoholic beverages during the Muharram processions (see Fruzzetti 1981: 104 and Saiyid *et al*. 1981: 127). Carnival is typically Trinidadian and many of its performance items, notably calypso and steelband, continue to be associated almost exclusively with Blacks, and the event as a whole is still known as the '*creole* [black] *bacchanal*' (Manning 1989: 141). There is no question that the Hosay is becoming a second 'creole bacchanal' and Shi'a informants recognize that changes have been occurring over which they seem to have little control:

> I would say it started about twenty years ago. The carnival atmosphere started creeping in, into the Hosay, the commemoration of the martyrdom of Imam Husain. The carnival spirit got into it more and more until it has completely taken over; completely taken over the Hosay celebrations now whilst it is being in the streets.
>
> We are six families, say with 25–30 people each, some 200 people – could we stop 30–40,000 people from drinking and dancing? Not even the police could stop them! No, not even the law could stop them – we

cannot! You dare not open your mouth to tell anyone anything, they will curse you; they will want to beat you.

In discussing their loss of control of the situation, several older Shi'a informants had nostalgic views of the colonial past, i.e., prior to 1962, when the British were in charge of public order; views which, however, are not completely borne out by the historical record as noted above with regard to the Muharram massacre of 1884 and other instances of colonial brutality and injustice during the indentureship period (Singh 1988: 1–36).

When Whites were here, there were rules and laws that prevented joyful behaviour. They respected our religion and didn't allow others to ruin it.

Another comment notes:

When I was a little boy we had the protection of the mounted police and we had very good behaviour. There was no dancing and getting on, on the street. We had very good behaviour. And, at one time, we had a South African Inspector in charge of the Mounted Police Branch. He would only allow the people directly connected with the celebration – or the observance, whatever you want to call it – to be allowed on the streets and the onlookers would have to be on the sidewalks . . . He was very strict about it and I wish they could come back now. But you can't attempt to do something like that now. We will have riots; we will have riots if you attempt to do anything like that now.

Still another view:

When you get thirty or forty thousand people looking forward to the Hosay celebrations – in St. James – the government cannot do anything to annoy a crowd like that, you know what I mean. Because any government, any government that comes into power in Trinidad, is always thinking about getting votes to form the next government.

CULTURAL HERITAGE AND CONTESTED MEANINGS

Clearly, the Shi'a are aware that they are losing control of being able to define the meaning of the public performances of the Muharram rituals. They admit they cannot stop the tens of thousands of spectators from doing what they wish during the Hosay. They recognize as well that social dynamics within their own community, and the larger society of which they are a part, have gone a long way in helping to reduce their control of the situation.

Many young East Indian Shi'a, for example, do not wish to carry on the Muharram rituals of commemoration. Nor are many of them, especially the secularly educated, strong in their Muslim faith. One young woman noted that neither she nor her brothers are interested in helping their father continue his *ta'ziyah* tradition and 'this bothers him a lot'. Young Indian boys do not wish to learn how to make and care for the drums, nor do many of them wish to continue the drumming itself, both of which activities are quite arduous. More and more young Afro-Trinidadians, then, are being brought in for this purpose, adding even further to the multi-cultural aspect of the Hosay. Women no longer weep or sing the *marseeha* and songs of lamentation for Imam Husain during the processions, since the younger generation does not speak Urdu and have not learned the traditional laments. Hence, 'Today, there is nobody remaining to do it; my nieces, the younger ones, walk behind the *ta'ziyah* but all they think about is what outfit they are going to wear – because the young ones are looking for boys.'

Members of the older generation believe that if they do not continue to construct the *ta'ziyah* and organize processions some evil or illness will befall the family. The younger generation listens to such explanations, however, with great scepticism and scorn. As well the younger generation does not accept the stories that are told of miraculous cures which occurred when promises were made to support the Hosay by building the *ta'ziyah* or by making financial contributions for its continuing success or the strong belief among many of the old timers that Imam Husain will reward, in this world, those who actively sustain the Hosay. Vows are made by individuals – Shi'a as well as non-Muslim Hindus and Afro-Trinidadians – that if a desired request is fulfilled, they will make a promise to support the Hosay in some way. The younger, more educated generation, view these explanations and practices as 'superstitions', which adds to their disenchantment and lack of enthusiasm for the Hosay.

Increasingly as well, the younger generation does not wish to be bound to marriages within the East Indian Shi'a community. Marriages with different racial, ethnic and religious groups, [especially Catholic, which accounts for about 37 per cent of the population against 6 or 7 per cent Muslim] are not at all uncommon, adding to a further weakening of support for the Hosay. One *ta'ziyah* builder noted: 'You don't get many pure Indians . . . my elder brother was married to a Negro girl, they have Negro children. In our family we have Indians, we have Negroes, we have Syrians, we have Portuguese, we have everybody.' Older generation parents do not like the changes that are occurring but feel they can do little about inter-ethnic and inter-religious marriages. They are especially concerned about the religious training of children: 'But she keeps up her Islamic things and he keeps up his Hindu practices. The problem arises with the children – in bringing up the children.'

Ironically, while racial and ethnic intermarriages are lamented on the one hand, on the other some of these same Indian Shi'a informants view what is happening as an affirmation of the liberal-mindedness and multiculturalism of Trinidadians: 'If, throughout the world you had more people like us, or the way we think, you would have a much better place to live.'

In addition to changes in the social dynamics of the Shiʿa community, the supporters of the Hosay also contribute in other ways to their loss of power in defining the situation. Seemingly, however, they are not aware of the implications of their actions. They are, themselves, facilitating the re-negotiation of the meaning of the Muharram commemorations by using concepts, patterns of behaviour and images and symbols derived from the wider society's carnival domain, as well as from the field of popular culture, rather than from a strictly Shiʿa religious sphere.

For example, the phrase 'coming out' is used by the Shiʿa in reference to the *taʿziyah* making its public appearance. It is a term borrowed from carnival referring to the costumed bands of maskers who enter the public arena after leaving their yards. The 'yards', another carnival term, are private places where both the *taʿziyahs* and the carnival costumes are made in secret, as well as where the steel-bands practise. All of these groups come out of the yards and present themselves, on their respective occasions, in their full colour and regalia. The use of such terms by the Shiʿa invites others to define the situation as an aspect or extension of carnival. These 'others' also use concepts, such as 'bacchanal', 'fête', 'jump-up', 'shake-up', 'ball', for characterizing Hosay which gives further legitimacy to the redefinition as a fête or carnival-type occasion. As well, the multi-racial team approach and assembly-line techniques which go into the making of the *taʿziyah* resemble the processes of the carnival/*mas* camps and yards (Bettelheim and Nunley 1988: 128, Figure 99). The fact that Afro-Trinidadians not only participate in the making of the *taʿziyah*, moons and drums but are encouraged to take over the drumming processions themselves adds to the public, participatory character of the Hosay. The cues given off indicate that it is not an exclusive ritual but a public performance, open to all. The bright colours and ornamentation of the *taʿziyah* and the moons also adds to the carnival, fête-like atmosphere. In addition, both the moons and the *taʿziyah* are recognized as innovative, creative works of art to be admired as objects in and of themselves independent of their religious meaning to their builders. Some Sunnis have told me that they participate in the Hosay in order to see the beauty of the *taʿziyahs*, following them each year as they become more elaborate and imaginative; while acknowledging that they try to avoid being caught up in the fête atmosphere. As in carnival, there is strong competition between the designers of the *taʿziyahs* for the most attractive and innovative Hosay which the spectators informally evaluate and rank. Such competitiveness is the main reason for secrecy in building the *taʿziyah* as it is in carnival. The drumming groups representing each *taʿziyah* family also compete with each other in exactly the same way that the steel-drum (Pan) bands compete during carnival. It should also be noted here that the Hosay drumming

made an important contribution to the development of Trinidadian steelband music. J. D. Elder, quoting W. Austin Simmonds, speaks of the
development of the steelband in the 1940s and notes that

> Violence led finally to a legal ban on this type of music. It was considered
> the music of the slums and only vagabonds played and enjoyed it. Once
> again, a new channel, a new outlet for the musical aspirations of an
> inherently musical people had to be found. This time it was the East
> Indian Husain Festival that came to its rescue.
>
> The East Indian indentured labourer was guaranteed religious free-
> dom . . . his drum festivals were never banned in Trinidad. Therefore at
> the annual Husain Festival . . . elaborately made temples of paper and
> bamboo are paraded through the streets to the accompaniment of
> drums. Indian drums made of goat skin heads on tubular wooden bodies
> are hung from the waist by leather thongs. . . . Simmonds argued that
> this influenced the earlier clandestine steel drummers to discard their
> tubes and iron bars and to use the tops of paint pans and other drums
> hung from the waist, e.g., the early 'cut and tumble' drummers of the
> BAR-20 a famous 'band' of Port-of-Spain, later drums were hung from
> the neck.
>
> Soon government authorities set up a committee to release the drum-
> mers from their legal ban and to develop this indigenous talent. . . . On
> the night that Governor Shaw danced to the strains of the steelband, and
> called for more . . . Steelband music had arrived.
>
> (Elder 1969: 19)

Popular names such as 'Conan', 'Rock and Roll', and 'Poison' which are
painted on the *tassa* drums, as was mentioned earlier, are not only copied
from the steel-drum/calypso domain and the field of popular culture, but
also further invite the redefinition of the situation from that of a religious
ritual to that which is secular, joyful and fun.

In trying to maintain some degree of control in defining the Hosay
situation, many Shi'a are redefining the meaning to suit the changed
circumstances. All acknowledge there is no joy in the death of anyone,
especially a revered descendant of the Prophet. Yet Husain's death and
sacrifice was instrumental in saving Islam, in preserving the true faith from
the corruption of Yazid. 'He died to protect Islam and his death should be
marked both by sorrow *and* happiness . . . So the atmosphere of elation
which is generated by those Muslims who participate in the Hosain festival
is definitely justifiable' (Ali 1990). This re-focus away from what had been
a tragic commemoration (the weeping and the singing of *marseeha*/tragic
lamentations) to one where joy is at least an acceptable additional value is
partially an attempt to regain control from the crowds; or at best an
accommodation to the inevitable.

Nevertheless, it is very likely that as the younger generation of educated

East Indians continue to move away from supporting the Hosay, it will continue to be taken over by others and continued as one of the major fêtes and festival occasions of Trinidad. One builder of the *ta'ziyah* noted: 'Changes are taking place with this commemoration; but the changes that are taking place will see the *ta'ziyah* become more oriented to the island's culture than to a select few . . . it has become part of Trinidad culture.'

A major problem facing the Muslim community is the uncertainty and ambiguity of their self-identity and heritage. Many of them seem to have a problem in being 'Indian' and 'Muslim' in a 'Trinidadian' context; an ambiguity which seems to have a great deal to do with the international revivalist movements within Islam, especially the success of the Islamic revolution in Iran.

The majority traditional-conservative Indian Muslim community in Trinidad exists with two apparently contradictory pulls on his [*sic*] consciousness and identity: that of being Indian, his race and that of Islam, his religion . . .

The Indian Muslim ambivalence has had its logical conclusion among the younger generation of Indian Muslim organizations. There is now a repudiation of their Indianness, of Indian identity, of self and hence a rejection of their conservative-traditional elders and organizations (TIA, ASJA, TML) [i.e, the Tackweyatul Islamic Association, the Anjuman Sunnatul Jamaat Association and the Trinidad Muslim League, respectively; Kasule notes that the TML is '*Ghair Muqallid*, i.e, does not belong to any of the four orthodox schools of law' (1986: 204)] who are now viewed as being too Indian, meaning 'Hindu'. They submerge themselves with a new Islamic personality, identity and consciousness, a new self. Pure and fundamentalist Islam creates in the Indian Muslim a new Islamic personality, one which rejects all aspects of Indianness – his historical experience as an Indian, Indian cultural survivals. These are now viewed as un-Islamic. There is a denial of race in this new Islamic theology; it becomes insignificant, even non-existent . . .

(Ryan 1991: 113, citing the Indian Review, August 1990)

Muslims in Trinidad generally feel a greater affinity for Hindus who make up the majority of fellow Indians than they do for other ethnic groups. Despite this, however, laments are expressed that this has led to the assimilation of Hindu practices into Muslim rituals and festivities (Ryan 1991: 114); an apparent attack on the Hosay festival.[15] Kasule notes that '95% of Trinidadian Muslims adhere to Islamic practices and teachings as they were imported from India a 100 years ago. Some of these may not be acceptable on valid theological grounds . . . Any attempt to correct even misconceptions and malpractices has been resisted' (1986: 201).

Thus, from the perspective of the Sunni, one of the problems with the Shi'a, aside from traditional Sunni dissatisfaction with their emphasis on the 'Alids and the consequent veneration of the Imams, is the association of the Hosay with Hindu religious and cultural influences; influences from a religion long felt to be idolatrous. The varying religious interpretations of the symbolism and meaning of the Muharram rituals[16] is thus not only a long-standing theological debate but one that is now also tinged with the problematic question of the Trinidadian Muslim's Indian heritage; a heritage and way of life now subject to scrutiny as never before.

At another level, this doctrinal conflict surfaces in Trinidad with regard to the representation of Islam to the wider social and political community. That is, it centres on the conception of the 'proper' image of Islam and which group shall represent that image to the government and to the world.

The leadership of the Sunni Muslim community tends to be wealthy and religiously conservative, with an organizational base in the Anjuman Sunnatul Jamaat Association of Trinidad and Tobago (ASJA), the largest and most powerful Islamic organization in the country (Kasule 1986: 203). They maintain a good deal of control over the Muslim community and its ideological direction. Part of their power and influence in the community centres about their ability to acquire assistance, in many forms, from the international Muslim community, especially Saudi Arabia and Egypt while rival Muslim groups, (especially the Afro-focused Jamaat al Muslimeen), tend to receive aid from Libya and other such revolutionary inclined Muslim states. Many of these conservative leaders fear the possibility of an Iranian-style Islamic revolution led by groups such as the Jamaat al Muslimeen; a concern not without some empirical justification given the attempted coup by that group in July 1990. Thus, they fear for their own power and conservative influence in the local Muslim community, especially among the youth.

While the Trinidadian government recognizes the Sunni ASJA as the official spokesgroup of the Muslims in the country, it nevertheless highlights the Shi'a Hosay festival in its tourist brochures. The Trinidadian government, especially since the decline of oil revenues, has turned to tourism to gain needed foreign currency and has not hesitated to exploit its 'natural' cultural resources – the cultural performances and tourist 'productions' of its heterogeneous society. Indeed, it is seeking an authentic cultural mandate which it can call its own in the competition for the international tourist dollar. Carnival and the music of the steel-band or 'Pan' are two of the most important ethnic practices which have become objectified and displayed as heritage objects, distinctive of Trinidad as a national entity. 'Carnival and Jonkonnu are unashamedly Afro-Creole or Euro-African expressions, claiming a particular authenticity over Divali (Festival of Lights) and Hosay as genuine ancestral Caribbean expressions' (Nettleford 1988: 193). Thus, while Carnival is largely an Afrocentric spectacle reflecting the very essence of the Trinidadian colonial experience with its borrowings from the French carnival and *cannes brulées/canboulay*, the Hosay represents to the government the Indian and, by extension, the broader multicultural unity of the country and hence a value to be exploited by the government. The Hosay is now also, as noted earlier, the second most important cultural festival in Trinidad. With government Tourist Office sanctioning given to this ritual and its associated creolization process, the Hosay is increasingly becoming a 'temple of authenticity', to use Handler's term (1986).[17] In many respects the *ta'ziyah* has become a moving, processional museum display; an objectification not only of the architectural beauty, colours and display of the *ta'ziyah*, but also, and more importantly, the embodiment of the ethos of the 'fête' – the oneness and brotherhood of a heterogeneous society. Indeed, *ta'ziyahs* have been produced for museum displays at the National Museum in Port of Spain as well as becoming part of the St. Louis Art Museum exhibition *Caribbean Festival Arts: each and every bit of difference* (Nunley and Bettelheim 1988). It has even been used to celebrate Trinidad's national day of Independence:

Another part of Trinidad and Tobago has been capturing the hearts of New Yorkers. This time, it's the Hosay. On August 31, while this country celebrated its Independence [i.e, Trinidad], scores of Yankees looked on and paid tribute to the country's Hosay which was displayed throughout the streets. In fact, so pleased were the Americans that local Hosay builder Gould Mohammed, who has been travelling to the U.S. for the past eight years, was recently presented with two trophies in appreciation of his outstanding contribution to Hosay in that country.
(*Sunday Guardian*, 16 October 1988)

The Shi'a, for their part, join their Sunni brothers in seeing such objectifications as a 'mockery'. One Shi'a *ta'ziyah* builder, in turning down an offer to build a *ta'ziyah* at a time other than Muharram, said:

I personally would not be able to look after that because then I would be making a mockery of what I believe in; of what I stand for. The *ta'ziyah* is something I believe in, my heart, my soul, my everything is in it and I'm not going to make a mockery of it by going and building a *ta'ziyah* at any time of year – just for a show . . . no, no, no!

The symbolism associated with the Hosay in Trinidadian commemorations is multivocal and polysemic, i.e., it is open to numerous interpretations depending on one's cultural and historically conditioned predispositions. Each of the social groups discussed has its own view of what is really true and authentic about the occasion, and attempt to make their definition of the situation prevail.

What is presently occurring then is an implicit process of negotiation which is defining and socially creating the reality of Hosay in the nation-state of Trinidad.[18] In many respects the Hosay is a microcosm of the 'politics of cultural struggle' (Williams 1991: 3) through which a former colony attempts to assert its national identity on the world stage. The negotiation and debate which the people of Trinidad are engaged in at the moment is similar to one which was argued, and lost, in Guyana over the same Muharram ritual (Williams 1990; Mangru 1993). That is, how to take elements of a historically produced heterogeneity, expressed in one instance in the culturally authentic Hosay festival, and blend it into a homogeneous national consciousness; without, at the same time, devaluing them or denying the original source of their contribution. In Guyana, the Sunni Muslim community was able, in the 1930s, to put an end to the *tadjah*, as it is known in Guyana, because they felt it was a mockery of Islamic values and a misrepresentation of their conception of Islam. They used their political power to force the government to ban the commemorations and processions (see Mangru 1993; Williams 1990; Bettelheim and Nunley 1988). Fox, in whose edited book the article by Williams appears, states that 'given the compartmentalized ethnic "traditions" sponsored by colonialism, Muslims were still thought to have rights over this part of Guyanese national culture' (1990: 9) and further he notes that 'Williams presents a case of "malpractice": a Guyanese national cultural practice is judged inauthentic and ruled out of existence as ethnic populations contest over cultural heritage'. What is interesting about Fox's comments and those, of course, of Williams, is the question: who 'owns' the 'rights' to a religious ritual? It may seem like a patently ridiculous question on the surface, but the issue of authenticity and multivocality lies at the very heart of this question, for if various religious and ethnic groups participate in a ritual such as the Hosay and give it idiosyncratic meanings, is it then not 'theirs', as well as belonging to those who organize and sponsor such rituals, who have a different meaning of its 'truth'? Has it not become, as Fox phrases it, a 'national cultural practice'? (see Cohen 1993: 75–7; Harrison 1992; Merryman 1986). In a very real sense the Hosay is an articulation of social and cultural differences and similarities and in the discursive process a ritual and social world is given meaning; but a meaning which is always contestable and open to re-articulations. It is a never ending process of negotiation. What it was in India, it is not today; and what it is today, it will not be tomorrow, although in that process various participants try to fix its meaning to reflect their view of the world.

With Afro-Trinidadians actively participating in the Hosay and turning it into a fête, they are, by their actions, saying they have a society which is free, pluralistic and 'of the people'; one which, at least on the surface, harbours no hostility between the 'races' and is religiously tolerant. The fête is the very embodiment of brotherhood and sisterhood; a Trinidadian way of obviating and reducing tensions and conflicts.

It can be said that the keystone of Creole culture is the festival or 'fete', culminating in the biggest fete of all, Carnival. A fete can be anything from a drink of rum and a quiet card game, to a bongo wake, to an elegant house party, to the two-day delirium preceding Lent to a month-long binge. But fete is what makes life worth living; it is the focus of Trinidadian culture. When the 'brown coolies' arrived, the Negroes soon discovered that they too had fetes. What gulfs existed between cultures and religions were bridged by enthusiasm for the fete, and little by little, through participation and conscious and unconscious mutual borrowing, the fetes of the two people have grown to have many features in common. These fetes provide an invaluable meeting-ground of common interest and understanding among all Trinidadians.

(Crowley 1954: 202)

In a secular sense, the Hosay, as a fête, is the affirmation of what the practitioners of Islam – an ecumenical Islam – have not been able to do among themselves – namely, foster a sense of togetherness and harmony in Trinidadian society. A new, socially constructed reality is in the process of creation, with the Hosay at centre stage; but a reality that is part of an 'Age of Uncertainty and Incompleteness' (Ahmed 1992: 11).

NOTES

1 The majority of Trinidadians refer to the Muharram rituals as 'Hosay', or 'Hosse', a vernacular form of Husain. The word refers both to the physical structure of the replica of the tomb of Husain which is carried in procession, as well as to the event itself. Older generation Shi'a Muslims in Trinidad who enact the Muharram rituals tend to follow the usage in India and use the Arabic word *ta'ziyah*, literally meaning 'mourning, condolence', for the tomb replica. It is pronounced in the Trinidadian patois as 'tajah' 'tadjah', 'tadjieh', 'tazia'. In Guyana it is known as 'tadjah' (Mangru 1993; Williams 1990).

2 The word 'festival' is in common use in much of the literature on Muharram rituals. Non-Muslim Trinidadians themselves refer to the Hosay as a 'fête', originally from the French meaning 'festival'. Fruzzetti also uses 'festival' in discussing her research on the Muharram rituals of India, but notes that she does so because it is a translation from two Bengali terms *utsob* (1981: 91, fn. 1) and *porob* (1981: 107). Herklots' translation of Ja'far Sharif's *Islam in India or the Qanun-i Islam* titles Chapter XIV 'The Muharram Festival' (Sharif 1972: 151), while Bettelheim and Nunley title their chapter, 'The Hosay Festival' (1988: 119). Trinidadian Shi'a dislike the term.

3 The issue of 'ownership' of intellectual property, such as rituals and ceremonial performances such as carnival, is the topic of a number of recent books and articles. Harrison (1992; 1993) discusses the theoretical implications of property rights in ritual symbolism in a comparative perspective, while Abner Cohen (1983; 1993) explores the politics of carnival and the issue of property rights in his account of the Notting Hill Carnival in London. He notes that local West Indians explicitly claim 'ownership' of carnival: 'Carnival is part of the cultural and artistic expression of the slave community. . . . It is an outward expression

of everything that is West Indian' (1993: 76). See also, Coombe (1992); Graham (1987) and Merryman (1986).

In nineteenth-century British Guiana, during a trial of a group of Creoles who had held their own *tadjah* [Hosay] ceremonies, in which they incorporated African rites which the law did not permit, the British Magistrate censured them 'for observing a ceremony which had absolutely nothing to do with their cultural traditions, as they apparently had no similar saintlike hero, whereas the Indian *tadjah* was institutionalised' (Mangru 1993: 22).

4 The 1990 coup attempt in Trinidad was organized by a group of Muslim Afro-Trinidadians (the Jamaat al Muslimeen) who have been trying to resurrect Islam among Blacks and to restore pride in their ancestral Muslim heritage (see Ryan 1991).

5 'The celebration of Hosein, involving large numbers of Indians and working class Creoles, began to cause anxiety in the early 1870s, because of the allegedly increasing tendency to riotous behaviour. The anxiety was increased in the 1880s, when discontent among the estate-resident Indians was widespread because of a reduction of wages and the lengthening of tasks. Further, police action against Carnival in 1881–4 prepared the way for the authorities to move against Hosein. The Hamilton Report on the 1881 Carnival riots had made the point that Hosein should also be regulated to prevent it from developing into a disorderly affair like Canboulay. Hamilton thought that it would be a grievance if any privilege, such as the right to carry torches on a public street, was given to the Indians but withheld from the Creoles. Accordingly, regulations were issued in 1884 to prevent Indians celebrating Hosein from entering Port of Spain or San Fernando, and from going along any public highway in procession. Excitement among estate-resident Indians mounted, the authorities prepared for confrontation, and the result was a major disaster in San Fernando, where 12 Indians were killed and 104 injured. Despite this massacre, the Government was determined to enforce the regulations rigidly in 1885 and subsequently, and the celebration of Hosein between 1885 and 1900 was restrained and orderly. One of the objects of the 1884 regulations was to prevent Creoles from participating in Hosein, and gradually after 1885 they withdrew from it' (Brereton 1979: 183).

6 This is based on explicit statements by several members of different families presently involved in constructing the *ta'ziyahs*. Singh, on the other hand, notes that there are twelve Shi'a families remaining in the St. James area (1988: 41, fn. 141).

7 The crescent-shaped Moon of Husain and Moon of Hasan are built of bamboo sticks which radiate out from a central supporting pole carried in a waist-pouch by a handler. The frame is covered with cardboard and decorated with tin foil, cloth, mirrors and other reflecting objects. Along the crescent curve, sharp blades are inserted between the material, projecting in a sort of spiked effect symbolic of the battle of Karbala. Peacock feathers add to the display, while decorative, coloured rosettes are interspersed among the mirrors. The Moon of Husain is always red, symbolic of the blood he shed for Islam; while the Moon of Hasan is coloured green, symbolic of his poisoning. The cadence of the procession's drums govern the motion of the 'dancing' of the moons, inspiring each moon to jump and move rapidly about requiring great strength, stamina and dexterity. Since the procession takes some $3\frac{1}{2}$ hours to proceed to its goal and another $3\frac{1}{2}$ hours to return, individuals take turns 'dancing' the moon for which, they believe, they receive religious blessings.

The moons may be based on the *nal sahib*, or 'sacred horseshoe' symbol used in the Muharram processions in India (Bettelheim and Nunley 1988: 131; see also Sharif 1972: 162 for a detailed discussion of the *nal sahib*).

8 In the Hosay processions at present in Port of Spain, the Village or Panchayati *Taʿziyah* takes the lead, as noted. However, one of the *taʿziyahs* is made by a family in the Cocorite suburb of Port of Spain and must make a long journey to join the procession at its staging area in the St. James district and proceed with it to its final destination, the Queen's Royal College grounds and then return home. Because of a government curfew by which time all processions must be off the streets, the place of precedence is reversed on the return journey with the Cocorite *taʿziyah* taking the lead from the Village *Taʿziyah* in order to reach home by the curfew time.

9 Tin foil used to be imported from England and Germany and sold in local bookstores. However, since the oil crisis of the 1960s and restrictions on foreign exchange, tin foil is no longer imported and individual families must find their own means to acquire this essential item. Most obtain it through relatives in the United States, who send it to them and for which they pay the required customs duties. Despite the importance of the Hosay as a tourist attraction, there is no direct or indirect government support for this 'festival' nor its needed supplies.

10 The *panchayat* coordinates Hosay activities among the families and liaises with municipal authorities to ensure that no problems arise. It also ensures that any conflicts between families find their expression in the drumming and not in any overt hostility. The *panchayat* is made up of six representatives, one from each family. Although the *panchayat* has a venerable history in Indian society as essentially a council of elders in village communities, the immediate precedent for this was the requirement established in Ordinance No. 9 of 1882: 'Indian immigrants living on any plantation or in any village intending to celebrate the Mohurrum Festival . . . must choose from amongst themselves headmen, not exceeding six in number, whose duty it will be to regulate, control and take charge of any such procession' (see Singh 1988: 80).

11 While the first ten days of Muharram are very important, the most significant days are the eighth to the tenth as these recall the imminent battle at Karbala, culminating with Husain's death on the tenth. It is during these days and nights that the procession takes place.

The eighth of Muharram is known as flag night. The flags are understood to represent the standard bearers of Husain; the people who are going to be with him and support him as he prepares to go into battle. Two days later the flagpoles are destroyed and the cloth flags themselves are used to tie the *tassa* drums around the necks of the drummers as they symbolically go into battle on the tenth of Muharram. On the evening of the eighth, the flags, which had earlier been prepared, are brought onto the *chauk* (a consecrated area of the yard on which prayers are said) and the evening prayers are performed. At about 11:00 p.m. they leave the yard and 'come out' into the streets for the procession of flags which continues until 4:00 a.m. which is the time set by the government for the procession to be off the streets. At this time they return to their yards and place the flags again on the *chauk* until the next evening.

Each *taʿziyah* builder has two flags which represent the family and are often carried by a prominent woman member of the family in the procession. Almost all of the flags are consecrated to the procession and emblematic of a vow by family members or anyone else in the community, including non-Muslim Afro-Trinidadians and others. In recent years so many flags have been consecrated, and so few people are there to carry them in the procession, that a wheeled platform, known as a *katieh*, is built on which the flags may be placed in a raised position, to highlight the number of supporters of Husain in his time of need. There is a widespread belief in the community – both Shi'a Muslim and non-Muslim – that support for Husain and, therefore, the Hosay, will bring blessings and help to the individual and his or her family.

The next night, the ninth, is known as 'Little Hosay Night'. At about the same time in the evening (11:00 p.m.), small (about six feet in height), less elaborately decorated, *ta'ziyahs* said to represent the tomb of Hasan, Husain's brother, 'come out' from the yards and are paraded on the streets along with the flags. The two moons of Husain and Hasan also make their first appearance at this time and when the two moons meet in the procession each of the moons touches the other in a symbolic kiss of brotherhood and solidarity. The procession again continues until 4:00 a.m.; but all of the flagpoles must be destroyed by 6:00 a.m., with the exception of the cloth flags themselves and the *alams*, or battle symbols, which top the flagpoles.

A few hours later, which is the later morning of the tenth, the main procession begins with the parading of the big *ta'ziyahs*, the moons and the beating of the battle drums. The *ta'ziyahs* 'come out' at 12:00 noon and join together in their pre-planned order of seniority and join with the Moons. The Moon of Hasan touches each of the *ta'ziyahs* as it passes by in a symbolic kiss believed to release the spirits of the brothers. They parade through the streets of the St. James district on their way to the Queen's Royal College Grounds, which is their destination. Queen Victoria allowed the *ta'ziyah* organizers to consecrate a small area on the grounds of the College as the Karbala – the place at which Husain and his followers met their deaths; and it is to this place that the procession proceeds. They arrive about 3:30 p.m., have a prayer service for a half hour and then make their way back along the same route to their individual yards where they arrive about 7:00 p.m. At this point, on the evening of the tenth day, the *ta'ziyah* is considered 'dead', and the period of abstinence at an end. Three days later, a day known as *tija*, the *ta'ziyah* is chopped and broken apart with axes, saws and hammers and the pieces placed in trucks and transported to the shoreline of the Gulf of Paria where the pieces are placed in the water and allowed to drift out to sea. The Hosay is thus ended for another year.

12 'Pan' is the commonly used term in Trinidad for the steel drum when used as an instrument played by the steelbands. It derives from the earliest attempts to make music from metal containers such as old pots, pans, garbage cans, and empty biscuit containers (Simmonds n.d.: 8). *Tassa* drums are small clay or wooden drums, covered with goatskin, which are hung from the neck and played with the hands. They are used to complement much larger drums used in the Muharram processions and together symbolize battle drums putatively associated with the battle at Karbala.

13 One elderly informant recalled that in his youth 'they used to – here in the district of St. James – at each corner during the Hosay processions, you would find someone with sweetened water – water sweetened with sugar – giving to everyone who was there; calling out 'Have a drink', 'Have a drink', and the significance was the remembrance of those who were denied water to drink. Now people want beer, they want beer and coke and rum; nobody wants water'.

14 The 'forty-day *ta'ziyah*' was reported by informants to refer to *ta'ziyahs* that were built in the countryside in the past (emphatically denied for the St. James area of Port of Spain) and displayed on the fortieth day after 'Ashura. It was built for display at rum shops and a 'big fête was held that day with the rum shops open and you sell any amount of rum because the Indian people like to drink a lot of rum. This used to happen, but it has stopped. There is only one

place – no, there are two or three places now – building forty-day *taʿziyahs*. One that is being built in Tunapuna, but this has no rum-drinking business with it; no rum shop business. There is one being built in Tacarigua; again no rum drinking business; and I think there is one being built in Cedros'. In Iran the fortieth day after Imam Husain's death falls on the twentieth of Safar, the second month of the Muslim calendar and is a day of tragic commemoration. Mangru also discusses the association of the *taʿziyah* with rum shops in former British Guiana (1993: 14–15).

15 In his studies of Muharram rituals in Hyderabad, Pinault notes 'the obvious influence of Hindu ritual on Hyderabadi Shiite observances. This is understandable given the overwhelmingly Hindu milieu in which Hyderabad's Shiites have survived. Reform-minded Muslims sometimes complain of this persistent influence. Shiites whom I questioned, however, described this syncretism as a kind of strength: the external borrowing from Hinduism, they said, helped attract the many Hindus who visit Hyderabad's Shiite shrines and offer homage to Husain during the month of Muharram' (1992: 61–2; see also his chapter 'Muharram Liturgies and Hindu-Muslim Relations in Hyderabad', pp. 153–65).

16 It is important to point out that throughout the Muslim world the Sunni commemorate, in various ways, the death of Husain at Karbala. It is seen as a distinct tragedy in the history of Islam and even such great scholars as Abu Hanifa and al-Shafiʿi, founders of the two major schools of Islamic law and interpretation, wrote poetic elegies of Husain and the martyrs of Karbala (see Mahdjoub 1988). Nevertheless, there has historically been strong antagonism between Sunni and Shiʿa.

17 Apart from Handler's phrasing here, many non-Muslim participants in the Hosay themselves refer to the *taʿziyah* as a 'temple' or 'church'. Its architectural features often resemble a mosque with minarets and domes and they also know it as an object which is accorded respect, veneration and 'sacredness'.

18 'The tadjah at Edinburgh Village, Chaguanas, was actually designed and executed, and the ceremonies carried out by a pious Hindu, Baboolal Lahouri, who was also responsible for the *Ramleela* held there the month before. At both fetes the bass drum was played by a Barbadian Negro complete with "limeskin" hat. The local sadhu explained that although the Muslims had introduced the fete, the Hindus had taken it up. He added that of the two brothers, Hasan and Hosein, one had been a Muslim and the other a Hindu, and they died together battling over their Faiths. People now make the tadjahs to commemorate their deaths, and "to show we should all live in unity together . . ." ' (Crowley 1954: 207).

REFERENCES

Ahmed, A. S. (1992) *Postmodernism and Islam*, London: Routledge.

Ahye, M. (1978) *Golden Heritage: The Dance in Trinidad and Tobago*, Republic of Trinidad and Tobago: Heritage Cultures Ltd.

Ali, Shair (1990) 'Hosay: Symbols of Martyrdom', in *Trinidad Guardian*, 17 July 1990.

Bettelheim, J. and Nunley, J. (1988) 'The Hosay Festival', in J. Nunley, and J. Bettelheim (eds) *Caribbean Festival Arts*, Seattle: University of Washington Press.

Brereton, B. (1979) *Race Relations in Colonial Trinidad 1870–1900*, Cambridge: Cambridge University Press.

Chelkowski, P. (1979) *Ta'ziyeh: Ritual and Drama in Iran*, New York: New York University Press.

— (1986) 'Popular Shi'i Mourning Rituals', *Al-Serāt* XII, 1: 209–26.

Cohen, A. (1983) 'Drama and Politics in the Development of a London Carnival', in M. J. Aronoff (ed.) *Culture and Political Change*, New Jersey: Transaction Books.

— (1993) *Masquerade Politics: Explorations in the Structure of Urban Cultural Movements*, Oxford: Berg Publishers Ltd.

Cole, J. (1988) *Roots of North Indian Shi'ism in Iran and Iraq: Religion and State in Awadh, 1722–1859*, Berkeley: University of California Press.

Coombe, R. (1992) 'Author/izing the Celebrity: Publicity Rights, Postmodern Politics and Unauthorized Genders', in *Cardozo Arts and Entertainment Law Journal*, 10(2): 365–95.

Crowley, D. (1954) 'East Indian Festivals in Trinidad Life', in *Caribbean Commission Monthly Bulletin*, VII April: 202–8.

Elder, J. D. (1969) *From Congo Drum to Steelband*, Trinidad: University of the West Indies.

Fox, R. G. (ed.) (1990) *Nationalist Ideologies and the Production of National Cultures*, American Ethnological Society Monograph No. 2, Washington, D.C.

Fruzzetti, L. (1981) 'Muslim Rituals: Household rites vs. Public Festivals in Rural India', in Imtiaz Ahmad (ed.) *Ritual and Religion Among Muslims in India*, New Delhi: Manohar Press.

Gaborieau, M. (1985) 'From Al-Beruni to Jinnah: Idiom, ritual and ideology of the Hindu-Muslim confrontation in South Asia', *Anthropology Today* 1(3): 7–14.

Graham, M. (1987) 'Protection and Reversion of Cultural Property: Issues of Definition and Justification', in *International Lawyer*, 21(3): 755–93.

Handler, R. (1986) 'Authenticity', *Anthropology Today* 2(1): 2–4.

Harrison, S. (1992) 'Ritual as Intellectual Property', *Man (N.S.)*, 27(2): 225–44.

— (1993) 'The Commerce of Cultures in Melanesia', *Man (N.S.)*, 28(1): 139–58.

Hill, E. (1972) *The Trinidad Carnival: Mandate for a National Theatre*, Austin: University of Texas Press.

Hjortshoj, K. (1987) 'Shi'i Identity and the Significance of Muharram in Lucknow, India', in Martin Kramer (ed.) *Shi'ism, Resistance and Revolution*, Boulder, CO: Westview Press.

Hossain, S. (1990) 'Ta'zia: Ephemeral Architecture in India', in *MIMAR: Architecture in Development*, 35, June 1990: 10–17.

Jha, J. C. (1973) 'Indian Heritage in Trinidad, West Indies', in *Caribbean Quarterly*, 19(2): 28–50.

— (1974) 'The Indian Heritage in Trinidad', in J. LaGuerre (ed.) *Calcutta to Caroni – The East Indians of Trinidad*, London: Longman Group Ltd.

Kasule, O. (1986) 'Muslims in Trinidad and Tobago', in *The Journal: Institute of Muslim Minority Affairs*, 7(1): 195–213.

Mahdjoub, M. (1988) 'The Evolution of Popular Eulogy of the Imams Among the Shi'a', in S. A. Arjomand (ed.) *Authority and Political Culture in Shi'ism*, Albany: SUNY Press.

Mangru, B. (1993) 'Tadjah in British Guiana', in F. Birbalsingh (ed.) *Indo-Caribbean Resistance*, Toronto: TSAR.

Manning, F. (1989) 'Spectacle', in *The International Encyclopedia of Communications*, Oxford: Oxford University Press.

Merryman, J. (1986) 'Two Ways of Thinking About Cultural Property', *American Journal of International Law*, 80(4): 831–53.

Mintz, S. and Price, R. (1976) *An Anthropological Approach to the Afro-American*

Past: A Caribbean Perspective, Philadelphia: Institute for the Study of Human Issues.

Momen, M. (1985) *An Introduction to Shi'i Islam*, New Haven: Yale University Press.

Nasr, S. H. (1966) *Ideals and Realities of Islam*, London: George Allen & Unwin Ltd.

Nettleford, R. (1988) 'Implications for Caribbean Development', in J. Nunley and J. Bettelheim (eds) *Caribbean Festival Arts*, Seattle: University of Washington Press.

Neubauer, E. (1972) 'Muharram-Bräuche im heutigen Persien', *Der Islam* 49: 249–72.

Nunley, J. and Bettelheim, J. (eds) (1988) *Caribbean Festival Arts*, Seattle: University of Washington Press.

Palmer, R. (1979) 'Artistry in Religious Ritual', in *The New York Times*, 5 April.

Pinault, D. (1992) *The Shiites*, New York: St. Martin's Press.

Rodney, W. (1981) *A History of the Guyanese Working People 1881–1905*, Baltimore: Johns Hopkins University Press.

Ryan, S. (1991) *The Muslimeen Grab for Power: Race, Religion and Revolution in Trinidad and Tobago*, Port of Spain: Imprint Caribbean Ltd.

Saiyid, A. R. assisted by P. Mirkhan and M. Talib (1981) 'Idea and Reality in the Observance of Moharram: A Behavioural Interpretation', in Imtiaz Ahmad (ed.) *Ritual and Religion Among Muslims in India*, New Delhi: Manohar Press.

Schechner, R. (1976) 'From Ritual to Theatre and Back: The Structure/Process of the Efficacy-Entertainment Dyad', in R. Schechner (ed.) *Essays on Performance Theory*, New York: Routledge and Kegan Paul.

Sharif, J. (1972) *Islam in India or the Qanun-i-Islam* (translated by G. A. Herklots), New Delhi: Oriental Books Reprint Corp.

Simmonds, W. A. (n.d.) ' "Pan" – The Story of the Steelband', BWIA International, A Sunjet Publication.

Singh, K. (1988) *Bloodstained Tombs: The Muharram Massacre 1884*, London: Macmillan Caribbean.

Smith, R. J. (1963) *Muslim East Indians in Trinidad: Retention of Ethnic Identity Under Acculturative Conditions*, University of Pennsylvania, Unpublished Ph.D. Dissertation, Ann Arbor: University Microfilms, Inc.

Thaiss, G. (1972) 'Religious symbolism and social change: the drama of Husain', in N. Keddie (ed.) *Scholars, Saints and Sufis*, Berkeley and Los Angeles: University of California Press.

van der Veer, P. and Vertovec, S. (1991) 'Brahmanism Abroad: On Caribbean Hinduism as an Ethnic Religion', *Ethnology*, 30(2): 149–66.

Williams, B. F. (1990) 'Nationalism, Traditionalism, and the Problem of Cultural Inauthenticity', in R. G. Fox (ed.) *Nationalist Ideologies and the Production of National Cultures*, A.E.S. Monograph Series No. 2. Washington, D.C.

—— (1991) *Stains on My Name, War in My Veins: Guyana and the Politics of Cultural Struggle*, Durham and London: Duke University Press.

Wood, D. (1968) *Trinidad in Transition: The Years After Slavery*, Oxford: Oxford University Press.

Yang, A. A. (1980) 'Sacred Symbol and Sacred Space in Rural India: Community Mobilization in the "Anti-Cow Killing" Riot of 1893', *Comparative Studies of Society and History*, 22(4): 576–96.

Chapter 4

How to be Islamic without being an Islamic state

Contested models of development in Malaysia

Judith Nagata

INTRODUCTION

The 'new world order' has almost as many constructions today as there are states. Whatever the political boundaries of the moment, a state must chart its path and cultivate its needs and image in an international arena, while continuing to manage its internal affairs and populations as a political, administrative and legal unit. Some religious and ethnic populations, however, span state boundaries. Population mobility and lack of proper fit between religious or ethnic communities and established political units have contributed largely to the dynamics recorded as politics and history, and to the condition of the world, both pre- and postmodern. What separates the pre-modern from the modern era is the arrival on the world stage of the political fabrication known as the nation-state[1] which, as Anderson (1983) and Gellner (1983) among others remind us, effectively imposed upon the communities of the world a set of administrative modules obsessed with the creation of cultural and linguistic homogeneity by means of bureaucratic efficiency and control of critical social and educational institutions. The nation part of the hybrid, however, while providing ideological focus and justification, was often as much a wishful fiction as based on historiographically verifiable fact.

'Nationalism' became a convenient rallying cry for state cohesion and mobilization. In fact, few states, past or present, have achieved a perfect fit between territorial boundaries and the single nation ideal. Internally, the 'misfits' or (national) minorities may be subject to procrustean policies of assimilation or to various forms of discriminatory action and status. The point is that any selected cultural, ideological or religious group can serve as an alternate to a 'national' model when politicized as the foundation for systems of affirmative action in which some citizens are privileged over others. Where such privilege is legally and constitutionally re-inforced, in a potent combination of means and ends, the state acquires a double-pronged control over its diverse citizenry.

The changing world of ideas of Enlightenment Europe that spawned the 'nation-state', often characterized as central to 'modernity', also gave rise to new notions of universal standards and measures of morality, human rights, dignity and political status (civil rights) detached from particular religious or cultural foundation (cf. Gellner 1992), applicable in all times and places. Thus the minorities marginalized in the newly-defined nation-states simultaneously acquired a new moral armamentarium against the particularistic bases of their homelands.

Many of these contradictory ideals were eventually carried to colonial shores by Europeans who left a legacy of western-style courts and legal codes set within their often arbitrarily crafted colonial states, now also called 'nations'. For their successors, when independence finally arrived, the colonially bequeathed confluence of peoples, religions, legal codes and political statuses was a test of their administrative, judicial and myth-making capacity, in their quest for a version of nationhood. A patchwork of unresolved cultural conflicts, legislative jurisdictions and ethical codes persist to the present, as many ex-colonial countries face the consequences of their inheritance, and each in its own way, seeks a solution. Today, inspiration for these solutions comes from a variety of sources, some relating to domestic events and conditions, others the resultant of forces from the world beyond. Commitments to economic modernization must often be weighed against other, less material, but equally compelling ideological gratifications, which may draw upon the more ancient 'imagined' communities of ethnicity and religion.

The rapid pace of the realignment of states following each of two world wars and culminating in the monumental reassortment of peoples and territories in the post-Communist makeover, creates ever evolving opportunities for new alliances to be formed and lacunae to be filled. For the new, as well as for older, continuing states, this can be a time to choose new political partners, pick over a variety of ideological offerings and to design a new system. Choices made in the international arena need to be justified to constituencies at home who in turn may have their own ideas about foreign policy and their image abroad.

One of the 'older' imagined communities, resurrected in various contemporary formats in the brave new world order is the Islamic *ummah*. Islam as an ideology of renewal has been gathering momentum in the Middle East and North Africa since the mid-nineteenth century, but the Islam that strikes chords in the world today is associated with the so-called 'resurgence', which moved to centre stage in the 1960s and 1970s. This marks the point at which contemporary Islam seriously became a player in the international political domain, seeking power both as an end in itself and as the means of spreading an Islamic way of life. Among the forerunners in the nineteenth century of what was to crest as a wave of pan-Islamism later, were the followers of Muhammad Abduh, whose sensitivities to the seeming paralysis of Islam to resist or overcome the effects of modernization planted in a colonial Egypt were reflected in writing which further inspired others to follow a more active path. The succeeding generation of Muslim intellectuals produced such spokesmen as Jinnah and Mohd Iqbal in India, whose design for what was to be Pakistan was essentially modern. The successors to these men, however, again reversed the trend, seriously questioned the march towards a world of secular nation-states, and abandoned the attempt to reconcile these with their faith. Instead, such leaders as Hassan al-Banna and Syed Qutb, with their Al-Ikhwan al Muslimin in Egypt, and Abdul A'la Maududi with his Jamaat-e-Islami in Pakistan, promoted the restoration of religious authority and standards in direct opposition to the incumbent regimes. Islamic movements in other states directed their attack on the centres of power, with the aim of taking political control and the creation of an Islamic state, as achieved in Sudan and as attempted in Algeria. The influence of some of these movements extends far beyond their countries of origin; in this very extra-territoriality lies much of their real power.

Islam today is the official religion of twenty-four world states and the religion of over 90 per cent of the populations of Saudi Arabia, Egypt, Iraq, Iran, Pakistan and Bangladesh and the dominant faith in officially secular Indonesia and Turkey. There are far fewer fully declared Islamic states; the reality is more elusive than the ideal. For the remaining Muslim states, the challenge is to establish how and how far to express their Muslim identity and character without losing sight of the interests of other constituencies in their own countries and of both Muslim and non-Muslim countries and politics outside. For many leaders, this calls for creative and timely planning, a mixture of pro-active and reactive policies and a supreme command of the political skills to project several different roles and images in different settings.

A common feature of the Islamization process is a drive to eliminate discrepancies between different standards and sources of authority, by realigning the administrative political unit with the religious. For outsiders, this can be described as the politicization of religion, but for Muslims, whose faith sets no clear boundary between secular and sacred, including in the political realm, this merely represents a step closer to the ideal of the Islamic state.

All existing multi-ethnic, multi-religious states where Muslims are numerically dominant and Islam the official religion are faced with in-built contradictions. The alternatives are either a policy of assimilation by conversion of the non-Muslim populations, or the creating of a separate, usually subordinate, citizenship status and/or system of quotas, such as the *dhimmi* model of a plural society, whose prototype is that of Medina at the time of the Prophet. Ruled according to Islamic principles, the early Medina regime also allowed freedom of religious practice for Jews and Christians as People of the Book or *kitabiyyah*. The political disabilities, however, were substantial, offering only limited physical protection and a strong encouragement to convert to Islam, as in Iran or the contemporary Sudan (cf. An-Naʿim 1988). By most 'modern' standards of justice and universal human rights, such multiple grades of citizenship are discriminatory and unacceptable and it is hard to reconcile the *dhimmi* system with a constitutional government, an independent judiciary and open, democratic political process. In designing their future, present or aspiring Islamic states must come to terms with the inevitability of challenge from international bodies as well as from non-Muslims within their borders.

MALAYSIA: THE CONSTITUTIONAL AND LEGAL SITUATION

A portrait of Malaysia as a state[2] reveals a number of seemingly discrepant characteristics. Although not an Islamic state, Islam is Malaysia's official religion, professed by 52.9 per cent of the population, most of whom are Malays.[3] The substantial non-Muslim populations are largely of immigrant stock, and part of the legacy of earlier colonial labour policies. The other part of that legacy lies in the structure and character of the state that was designed at the time of Independence in 1957. Until then, Malaya, as it was then known, consisted of nine traditional Malay sultanates, whose rulers had, through colonial treaties, abrogated most of their real political powers for a more symbolic role as 'Heads of Malay religion and custom' in their respective domains. In this capacity, they became titular heads of the Islamic religious councils concerned with the administration of Shariʿah law, issuance of *fatwas* and control of matters pertaining to religious lands and bequests, independently in their respective states.

Prior to British intervention, each state had practised a mixture of Malay customary law (*adat*) and a selection of Islamic laws, which sometimes extended beyond the realm of personal law to procedures of trade, theft, alcohol and sexual offences and homicide (Hamid Jusoh 1991:xiiiff.). However, there is no clear record of recognition of a full Muslim criminal (*hudud*) code in pre-colonial times. Under British rule, there was a trend towards bureaucratization of the states' religious courts (Roff 1967), partly as a means of control, although total standardization between them has never been achieved to this day. The close identification of Islam, royalty and Malayness was one of the enduring products of colonial policy, with the first two becoming essential symbols of the latter in an unbreakable trinity.

The federation forged at Independence drew together for the first time all the populations of the original royal states and two non-royal Straits Settlements, under a constitution in which it was specified that: 'Islam shall be the religion of the state of Malaya, but nothing in this article shall prevent any citizen professing any religion other than Islam, to profess, practise and propagate that religion, nor shall any citizen be under any disability by reason of not being Muslim' (Report of the Federation of Malaya Constitutional Commission, 1957:99). At this time, it was the intention of the framers of the constitution that Islam's 'official' role would be principally confined to ceremonial purposes and public occasions, and that otherwise, the federation would remain a secular state (Mohd Suffian Hashim *et al.* 1978), as affirmed by the first prime minister, Tunku Abdul Rahman (Hamid Jusoh 1991:99).

Although this left intact the administration of Shari'ah law by the religious courts under the authority of the sultans in their states, it was made clear in Article 4(1) that the constitution is the supreme law of the federation, and that any law passed subsequently, if inconsistent with the constitution, will be void, and further, by Article 75, that all individual state laws must be consistent with federal law (Hamid Jusoh 1991:33). Furthermore, where the powers of the religious and secular courts conflict, the former shall be subordinate to the latter (Hamid Jusoh 1991:46), and although in 1988 an amendment to the federal constitution reduced somewhat the power of the secular courts to interfere in Shari'ah matters, many cracks of uncertainty still remain.

In one measure to reduce some of the variability[4] of religious court operations and rulings in different states, the federal government in 1974 excised a new Federal Territory under its direct administration in which to cultivate its own religious council and Office of Islamic Affairs (Pusat Islam) under a Department of Religious Affairs in the Prime Minister's Office. These bodies also try to co-ordinate religious affairs of national importance, such as the dates of the fasting month, and they attempt to streamline laws pertaining to marriage, polygamy, divorce and the collection of the religious property tax, *zakat al mal*.

Parallel to the Shari'ah courts at the state level operates a system of secular courts, concerned with all other aspects of civil law, including special juvenile and native courts. At this level, there is an approximate correspondence between the offices of magistrate and religious judge (*kathi*). Beyond these are two courts of appeal, the High and Supreme Courts, for which the Shari'ah has no equivalent. Thus any appeal from a Shari'ah decision, or arising out of a disputed jurisdiction, as over land or property, must be heard in a secular court, although appropriate Muslim jurists may be consulted. Within the jurisdiction of the Shari'ah in the Malaysian states are matters of marriage, divorce, legitimacy, family property and inheritance, religious rituals and observances, including the fast, administration of religious taxes, charities, lands and mosques, for all Muslims. For most practical purposes, this may be considered the equivalent of personal civil law.

By and large, matters falling under the Muslim version of criminal law (*hudud*) remain under the jurisdiction of the secular courts, although some amendments in 1985 and 1988 transferred to religious courts certain additional offences which in the federal criminal code carry lesser penalties, such as alcohol consumption and sexual misconduct (*zina*). Generally in Malaysia, the full criminal portion of Islamic laws lies outside the authority of the religious courts. In Islam, *hudud* is normally considered to cover six major areas: theft; rebellion or highway robbery; illicit sex; false accusation against someone of having illicit sex; drunkenness; and apostasy (cf. An-Na'im 1986). For the implementation of complete *hudud* law in any Malaysian state, a major constitutional amendment would be required, if only because some of its provisions and penalties would be 'inconsistent' with current federal laws. Other problems will be taken up below.

Recalling once more the demographics of Malaysia's ethnic and religious populations, that the Muslims account for little over fifty per cent of the total, and given the constitutional guarantees of religious freedom for non-Muslims, it follows that Shari'ah law applies to just over one half of all Malaysians. At present, Malaysian citizens are differentially administered under two separate systems in terms of personal and family law, with the non-Muslims subject to federal Marriage and Family Ordinances. It also follows that, as Malaysia lacks a *dhimmi* tradition, were full *hudud* laws to be applied, some decision as to the legal liability of non-Muslims would be necessary. Assuming the required constitutional amendments, were *hudud* to replace the secular codes and courts, it would thereby eliminate the problem of parallel, overlapping or competing legal systems, but would also subject non-Muslims to an alien religious law. A *dhimmi* alternative on the other hand would guarantee at least some[5] non-Muslims a measure of internal religious and community autonomy and security of person and property, but not full participation in public and political affairs of the state, nor would they enjoy the right to positions of authority over Muslims. By today's 'modern' international standards, such a step would undoubtedly be seen by many inside and outside the country as contravening both established constitutional and also basic civil and human rights. Domestically too, it would be an administrative challenge, especially as the different religious populations are not territorially discrete, to operate two separate criminal codes. As with the present system, a *dhimmi* 'solution' would generate substantial problems of its own.

Another major problem of the implementation of Shari'ah law anywhere is that, while it aims to regulate the entire range of human and social activities, from personal to criminal, it has never yet been completely codified according to the canons of most modern law. Several Islamic scholars have pointed out (cf. Schacht 1960; An Na'im 1988) that Shari'ah is more a doctrine and a method than a systematic code, a variety of exegesis. To this is added the ongoing debate over what is divine and what is human law, which hinges on the relationship between the text of the Qur'an and the Sunnah or Hadith, especially where these contradict.[6] Even for Islamic jurists of the same 'school' or *mazahab*,[7] the situation provides endless opportunities to engage in religious casuistry over legal decisions. Similar problems confront all existing Islamic states, and those in the process of Islamizing their legal systems, so that Islamic law acquires distinctive 'national' characteristics in each country. Finally, a perennial issue, often debated in Malaysian circles, revolves around the question as to how far contemporary societies may creatively adapt laws and customs which evolved in the unique historical and cultural context of seventh-century Arabia, to the needs and circumstances of a twentieth-century Southeast Asian setting.[8]

MALAYSIA: THE POLITICAL SCENE

Unceasingly since Independence, Malaya/Malaysia has been engaged in a process of state building and consolidation. To the extent that the country aspires to be a 'nation-state', the national focus has always been Malay, and the constitution clearly establishes the primacy of Malay status in a number of provisions and policies.[9] While the constitutionally defined characteristics of Malayness – by language, custom and (the Muslim) religion – are essentially cultural, thus theoretically permitting assimilation of immigrants and minorities (to Malay status) according to the classic ideal, in practice, informal social mechanisms prevent full acceptance of culturally qualified non-Malays.[10] From another perspective, the constitution also requires that Malays be Muslims, as a condition of ethnic recognition, and a non-Muslim Malay is thus a legal anomaly. Malays therefore are the only Malaysians to enjoy no freedom of religious choice or practice, a price paid for political perquisites and ethnic protection. Malaysia thus remains a plural state, whose principal political parties are also ethnic based. The ruling coalition (Barisan Nasional) which has ruled in substantially the same format since Independence, consists of a core of the United Malays National Organization (UMNO); the Malaysian Chinese Association (MCA); and the Malaysian Indian Congress (MIC), to which are added from time to time other parties. Among the permanent opposition parties are the largely Chinese Democratic Action Party (DAP); a splinter party from UMNO, known as Semangat 46, led by a Malay prince; and an attenuated multiethnic Peoples' Party (Party Rakyat). The other principal opposition player is the Pan-Malayan Islamic Party or PAS, which keeps the UMNO constantly on its moral and religious toes, and which at present, in alliance with Semangat 46, is the ruling party of the heavily Malay northeastern state of Kelantan. In its early years, beginning in 1951 as Hisbul Muslimin, PAS was more concerned with the promotion of Malay interests, an ethnic party legitimated by the moral force of Islam. In this guise, it briefly, in the 1970s joined the UMNO-dominated political coalition, the National Front. Today, it officially denounces ethnic chauvinism as a form of *assabiyah*, and has become the protagonist of an Islamic state, in which more universal principles of (Islamic) justice (*keadilan*) for all would replace sectional biases. Over the past twenty years, PAS has augmented its national membership by recruitment of past leaders of some of the resurgent Islamic (*dakwah*) movements which arose in Malaysia in the early 1970s,[11] but which have always lacked an independent political base. Several current PAS leaders were originally exiles from the Angkatan Belia Islam Malaysia (ABIM), itself born as a Malay nationalist student movement, and later adopting a more non-ethnic, pan-Islamic stance. In 1982, however, ABIM's founder, star performer and personal embodiment, Anwar Ibrahim, stunned his followers and the country by relinquishing his creation and joining UMNO, the erstwhile enemy. In a single move, UMNO raised its Islamic credibility rating, while ABIM thereafter lost most of its momentum, settling in to a more docile existence as an educational and publishing organization, espousing a moderate, more innerworldly religious viewpoint conveniently compatible with that of UMNO's own public religious posture. Hence the exit of some of ABIM's more activist and ideologically committed members to PAS.

As the senior incumbent party in the state of Kelantan, PAS pursues its opposition to UMNO in a crusading spirit of moral religious righteousness as the true protector of Islam in Malaysia, a counterpoint to the allegedly materialistic and corrupt agenda of a federal government seduced by the blandishments of a decadent 'Christian/Zionist' west. While publicly vilifying the goals of the Prime Minister's vision of full industrial development by the year 2020 (under the slogan, Vision 2020), PAS is as much concerned over the means to that end, as the end in itself, for PAS shows little evidence of opposing economic success or wealth *per se*. The public battle is as much moral and verbal as substantive, and its score depends heavily on the rhetorical and casuistic skills of *ulama* spokesmen on both sides.

PAS's immediate programme, under its President who is a member of the *ulama* in his own right, is the creation of an Islamic state for Kelantan, the 'verandah of Mecca' (*serambi Mekkah*) of which he is also chief minister. Avowedly, this would also be his ultimate goal for all of Malaysia, were PAS ever to come to power nationally. This issue of the Islamic state has become the principal ideological focus of the opposition with UMNO and the federal centre, while raising serious legal and constitutional questions for the country as a whole. The religious gauntlet is down, and both sides conduct themselves as defenders of the faith over every public policy, in a game known locally as *kafir mengafir*, or mutual excoriation as infidels.

Now that PAS has been in power in Kelantan since 1990, the question arises as to why the party has been so dilatory in the first step in its Islamization programme, the implementation of *hudud* law in its domain.

On several occasions, (e.g. in January, April and November 1992), UMNO has openly challenged PAS to follow its rhetoric with action, although probably more by way of irritation and goading, since it is recognized by both sides that such a move would require a constitutional amendment, in which all national parties, including non-Muslims, would have a vote. Three times PAS has presented a draft proposal for the introduction of *hudud* law to the Kelantan state assembly, the latest in March 1993, being tabled before the sultan. Each time, however, the motions have been withdrawn on 'technical grounds' (cf. *New Straits Times*, 17 March 1993). PAS spokesmen claim that more time is needed to inform and educate non-Muslims in matters of *hudud* law, and even suggest that some Muslims themselves are not yet sufficiently religiously mature, requiring more preparation. Premature implementation would be comparable to trying to 'pour water into a vessel full of holes,' to use PAS's metaphor in its publication, *Harakah* (21 August 1992). Both parties, PAS and UMNO, hedge the stalemate with a need for 'further studies' (*Harakah* 9 September 1992). To this end, UMNO marshalls its stable of constitutional experts and sympathetic *ulama* at the centre, to demonstrate the legal complexity of the issue, defying swift resolution (*Berita Harian* 26 August 1992). In its publication, *Risalah* (July 1992), ABIM likewise lays out an elaborate and cautious set of preconditions for *hudud* implementation; it expresses concern over human rights and justice, a need for careful examination of the scriptures and the necessity for preparation of both the *ummah* and of non-Muslims, but leaves readers to draw their own conclusions. In support of its own measured approach, UMNO is represented by a corps of selected *ulama*, seconded from local universities, or working as bureaucrats in government-funded Islamic institutions, who make fine distinctions between 'believing in the correctness of *hudud* and its correct implementation' (*Berita Minggu* 10 August 1992); the necessity for waiting until all the preconditions are in place; and generally dismissing the opposition's proposals as '*hudud* PAS' not '*hudud* Islam'.

In effect, all the public political players in Malaysia's *hudud* debate appear to be prevaricating. It is possible that the federal government hopes to keep the *hudud* ball in the air until the next national election, on the gamble that PAS will lose its control in Kelantan and on the assumption that as yet PAS leaders, many of them *ulama*, are insufficiently prepared or administratively too inexperienced to take the unprecedented plunge.

Even some ordinary Kelantanese Malays are apprehensive as to the full implications of *hudud*. While they are prepared to accept such measures as tighter enforcement of dress codes for women, and the closure of drinking and gambling establishments, some uncertainty over the legendary chopping off the hands of thieves and stoning of adulterers cannot easily be dispelled. Against these familiar and much flaunted examples, *hudud* supporters reassure the doubters that such penalties would be applied only after exhaustive investigations, that they are intended as deterrents rather than punishments, hence would reduce crime, and that they are no harsher than the effects of long-term incarceration and other penalties of the secular courts. The crowning, unassailable argument is that *hudud* represents divine law, beyond human manipulation. But even divine law is not so easily determined and there continue to be lively disputes among Islamic scholars over the inflation of the Hadith, as a source of legal inspiration, and of the legitimacy of interpretations (*tafsiran*) handed down over the centuries, without reference back to the original source. Whereas the infamous stoning of sexual offenders is based on the traditions of the Hadith, the original scriptures, as one renegade Malaysian scholar reminds us, are more humane, and no such dire penalties are specified in the Qur'an (Kassim Ahmad 1986).

The other pressing issue in the *hudud* debate concerns the status of non-Muslims, who in Kelantan represent a minority of barely three per cent. PAS has made it clear that it intends its law to cover all residents of Kelantan, regardless of religious or ethnic origin, and has made no mention of any *dhimmi* provision. Understandably, the non-Malay political parties at all levels are determined to forestall such plans through constitutional and political lobbying at the centre, while the principal non-Muslim religions are also mobilizing for the defence, partly through a representative Malaysian Consultative Council of Buddhists, Christians, Hindus and Sikhs (MCCBCHS).

One other minor alternative to the current political status quo deserves mention, more as a variant Islamic lifestyle than a serious political player in Malaysia. This is one of the remaining *dakwah* movements, Darul Arqam, which emerged at the same time as ABIM in the late 1960s. Arqam is unique in Malaysia in its attempt to follow an exemplary Muslim community way of life as decreed by the Prophet. Many Arqam members reside in separate settlements where emphasis is placed on economic self sufficiency, restricted material needs, egalitarianism through redistribution of resources (*ma'ash*), and religiously correct family and gender relations, including polygamy (Muhd Syukri Salleh 1992). Arqam runs its own schools, clinics, shops and manufacturing businesses, printing presses and even manages trading and entertainment networks, all based on the principles of Islamic purity (*halal*) and of independence from *kafir* association including political groups. Arqam could be presented as a non-politicized form of Islamic existence, harbouring no designs either to take over the state or to co-operate with one so in league with Chinese and other unbelievers. A brief flirtation with PAS in Kelantan was abandoned after a few months.

One of Arqam's strengths lies in its enthusiastic proselytization through *dakwah*, which is pursued in the manner of a Sufi brotherhood or *tarekat*, through personal contacts at the grassroots level, and recruitment through educational institutions and by marriage whereby Arqam males attract and maintain wives polygynously in several different settlements in Malaysia and overseas. On the basis of numbers alone, Arqam's success appears modest, with about 6,000 members and sympathisers in Malaysia and possibly 2–3,000 more overseas (Muhd Syukri Salleh 1992), but in terms of quality, most members are drawn from highly educated, professional and technically sophisticated young graduates, with energy and enthusiasm to match. Its character has been compromised, however, in the view of most state and federal religious bodies in Malaysia by the messianic claims of its leader, Ustaz Ashaari, and the allegations by some Arqam deserters of the totalitarian and even deviant 'magical' practices of its leaders (cf. Mohd. Rushdi Yusuf 1990). These have led to the banning of Arqam operations in much of Malaysia, on grounds of 'heresy' and even 'Shi'ite tendencies', forcing Ashaari to relocate his headquarters to South Thailand and to concentrate expansion overseas, in Indonesia, the Philippines, China and now on the new territories of Central Asia, especially Uzbekistan. In its zeal to control or restrict any potential Islamic opposition within the country, Malaysian religious authorities, under federal prodding, have in fact driven the movement underground and overseas, where its informal political success in a longer term may in fact be enhanced. Within Malaysia, another government weapon against anticipated religious opposition, is to make its own definition of 'heresy' and to implement this through the *fatwas* of its own co-opted *ulama* and religious courts, including the Pusat Islam.

It should be apparent that the role of the *ulama*, as scholar-guardians of Islam, and as gatekeepers and exegesists of the textual and historical treasury, so essential to legitimate any major policy, cannot be over-estimated. Over centuries, pronouncements and interpretations (*tafsiran*) by recognized scholars have carried the tradition from one generation to the next and formed the basis of a consultative role to political regimes. This, and the generally great reverence with which they are held by the Muslim public, has endowed them with formidable moral and political power, a sort of fifth column or power behind the throne. For access to their privileged information and authority, every Muslim interest group in Malaysia needs it own cohort of *ulama* consultants and supporters, whether of the government bureaucratic, or more fundamentalist variety. Today, a growing number of non-Malaysian *ulama* from such countries as Pakistan and Bangladesh are developing profitable new careers in the International Islamic University in Kuala Lumpur, as informal consultants serving all shades of local public religious opinion, while others are seconded to government Islamic organizations such as the Islamic Dakwah Foundation. Professional religious consultancy is a growth industry, with a promising future for some time to come, as events unfold in Malaysia.

In what follows, I take up some of the most recent and contentious issues concerning the Islamic directions of the Malaysian state, and describe the manner of their presentation and legitimation by the various interest groups involved.

ECONOMIC POLICY

As noted, the technocratic federal government of Malaysia is committed to an aggressive capitalist-industrial form of modernity which locks it into co-operation with countries of the west and Japan. There is little evidence to suggest that PAS opposes development in principle, but in order to maintain its political opposition, it has much to say on the manner and ethics of development. More important is that both parties are seen by their respective audiences to be religiously correct, with the appropriate *ulama* and scriptural support.

There is no doubt that the *dakwah* movements of recent decades have left an indelible impression on economic policy, especially since Anwar's entry into UMNO, but they have by no means co-opted it. In 1983, with Arab consultants, an Islamic Bank was launched and more recently several private banks have begun to offer separate counters for Islamic and 'non-interest' services. This was followed by an Islamic insurance company (*takaful*), and a government-controlled Pilgrims' Savings Fund (*Tabung Haji*), although it is known that some of the investments of the latter are in the secular stock market. Despite the independent authority of the state religious councils in most Shari'ah matters, the federal Department of Religious Affairs is now attempting to encourage and co-ordinate the full payment of *zakat* religious taxes, which have in the past rarely been paid in full by urban, non-farmers on professional salaries, business profits or bank savings. Some Muslims, however, unswayed by appeals to ideas of 'Islamic justice and obligation', are voicing very secular concerns over what they see as a double income tax. Another resource under state authority is that of religiously-endowed *wakaf* land, donated by Muslim benefactors for mosques and Muslim welfare. Such lands have traditionally been immune from Land Office control, but the situation of many *wakaf* lands in potentially lucrative urban and industrial areas has inevitably led to pressures for their 'development', on the grounds that the income so derived would benefit indigent Muslims more than the meagre yields by present assessments. Resistance to such proposals has been raised vigorously by *wakaf* residents in cities such as Penang and Malacca, who fear non-Muslim interests behind the schemes. The evidence suggests, however, that it is the local state religious councils who are the entrepreneurs behind such plans, in conjunction with business colleagues. A recent case of contested *wakaf* land in Penang tested the jurisdiction of religious versus secular courts. After appeals, it was finally settled by the Supreme Court, with a ruling that, while the religious council has jurisdiction over such land, it has no right to subvert the original intent of the donation (*New Straits Times*, 3 September 1992). Since then, the same defeated religious council with the support of the finance minister, Anwar Ibrahim (his ABIM past well behind him), has announced the formation of a limited share company for the sole purpose of *wakaf* development. The ultimate fate of *wakaf* land will undoubtedly have much to do with UMNO politics.

With its New Economic Policy, the federal government has often been charged with being more pro-Malay than pro-Muslim. From the sidelines, PAS now claims a more universalistic notion of justice and redistribution of wealth free of the taint of ethnic chauvinism (*assabi'yah*). Quick to respond, minister of finance, Anwar Ibrahim draws on his ABIM credentials, when he was notable for his criticism of all brands of chauvinism. In his current capacity, Anwar redefines creation of wealth through development and growth as beneficial to all citizens in this pluralistic society including the poor of all religions, which allowed him to describe his 1992 capital investment budget as 'Islamic in spirit' (*New Straits Times*, 11 January 1993).

The most recent addition to the federal government's moral armamentarium was the creation in 1992, of a special Institute for Islamic Understanding (IKIM in the Malay acronym), a generously endowed religious think-tank whose president is the secretary of government in the Prime Minister's Office. To IKIM are seconded hand-picked 'senior fellows' from the local universities and private *ulama*. Their task is to find some common ground between Muslims and non-Muslims, academics and businessmen, Malays, Chinese and foreign investors, and to persuade all of the merits of the government's brand of economics. Their portrayal of Islam is one equally concerned with the world as with the afterlife, and to reassure non-Muslims of the painlessness of the government's Islamization policies. For the Muslim constituency, one of IKIM's dominant themes revolves around the question as to why Muslim countries today are so widely associated with 'backwardness' and carry a negative image to the world at large (cf. *Utusan Malaysia*, 22 November 1992). Muslims are reminded by the Prime Minister, through IKIM, that the dismal record at present contrasts starkly with the golden age of Muslim civilisation of the past, when Islamic medicine, science, astronomy, literature and art were the wonders of the world (*New Straits Times*, 4 July 1992), and this decline has left Muslims vulnerable to the immoral influences and attacks from the west. In a global perspective, therefore, it is incumbent on Malaysian Muslims to repolish their image, by encouraging competitiveness and achievement in science and business and all modern developments. Muslims should not be intimidated by fear of the afterlife (*akhirat*) alone, but should emphasize the needs of the here and now (*dunia*). Even the *ulama* are challenged to acquire 'modern' skills and knowledge, and to remain *au courant* with such contemporary problems as AIDS and scientific developments (*New Straits Times*, 26 July 1992).

For non-Muslim consumption, the message is one of 'correcting misconceptions and allaying fears over Islamic policies', as a means of distancing the government and UMNO from accusations of fanaticism (*New Straits Times*, 4 July 1992). IKIM has already held numerous workshops for local and foreign investors, including German and Japanese multinationals, explaining Malaysia's commitment to development, while presenting a non-threatening scheme of 'Islamic management' and advice as to treatment of Muslim employees (*Star*, 10 March 1993). The limits of exegesis in the IKIM world view are broad; its spokesmen claim to be solidly grounded in the scriptures and the Hadith, yet attempt to be universalistic, with something for everyone. IKIM, together with the other government Islamic foundations, has become the public moral counsellor to the assorted citizenry of Malaysia, using its access to the media sources at the government's disposal to pronounce on such matters as happy and caring families, moderation in festival celebrations and business ethics.

THE LIMITS OF THE SHARI'AH AND THE BOUNDARIES OF THE *UMMAH*

Confusion between Malay and Muslim 'nationalism' often pervades Malaysian political discourse. The constitutional conflation of Malay and Muslim identity, leading to the logical impossibility of being a non-Muslim Malay, when combined with the difficulties encountered by converts to Islam in acceptance by the Malay community, all suggest a privileging of a specifically Malay brand of Islam. Even the *dakwah* proselytizers largely confine their activities to the Malays. On the other hand, the tacit official approval of projects to convert non-Malays to Islam could be construed as an attempt to create a more pluralistic *ummah*. Programmes for the conversion of the aboriginal populations are also active, although the wave of converts of the 1970s seems now to have abated.[12]

Finance minister Anwar Ibrahim continues to evoke some of the ideals of his ABIM days when he was one of the first Malay leaders to advocate unity through Islam alone.[13] In the 1990s, he replays the theme of the universalism of Islam, which is consistent with a broader (though still not formally articulated) vision of an enlarged and more diverse *ummah* in Malaysia. This could have the double advantage of not encroaching on Malay identity and also of reducing the 'problem' of the non-Muslim population in the process of Islamization. Conversion, however, whether into Islam or out of it, creates legal as well as social problems. These arise particularly when families are religiously divided by conversion and have recourse to the courts. A number of recent cases in Malaysia involved conversion of minors to Islam against their parents' wishes. In one

Kelantan case, the unhappy Chinese parents appealed to a state civil court that their daughter, aged seventeen, had not yet reached the (constitutional) age of maturity (of eighteen), hence the conversion was invalid. The claim was rejected by the Kelantan state court, on grounds that every 'person' under the constitution enjoys freedom of religion, and since the girl was already seventeen years old, she should be allowed to exercise her rights. A second appeal to the Supreme Court, however, referred to the Guardian of Infants Act, upheld the convert's lack of majority and granted the appeal (Hamid Jusoh 1991: 85–8). In other states (e.g. Selangor), discrepancies have arisen between the Shari'ah's recognition of the age of maturity as coinciding with puberty and the eighteen years of the civil courts.

Comparable problems arise when a convert to Islam reneges on the faith. Where the individual is married, the Shari'ah has sometimes intervened unilaterally to annul the marriage, while the non-Muslim spouse seeks protection from civil codes and marriage ordinances, creating a legal impasse. When a single convert voluntarily withdraws from Islam, this has been construed as apostasy under Shari'ah law (*murtad*), although civil courts uphold constitutional freedoms of person and religion, and this too results in acrimonious wrangling. A prolonged case in 1992 became politicized, when a sixteen year old Chinese female convert to Islam subsequently reverted to her ancestral Buddhism and was accused of apostasy. At this point, the girl's parents invoked the aid of a Chinese political party (the DAP), which in turn unleashed a vituperative flow of accusations by PAS and other *ulama* that the DAP and other Chinese 'elements' had conspired to offer her financial inducements to renounce Islam (*Harakah*, 21 August 1992), and this was followed by further 'revelations' of a list of briberies in other comparable cases to seduce converts away from Islam (*Harakah* 21 August 1992). This evoked a series of counter-allegations by other new Muslims (known in Malaysia as 'new associates' or *saudara baru*, cf. Nagata 1978), over the lack of concern, goodwill or follow-up services provided by the converts' associations or by the Malay community generally (*Star*, 24 August 1992).

Even more intense emotions are generated over the idea of apostasy by Malays. Technically, *murtad* is part of *hudud*, and has not been prosecuted in Malaysia to date. Juristically too, there is disagreement over the appropriate penalty for *murtad*. Some jurists uphold the death penalty, based on the Hadith, where it is said to be recommended by the Prophet; others point out that the Qur'an is itself inconclusive on the matter, implying that punishment will be applied in the hereafter (cf. An-Na'im 1986). For Malays socially, however, *murtad* combines a heinous sin with abandonment of Malay status (by a combination of divine and constitutional laws). Recent reports of Malay students overseas converting or forsaking Islam through marriage, resulted in a massive mobilization by the federal religious department as well as those of many states, with much popular Malay support, to revoke the apostates' scholarships and to impose (unspecified) harsh penalties, and to ensure that all future government sponsored students be thoroughly prepared in their religion (*New Straits Times*, 23 June 1992; 1 July 1992). Not surprisingly, PAS also seized the opportunity to excoriate UMNO for its alleged laissez-faire attitude to the religious welfare of its scholarship holders. As attempts are made to chart a path between religious and other legal jurisdictions, no clear resolution emerges, except that there appears no definite trend towards an Islamic state.

One spin-off from the *murtad* dramas and of the *hudud* controversy generally is to reinforce the hostilities and constraints on Christian mission and other activities, and the growing polarization between Muslim and non-Muslim in Malaysia.

The other audience addressed by government and official religious circles, is the non-Muslim population. As long as Malaysia remains a parliamentary democracy, their alienation or subjugation is out of the question. The MCCBCHS religious coalition regularly sends deputations to various ministers and political parties, but has been informed by PAS that, since the other religions fail to specify their own penalties for crimes covered by *hudud*, they will by default have to follow those of the state in which they reside. Even some 'moderate' Muslim MPs have suggested that were they to vote publicly against *hudud* laws, they could be regarded as *kafir* or apostates themselves.

THE POSITION OF WOMEN IN MALAYSIAN ISLAM

It is clear that in the Malaysian (and UMNO) vision of development, women are expected to play a substantial role. Women are involved equally with men in higher education and overseas training programmes and are employed widely in public, private and professional sectors, which today includes two senior cabinet ministers. During the heady days of the early *dakwah* resurgence in Malaysia, many zealous women followers voluntarily adopted versions of the veil as a visible declaration of religious commitment (Nagata 1984; Zainah 1987). In response, government departments, including hospitals and schools, and most private employers, instituted dress codes of their own, which restricted more extreme forms of veiling lest it present a 'backward' image of Malaysia to the rest of the world. In keeping with these views, many religious publications representing officialdom written by *ulama* from IKIM and the ABIM journal *Risalah*, feature portraits of women who successfully combine a public career and personal modesty, and whose dress usually consists of a headscarf or attractively styled veil which does not cover the face, and a long, loose two-piece dress also in an appealing co-ordination of colours and textures. Today most Malay women have adopted some version of this style, to the point where it may be said to have become Malay national costume. The case studies in these publications also portray women who have achieved a balance between their profession and their role as a good Muslim wife and mother, and the general conclusion in the event of a conflict between the roles, is for the latter to be given priority.

PAS's view of the role of women in public life is less accommodating and it uses the issue to attack the Islamic character and commitment of UMNO and the government. While not totally opposed to women's working outside the home, PAS is more specific in its restriction to 'appropriate' occupations, such as the nurturant nurse, teacher or social worker. Moreover, PAS endorses a woman's right to adopt full *purdah*, in accordance with the scriptural injunction to cover her modesty (*aurat*) in public. In its own women's magazine, *Muslimah*, PAS features articles on women who successfully manage their public careers in full *purdah*, without compromising their efficiency. In the early 1990s, a number of women in Malaysia's universities, including the International Islamic University, as well as some in government offices, complained via the media of their being forbidden to cover their faces in these institutions, or to exercise their full religious freedoms and to follow divine law in protecting their modesty in a country where Islam is the official religion (cf. *Muslimah* April 1992: 7). One clerk in a government office, who was dismissed for continuing to wear full *purdah* in contravention of an official injunction, took her case to court. Interestingly, she chose a civil court and to be defended by a non-Muslim lawyer, on the grounds that her civil (occupational) rights had been violated. Her choice of process was determined by her own concern over sullying the image of, or exposing the (political) divisions within, local Islamic groups to the public which could be exploited by non-Muslims (*Ummah*, April 1992: 30–1). In the event, the plaintiff lost her case, even after an appeal to the Supreme Court, on the grounds of 'insubordination' by disobeying the government circular on dress codes (*Star*, 10 March 1993). Even in her defeat, however, the plaintiff felt vindicated to the extent that she had made a public statement of her faith and also shown the government to be less than Islamic in the process (*Dunia Islam*, April 1992: 66).

A recent significant development in relation to women in Malaysian Islam is a small movement of highly educated and articulate, professional and cosmopolitan women known as the Sisters in Islam. The Sisters' concerns extend from the male biases of the Shari'ah family court in Malaysia, to the very foundations and scriptural interpretations compiled by male exegesists over the centuries, over the position of women in Muslim society. For the Sisters, the only authentic source is the text of the Qur'an, while the authority of the Hadith is of uncertain, and sometimes contradictory status, due to the historical circumstance in which it was constructed. Aware of the sensitivity and innovativeness of their stand, the Sisters have prepared a meticulously documented and analysed reinterpretation of the Qur'an, which takes the text as a whole and in context, in an attempt to trace the evolution of ideas, and to extract the spirit of the message, in contrast to the customary exegetical method of selecting isolated verses to suit the (particular scholar's) argument of the moment. Through this latter method, the Sisters feel that generations of male commentators have created a distorted view of the status of women and injected greater inequality than the original text intended or even displays, when details of context, consistency and even grammar are taken into account (Amina Wadud-Muhsin 1992).

Even where the Qur'an places unequivocal constraints on dress and access to public office for women, the Sisters' argument centres on the universality of the scriptural message; in this spirit, it should not be expected that society be frozen in a seventh-century Arabian mould, but that it should be open to suitable adaptation to the needs of changing times and circumstances. In their statements, the Sisters are careful in making it clear that it is not Islam which oppresses women, but human beings in their weaknesses, who fail fully to understand Allah's intentions as revealed in the Qur'an, but who are bound by male peer pressure groups and build on each other's commentaries without referring back to the original sources. The Sisters draw attention to the fact that Islam actually upgraded women's status in contrast to that in the time before the Prophet (*jahiliyah*), but that this was not always duly reflected in later social developments. Predictably, the PAS constituency as well as many established *ulama*, sense a threat, not just to the status quo, but even to their own security as the gatekeepers of Islamic knowledge. One of the epithets now current, and used against the Sisters, is that they are 'anti-Hadith', which in Malaysia carries the implication of heresy. For the government, the Sisters' threat lies in their antipathy to the politicization of Islam, and to the excessive control by a small group of professional *ulama* whose priority is to protect their own interests and careers. To date, however, there has been no formal harassment of the Sisters, and indeed, one of the *ulama*, advisor to the Religious Affairs Department in the Prime Minister's Office, has defended them by recommending that they be judged by their *taqwa* (piety), and not their gender.

ROYALTY

In the traditional Islamic state, it is expected that the ruler be an exemplary Muslim, observant of the full Shari'ah law. The favourite Malaysian example of the ideal ruler is embodied in the Four Righteous Caliphs (632–61 AD), especially Omar, who reputedly dispensed full justice to Muslims and non-Muslims alike (cf. Chandra 1981).

Independent Malaysia combines its parliamentary democracy with a legacy of nine sultanates, of whom one is elected every five years as King of Malaysia. Beyond their role as heads of religion in their respective states, the sultans' real strength remains in their symbolic representation of Malay identity and power as the original and dominant people of the country. The constitutional monarchy, however, retains certain arbitrary powers which Chandra (1981) and others see as residues of the 'feudal' age. Loyalty to the person of the king and the elaborate trappings of pre-Islamic rituals and titles, lead others to say that 'we fear the king more than Allah' (*Berita Harian* 4 January 1993). Even the constitution article 181(2) affirms that no proceedings shall be brought in any court against the ruler of a state in his personal capacity, which means that rulers are in fact above the law.

A number of incidents over the past decade involving anti-social, corrupt and even criminal behaviour by some of the rulers[14] finally reached crisis point in late 1992, culminating in a parliamentary constitutional amendment to remove the sultans' legal immunity. The Prime Minister, the first in Malaysia not to come from an aristocratic or royal background,[15] was personally strongly committed to this move, although critics claim that the measure also strengthens his own powers. Despite their formal roles as heads of religion, the sultans' newly publicized lifestyle and character were quickly targeted as 'feudal' and 'un-Islamic' (*New Straits Times*, 26 January 1993), hence unfit for office and for the title *Baginda*, one also used for the Prophet.

The *muftis* and *fatwa* councils of several states have issued statements to the effect that stripping sultans of their legal immunity is in line with Islamic law and justice, and even the PAS Council of Ulama asserted that royals are not above the law, but all are equal before Allah (*Malaysian Business*, January 1993: 26). When the final parliamentary vote was taken, however, PAS voted against the constitutional amendments to abolish royal immunity, once again for political reasons. On this occasion, the pressure came from PAS's Kelantan state coalition partner, Semangat 46, whose head also happens to be the uncle of the present Sultan of Kelantan, and who became quite personally involved in the constitutional debate. In the final parliamentary vote, all Semangat MPs were absent from the house. Meanwhile, by way of self-justification, many rulers made emotional appeals to 'their' people, also in the name of Islam. Several made unprecedented visits to local mosques for Friday prayers and invited their subjects to special prayers and feasts at the palace, with the aim of creating an impression of their unity and solidarity before God. While the language was religious, an unspoken underlying theme of another kind of unity, of Malayness, was also present. Again, religious and nationalist sentiments are hard to disentangle in practice, and there remains a residue of royal power which no constitutional amendment can erase. For the federal government, however, the issue is clearer: the legitimacy of the Malaysian state is thoroughly secular even though many of its policies and characteristics are presented in Islamic clothing. In its latest stand-off with royalty, the rights of the people are re-defined in a civil, constitutional sense, with Islam as a social and political levelling mechanism.

FOREIGN IMAGE AND POLICY

Even as Malaysia tries to come to terms with its internal contradictions, it is ever conscious of its place in a wider world order, economically and politically. Sensitive to this, the Prime Minister has embarked upon aggressive and highly visible political forays into other world groupings, such as the non-aligned countries and relationships with other countries of the South and with fellow Muslim states, some of which can be played off against the 'developed' world.

From its own perspective, Malaysia's relations with the 'west' are highly ambivalent and sometimes defensive. Beneath the co-operation, it perceives a lurking 'orientalist' bias, which may be partly a projection of Malaysia's own uncertain identity. Western countries are portrayed alternately as role models to be emulated or rejected, as indeed are Muslim ones. In the positive mode, the Prime Minister rhetorically asks his countrymen (especially the Malays) why the Muslim people of today are less developed and enterprising, unable to co-operate among themselves or to gain respect for their achievements, 'like fruits floating haphazardly in the sea' (*Dakwah*, July 1992: 14). Such sentiments are more commonly heard where economic development is the theme and IKIM the sponsor, and resemble the original questions posed by such Muslim thinkers as Muhd. Abduh. Like Abduh too, the Malaysian leader ponders how Muslim countries can modernize without destroying the faith (cf. *Ummah*, 41:1992: 41ff).

It is but a short step from these attitudes to an assumption of hostility towards Muslims by the west (cf. *Dakwah*, April 1992: 13ff), readily vindicated by contemporary Middle Eastern politics, of a continuing holy war with Muslims as the victims (*Al-Islam*, February 1992: 11). Commentaries in the Malaysian Muslim media generally, see a conspiratorial trend in the (western) purveying of the term 'fundamentalist' as inherently sinister and threatening, associated with fanaticism (*Dakwah*, April 1992: 14). Ultimately, the only antidote to such sentiments lies in an assertion of self-esteem through the moral superiority of Islam over western materialism and decadence. The defenders of economic development are usually scrupulous in separating the west's technical and scientific contributions from its accompanying social and cultural shortcomings. Further compensation is sought from history, and the glories of the Islamic civilization in times past.

As for the present, Malaysia's relations with other Muslim countries and peoples is selective. Although formally a member of the Organization of Islamic Conference, Malaysia has a rather low opinion of that grouping, for its perceived indecisiveness and lack of co-ordination amid the compelling events of Bosnia, Somalia and the Gulf War. The Malaysian government generally tries to distance itself from the immediacy of local Middle Eastern politics, and some of its publications are critical of the disposition of Arab wealth, which does not necessarily appear to benefit the world's poorer Muslims. It is apparent, too that Iran is no role model for Malaysia ever since some of the *dakwah* movements openly declared their inspiration from the Iranian revolution. To this day, any behaviour or belief resembling Shi'ism is suspect, and the label is used pejoratively even inaccurately, to condemn any unacceptable group, such as Darul Arqam.

Unlike many 'developing' countries, Malaysia's relative prosperity and freedom from foreign debt allows it to chart its own course in the new emerging world order. One of these areas concerns international refugees. In early 1993, Malaysia took a pro-active stand on Bosnia, and, through the offices of ABIM, officially sponsored over 200 Bosnians who are now living and studying in Malaysia (*New Straits Times* 16 January 1993). It also launched a fund in aid of the Burmese Muslim Rohingya, in contrast to its record of rejection of ethnic Chinese and Vietnamese non-Muslim boat people in the 1970s and 1980s. In these scenarios, the labelling of populations invariably reflects religious identification: thus the Bosnian–Muslim–Serb opposition is described as a Christian–Muslim conflict, and the government of Burma as the 'Buddhist power of Rangoon' (*Dakwah*, July 1992: 17), as forms of holy war. Likewise, westerners are sometimes arbitrarily equated with Zionists and Christians although Anwar Ibrahim officially cautions against such 'appeals to slogans and rallying cries' (*New Straits Times* 11 February 1993).

The latest exercise in religious politics for Malaysia has been in the new Central Asian republics of Kazakhstan, Tajikistan and especially Uzbekistan, where it perceives a tempting vacuum. Political and trading overtures, followed by a prime ministerial visit to Uzbekistan mark this new alignment for the region's Muslim population and re-incorporation as members of the wider *ummah*. Also, in the name of the *ummah*, but outside the purview of the state, other Muslims, such as Darul Arqam, are forging their own independent connections with Central Asia, with emphasis on Uzbekistan. Whereas the Malaysian government treads carefully in religious matters, Arqam is at the centre of a lively religious revitalization in Uzbekistan, active in the restoration of mosques and resocializing the youth, especially those in the university in Tashkent, in their ancestral faith. Arqam sweetens its overtures with offers of small-scale trade and investments, fruits of its own economic enterprises, and has already opened a Malay restaurant and invested in property in Tashkent. PAS too sometimes tries to develop an independent foreign policy; it was initially as a response to goading by PAS that the Malaysian programme to aid the Bosnians was put into place, to pre-empt a similar plan being hatched in Kelantan. Once again, the Malaysian government's sense of religious correctness is propelled as much by the push of domestic politics as by the pull of international *ummah*.

CONCLUSION

Like many plural or multicultural states, Malaysia has yet to establish its fundamental image and identity. Until the end of the 1960s, most attention was directed towards the definition and universalization of Malayness, and subsequent economic policies supported this goal. Although much of today's public life in Malaysia is pervaded by the Malay language and culture and by a Malay political party, assimilation to Malayness by the immigrant populations, even through conversion to Islam, has never been encouraged.

Malayness is unimaginable without Islam, but the relationship has constantly been redefined. The relationship was redefined by the *dakwah* movements of the 1970s which pushed Islam to centre stage as the most visible pillar of Malay identity, but also triggered responses by the state and UMNO, in the form of greater public attention to Islam.

The *dakwah* episode represents a major paradox for Malay Muslims. Within Malaysia *dakwah* operated as a form of internal conversion, hence reinforced the boundaries between Malays and non-Malays, and highlighted the fact that Malays enjoy no freedom of religious choice, as the recent attention to apostasy testifies. On the other hand, *dakwah* also was a universalizing experience for Malays, who, through their networks with Muslims overseas, became part of an international religious community. Thus were the Malays projected on to a world stage, endowed with a presence beyond their homeland and nation state. For those Malays who continue to be active in such movements as Darul Arqam, and even for some PAS members, this transnational Islamic identity takes precedence over local citizenship, with its alleged dangers of *assabiyah*.

For the federal government, the path to its goal of economic modernity by 2020 is strewn with obstacles both national and religious and to overcome these it must be seen to join and promote them, if sometimes but symbolically. This has led to the 'holier-than-thou' contest of Islamic correctness and credibility between UMNO and PAS, with the former goaded to show its Islamic character, yet without being snared by attributions of 'fundamentalism' or 'fanaticism' intimidating to investors, developers or non-Muslims. To manage this delicate balance, Malaysia's government depends heavily on its co-opted ABIM leadership, on its own selected cohorts of Islamic scholars and *ulama*, and on its self-created federal departments of religious affairs and the public relations services of IKIM.

It does not necessarily follow that either a revitalized Malay or Muslim consciousness are anti-modern. They are neither inert pre-modern relics nor radical forces out of step with the times. Both are forces in a continuous process of re-creation and adaptation to events around them. They shape and are shaped by processes of modernization, economic and political. Today, the Malays are as much products of the New Economic Policy as its creators, and Malay identity centres on new bourgeois styles of life and consumption (cf. Kahn 1992). Yet UMNO and the government which feeds this community also depends on it for votes, hence must continue its affirmative action policies. However, the recent attacks by the federal government on Malay royalty do represent a bold and unprecedented transformation, not only in the direction of legal and constitutional modernity, but also in their symbolic relationship to Malay dominance, with public metaphors shifting from Malay to Islamic domains.

It is in the administrative arm of the state that UMNO retains the greatest control, by holding the constitutional key. The secular constitution is the legal fortress against unilateral implementation of *hudud* by PAS in Kelantan, although allowing the prime minister to make the appropriate verbal gestures with but minimal political risk. The constitution also defends individual rights and freedoms, including those of ethnic and religious minorities and of women. Much of the government's success in sustaining its own development programmes (and power) lies in its management of the legal system, with its complex heritage of conflicts and overlaps between religious and secular courts. However, many legal uncertainties and lacunae persist, even to the definition of the boundaries of the *ummah*, in the marginal cases of converts, mixed marriages and apostates, which test the limits of a multireligious society.

Such anomalies of court, code and religious status could be resolved by the arbitrary and unambiguous implementation of an Islamic state, a solution favoured by PAS in Kelantan. But the social and legal side-effects of such a move would only create iniquities of a different order and erase the entire character and spirit of the multi-ethnic constitutional parliamentary democracy with life-changing consequences for almost 50 per cent of the population, the non-Muslims. And for all its oppositional rhetoric, it is apparent that PAS has not yet prepared a full blueprint for its model Islamic state and *hudud* law. Any Islamic state route to assimilation and uniformity would threaten the economic development programme of the incumbent regime, and the base of its power and authority.

For the time being, the course of development for Malaysia in the immediate future appears locked into the compromise of pursuit of modernity under the cloak of Islamic correctness, and for every major policy to be authenticated by the appropriate religious spokesmen and *ulama*. This approach requires the almost impossible combination of appeal to investors from abroad, while maintaining an impeccable religious image with 'something for everyone' among the assorted Islamic and political interest groups at home. Achievement of this balance requires a substantial measure of authoritarianism in practice, but of a different order than that of an Islamic state. The state uses the *ulama* for its own purposes, but is reluctant to share power with them. It is a task fraught with contradictions, one familiar to other Islamizing states, as the case of Pakistan bears continuing testimony.[16]

The direction of Islamization in Malaysia at present bears more resemblance to a form of evolving civic religion, in which religion legitimates much of state action and policy, and transposes many of the interests of its people on to a sacred plane. In contemporary Malaysia this happens to be a thoroughly 'modern' form of Islam, in tension with competing, more 'fundamentalist' forms in PAS and some of the remaining *dakwah* movements. It represents a situation of uncertain and possibly temporary stability, which is ever vulnerable to destabilization as the result of unanticipated changes, either in the local political scene, or in the Muslim world community at large.

NOTES

1 In the 'pre-modern' era the legitimacy of states did not necessarily derive from a particular people. Thus ancient empires encompassed multiple 'nations' within their boundaries, in a free-floating pluralism, ultimately held together by the strength of a ruler, based on personal/feudal loyalty, coercive military force or myth of divinity. The idea of a people as a source of power and legitimacy is an idiosyncracy which arose in post-medieval Europe.

2 The federation of Malaysia today encompasses the Malay peninsula, which consists of nine original Malay royal states, plus the erstwhile Straits Settlements of Penang and Malacca; and the two states of Sabah and Sarawak of East Malaysia which joined the federation in 1963. Two years later, in 1965, Singapore seceded, thus reducing the proportion of non-Malay populations considerably. For reasons of space, this chapter will not attempt to cover East Malaysia, whose colonial history, demographic, political and cultural character differs substantially from that of the peninsula.

3 Owing to delay in publication of the 1991 census results, the population statistics available are still those of the 1980s. In West Malaysia, the ethnic proportions are officially 55 per cent Malay; 34 per cent Chinese; 12 per cent Indian; and one per cent 'other' (and unofficial updates do not indicate any major changes). It is important to recognize that up to 4 per cent of those listed as 'Malays' are in fact aboriginal people who are not Muslim (*Bumiputra* or 'sons of the soil'). Approximately 8 per cent of Indians are Muslim, while the non-Muslim population comprises 29 per cent Buddhist/Taoist, 7 per cent Hindu, 7 per cent Christian, 2 per cent 'folk', one per cent 'other' and 2 per cent 'no religion' (Department of Statistics, 1981).

4 Some of this variability is the result of differential interpretations (*tafsiran*) and court rulings by local *kathi*, and of accumulated *fatwas* in each state. The two

states without hereditary rulers (Penang and Malacca) are administered in religious matters directly by the King of Malaysia.

5 Strictly, such concessions apply only to members of 'religions of the Book' (*kitabbiyah*), viz. Christians and Jews, and then only to adult males. A third category of 'unbelievers' also exists, and it is not clear whether in Malaysia Buddhism and Hinduism would be classified as such, or whether, as scriptural religions, they would be distinguished from Taoism and local forms of 'animism'. Collectively in Malaysia, the latter would far out-number the original *kitabbiyah* or Christians.

6 The Shari'ah is more doctrine and method than code of law in the following senses (cf. Schacht 1960: 108; An-Na'im 1988: 56). Firstly, in the primary sources or text (the Qur'an), only eighty out of over 6,000 verses can be said to have direct legal significance. Second, some of these verses, especially when taken in conjunction with the Hadith or Sunnah (the deeds and sayings of the Prophet), are contradictory (e.g. over lashes or stoning for sexual offences, death or other penalty for apostasy). Third, the mode of application through exegesis by jurists (*tafsiran*) of different schools has led to diverse legal interpretations and approaches; some jurists maintain that continual reinterpretations in keeping with evolving societies are desirable, whereas others attempt to reconstruct the conditions of the original Muslim community of the first centuries after the Prophet as a permanent precedent, regardless of changing particulars of society and culture. As far as the Hadith is concerned, it must be remembered that this record was not finally compiled until the second and third centuries of the Muslim era (eighth and ninth centuries AD), thus restricting its authority as the ultimate Word of God or of the Prophet in legal matters. Finally, all jurists and *ulama* must defend their own legal credibility and authority by invoking a recognized religious/intellectual genealogy or scholarly tradition (*isnad*), and this has permitted a variety of different schools and rulings to emerge in practice. Thus it has come about over the centuries that Islamic legal rulings vary from state to state, as between Libya, Saudi Arabia, the Sudan, and between the local state religious courts of Malaysia.

7 Of the four major schools or *mazahab* recognized in the Sunni tradition, the Malays officially belong to the Shafi'e school, while a small minority of Indian Muslims follow the Hanbali tradition.

8 Until about the end of the ninth century AD, considerable flexibility of interpretation and legal creativity in the form of new precedents was permitted in the Shari'ah code (*ijtihad*). After this period, something of a 'freeze' set in, (*ijma*), accompanied by a more mechanistic adherence to established practice, which became ever more atavistic in the name of the 'original/fundamental' Islam.

9 Malaysia is ruled by a political coalition, the National Front (*Barisan Nasional*), of which one party, the United Malays National Organisation (UMNO), is the senior and whose head is normally the prime minister. The national language is Malay, and the tone of public culture and morality is increasingly infused with a Malay and Islamic ethos, while the symbols and institutions of royalty are a constant reminder of Malay hegemony. From 1970 until 1990, a general programme of affirmative action, known as the New Economic Policy (NEP), guaranteed favourable quotas for Malays in many educational and occupational arenas, and special financial assistance in many sectors of the economy. This programme was essentially renewed, with minor modifications, as the New Development Policy (NDP) in 1991, and has not reversed the trend towards state capitalism.

10 This is reflected in the situation of non-Malays who are fluent in the Malay language, who observe as much Malay custom as many Malay élites, and who have converted to Islam, but are nonetheless often marginalized as 'new associates' or in separate (Chinese) converts' Associations, as permanent anomalies (see Nagata 1978). Despite the continuing tacit encouragement of conversion to Islam, there is still relatively little provision for moral and other support of the converts in their life as non-Malay Muslims, and the existence of a new Muslims' welfare organization, Peretubuhan Kebajikan Islam Malaysia (PERKIM), has done little to clarify or alleviate this zone of uncertainty.

11 For the history and characteristics of the various Malaysian Muslim resurgent movements since the late 1960s, see : Nagata 1984; Husin Mutalib 1990; Zainah 1987; Chandra 1987; Jomo and Ahmad Shabery Cheek 1992; Muhd Syukri Salleh 1992; Mauzy and Milne 1983–84.

12 During the early 1970s several thousand Chinese, especially in urban areas of West Malaysia, attempted the conversion route to Malay status, in the expectation of some of the perquisites of the NEP, and at this time, the Muslim Converts' Association, PERKIM, under the active leadership of its founder, and ex-prime minister of Malaysia, Tunku Abdul Rahman, was quite supportive. At the same time, in the East Malaysian state of Sabah, an excessively zealous Malay chief minister made liberal use of state resources and authority to sponsor the conversion of many thousands of the aboriginal people to Islam, an enterprise which was also in direct competition with the Christian missions (Nagata 1984). It is generally acknowledged that many of these earlier converts have since lapsed in the wake of unfulfilled expectations.

13 At the height of their influence and activity, the major *dakwah* organizations in Malaysia tended to concentrate on the 'internal' conversion of born Muslim Malays. By contrast, the vision of Anwar Ibrahim, ABIM's founder and first President, was always broader than that of many of his grassroots followers; and Darul Arqam leaders today have increasingly turned to international expansion through *dakwah* directed also towards non-Muslims, as in Central Asia and the Philippines, sometimes cemented through marriage.

14 Another immunity also enjoyed by the sultans and covered by a Sedition Act, was from any public discussion or questioning of their role or from criticism of their personal behaviour, since it touched on the special status of the Malays, and was classified as a 'sensitive' issue. Once the events leading to the opening of the constitutional amendment were publicized and opened up to public scrutiny by the Prime Minister himself, however, a flow of past revelations and allegations was unleashed, from matters of involvement in illegal logging of tropical forests, to gambling, business corruption and physical violence towards the 'people' (*rakyat*). For several weeks, the government seemed to revel in publishing such cases, as one means of persuading the 'traditional' Malay of the flaws in the character of their monarchs, as simultaneously anti-modern and un-Islamic.

15 The other post Independence prime ministers of Malaysia were: Tunku Abdul Rahman, a prince of the house of Kedah, followed by Tun Hussein Onn and Tun Abdul Razak respectively, both scions of aristocratic families.

16 At the time of writing, in April 1993, the Malaysian Prime Minister and his wife completed their first visit to ('Shi'ite') Iran, the old role model of the early, more revolutionary ABIM. In addition to discussing trade between the two countries, inside sources revealed that one of the interests of Iranian leaders was to solicit advice from the Prime Minister's wife, as to ways and means of re-involving Iranian women in an economy suffering from loss of female

services. In Iran, as elsewhere (e.g. Central Asia), countries like Malaysia (and also Turkey) are regarded as viable models for economic development and forms of 'modernity' within an Islamic framework.

REFERENCES

Amina Wadud-Muhsin (1992) *Qur'an and Woman*, Kuala Lumpur: Penerbit Fajar Bakti Sdn. Bhd.

Anderson, Benedict (1983) *The Imagined Community*, Ithaca: Cornell University Press.

An-Na'im, Abdullahi (1986) 'The Islamic Law of Apostasy and its Modern Applicability: A Case from the Sudan, *Religion* 16: 197–224.

—— (1988) 'Mahmud Muhammad Taha and the Crisis in Islamic Law Reform: Implications for Interreligious Relations', *Journal of Ecumenical Studies* 25(1): 1–21.

Chandra Muzaffar (1981) *Protector? An Analysis of the Concept and Practice of Loyalty in Leader-Led Relationships Within Malay Society*, Penang: Aliran Publications.

—— (1987) *Islamic Resurgence in Malaysia*, Petaling Jaya: Penerbit Fajar Bakti Sdn. Bhd.

Department of Statistics (1981) *Population Census of Malaysia (1980): General Report*, Kuala Lumpur.

Gellner, Ernest (1983) *Nations and Nationalism*, Oxford: Basil Blackwell.

—— (1992) *Postmodernism, Reason and Religion*, London: Routledge.

Hamid Jusoh (1991) *The Position of Islamic Law in the Malaysian Constitution with Special Reference to the Conversion Case in Family Law*, Kuala Lumpur: Dewan Bahasa & Pustaka.

Husin Mutalib (1990) *Islam and Ethnicity in Malay Politics*, Singapore: Oxford University Press.

Jomo, K. S. and Ahmad Shabery Cheek (1992) 'Malaysia's Islamic Movements', in Joel S. Kahn and Francis Loh Kok Wah (eds) *Fragmented Vision: Culture and Politics in Contemporary Malaysia*, North Sydney, Australia: Allen & Unwin, (in association with Asian Studies Association, Australia).

Kahn, Joel (1992) 'Class, Ethnicity and Diversity: Some Remarks on Malay Culture in Malaysia', in Joel S. Kahn and Francis Loh Kok Wah (eds) *Fragmented Vision: Culture and Politics in Contemporary Malaysia*, North Sydney, Australia: Allen & Unwin (in association with Asian Studies Association, Australia).

Kassim Ahmad (1986) *Hadis: Jawapan Kepada Pengritik*, Kaula Lumpur: Media Indah.

Mauzy, D. and Milne, S. R. (1983–4) 'The Mahathir Administration in Malaysia: Discipline through Islam', *Pacific Affairs* 56(4):617–48 (Winter).

Mohd. Rushdi Yusuf (1990) *Darul Arqam: Antara Kebenaran dan Kekeliruan*, Kuala Lumpur: Penerbitan Kintan Sdn. Bhd.

Mohd Suffian Hashim *et al.* (1978) 'The Constitution of Malaysia: Its Development, 1957–1977,' Kuala Lumpur: Oxford University Press.

Muhd Syukri Salleh (1992) *An Islamic Approach to Rural Development: The Arqam Way*, London: ASOIB International.

Nagata, Judith (1978) 'The Chinese Muslims of Malaysia: New Malays or New Associates? A Problem in Ethnicity', in Gordon Means (ed.) *The Past in Southeast Asia's Present*, Selected Proceedings, Canadian Council of Southeast Asian Studies, Hamilton: McMaster University.

—— (1984) *The Reflowering of Malaysian Islam: Religious Radicals and Their Roots*, Vancouver: University of British Columbia Press.

Report of the Federation of Malaysia Constitutional Commission (1957), London: Colonial Office.

Roff, William (1967) *The Origins of Malay Nationalism*, New Haven: Yale University Press.

Schacht, Joseph (1960) 'Problems of Modern Islamic Legislation', *Studia Islamica* 12.

Zainah Anwar (1987) *Islamic Revivalism in Malaysia*, Petaling Jaya: Pelandok.

Chapter 5

The politics of Islamic fundamentalism
Iran, Tunisia and the challenge to the secular state

Fred Halliday

INTRODUCTION

The rise of Islamic fundamentalism has occasioned many, often contradictory, claims as to its significance for the contemporary world. Within the Islamic countries themselves there are those who argue that a new era of Islamic power is dawning – present in the rhetoric of the Iranian revolution, this theme has acquired apparent confirmation from the collapse of the Soviet Union a decade later, which was interpreted by some Islamists to show that the only contestatory ideology with a global potential is Islam. In the West, the 'challenge' of Islamic movements has been construed, variously, as the rise of a new threat equal to communism, or as part of a new pattern of world politics dominated by the 'clash of civilisations'.[1] For others, Islamic movements correspond to some new conceptual and even ethical epoch, one of 'post-modernity', in which the claims of rationalist discourse derived from the European enlightenment are no longer valid, as either analytic tools or moral guidelines.

The analysis that follows corresponds to none of these interpretations. The argument, whether made by Islamists or their enemies, that 'Islam' constitutes a strategic challenge to the West is nonsense – not least because of the weak economic condition of the supposedly menacing countries. The theory of a clash of civilizations operates with a deterministic concept of 'civilization', and understates the degree to which conflict is between peoples of similar orientation. As for the claim that the enlightenment project should be abandoned, there is in this a degree of exaggeration and projection – exaggeration of how supposedly 'new' much of the contemporary world is, and projection of what may be valid forms of literary analysis on to the very different world of social and political reality. The following analysis is by contrast neither apocalyptic nor 'postmodern': it is rather an attempt, using decidedly traditional and rational categories of analysis, to grasp the contingency, variety and indeed modernity of the Islamist upsurge. In this vein, I will begin with the most traditional approach of all, a dose of historical perspective.

The past decade or two have not been the first occasion on which forces claiming to represent 'Islam' have adopted an assertive international stance. The dynamic unleashed in Arabia in the seventh century of the Christian epoch took more than a millennium to spend itself and for today's boundaries to be drawn: if the Arabs were expelled from Spain at the end of the fifteenth century, the Turks sought to counter-attack in the sixteenth and subjected much of the Eastern Mediterranean and North Africa to their control. The siege of Malta in the mid-sixteenth century failed; that of Crete, over a century later, succeeded. Where Vittoriosa, Cospicua and Senglea held out, Chania, Rethimno and Heraklion succumbed – not least because of shorter Ottoman lines of communication. The Turks ruled Crete until 1898. Only at the end of World War I, when other empires had obtruded into the Mediterranean, did the last of the Islamic empires collapse. To the south-east a similar, long, confrontation was fought out between the Muslim and Hindu worlds, one that culminated in the establishment of the Moghul empire in northern India.

In this, as in so many other cases of international and confessional conflict, the past provides a reserve of symbols and fears, even if it does little to explain the resurgence of religious and ethnic identities. Both Muslims, and their non-Muslim neighbours in the Mediterranean and elsewhere, are aware of, and frequently invoke these precedents, to legitimate or discredit more recent manifestations of Islamic assertion.[2] But the earlier expansions of Islam – in the seventh to tenth centuries AD, with the Arab conquests, and in the sixteenth and seventeenth centuries with the Ottomans – took place in a very different context, for two evident reasons. First the historical context was one in which the industrial and military supremacy of the West had not yet been assured. To-day the Islamic states may present a rhetorical threat to the West, and may engage in individual acts of pressure, military or economic, against it: but the strategic situation is quite different. They are incapable of mounting a concerted challenge, let alone of redrawing boundaries. In this sense, those areas of Europe once occupied by, or threatened from, the south are to a considerable degree immune – the flow of migrant workers and the incidence of terrorism by Middle East groups being very different from the military and piratical attacks of previous centuries.

Secondly, the contemporary challenge of 'Islam' is, demagogy on both sides apart, not about inter-state relations at all, but about how these Islamic societies and states will organize themselves and what the implications of such organization for their relations with the outside world will be.[3] The dynamic is an internal, often destructively involutionary, one, rather than a continuation however remote, of the Arab and Ottoman conquests. As will be argued below, the more recent rise of Islamic politics in the states and popular movements of the Muslim world poses little threat to the non-Muslim world without; it is primarily a response to the perceived weakness and subjugation of the Islamic world, and is concerned with an internal regeneration. That this process is accompanied by much denunciation of the outside world and the occasional act of violence against it should not obscure the fact that the Islamic revival concerns above all the Muslim world itself. The question it poses is not, therefore, whether it threatens the outside world which, broadly speaking, it does not: but whether, in any of its variants, it can provide a solution to the problems which Muslim societies face today.

The 1990s provide, in some degree, an advantageous position from which to assess the causes and consequences of the rise of what is termed Islamic fundamentalism or 'Islamism'.[4] A decade and a half have passed since the most spectacular success of this movement, the advent to power of Ayatollah Khomeini in February 1979 and the establishment of the Islamic Republic of Iran. The passage of time allows of assessment of its achievement in two central respects: the construction of a post-revolutionary state, and the international impact of the revolution. The years since then have also seen the growth of fundamentalist movements in a number of countries, notably Algeria, Egypt, Jordan and Afghanistan.[5] The Iraqi invasion of Kuwait in August 1990, while initiated by a regime of decidedly secular and anti-clerical orientation, nonetheless served to mobilize Islamist sentiment in a range of countries in support of Saddam Hussein.[6] They have also been ones in which the several million Muslims of western Europe have become more organized and explicit in their Islamic identity. The Rushdie affair, which exploded in 1989 with Khomeini's condemnation of the writer to death, became a particular source of conflict and resentment.[7] Earlier emphases have now given way to a pursuit of identity, community and continued distinctness.

DISAGGREGATING 'ISLAM': FOUR GUIDELINES

This overview of developments since the 1970s may serve to illustrate some of the features of this international trend, but also to underline the dangers of simplification with regard to it. In the light of this diversity, and of the record of the past two decades, it is possible to make some general remarks about this current and to place it in some broader perspective. Four of these are especially relevant to any assessment of the current stage of Islamic movements.[8]

1   Islamism as politics

The terms 'revival' and 'fundamentalist' are misleading, since both refer to trends *within* a religion. This Islamic current involves not a revival of religious belief, but an assertion of the relevance of this belief, selectively interpreted, to politics. The Islamic movement has had a strong religious character: but it has not involved a movement of conversion, from other religions, or a return to belief by formerly Muslim communities who had abandoned their faith. Rather, it involves the assertion that, in the face of secular, modern, and European ideas, Islamic values should play a dominant role in political and social life and should define the identity of the Islamic peoples. If there is one common thread running through the multiple movements characterized as 'fundamentalist', it is not anything to do with their interpretation of the Islamic 'foundations', i.e. the Qur'an or *hadith* but rather their claim to be able to determine a politics for Muslim peoples. The central concern of Islamist movements is the state, how to resist what is seen as an alien and oppressive state, and how, through a variety of tactics, to obtain and maintain control of the state. In this perspective the rise of Islamist movements in the 1970s and 1980s bears comparison with that of tendencies elsewhere that deploy religious ideology in pursuit of other, nationalist and populist, political goals – in Christianity, Judaism, Hinduism, Buddhism.[9] Given the tendency of both Muslims themselves and those who write about 'Islam' to treat it as both a unitary and unique phenomenon, it would be prudent henceforth to check any generalization about Islam against the practices of those using other, non-Islamic, religions in a similarly political manner.

2 Variants of Islamism

Once this, essentially, political interpretation becomes clear, then it is more possible to identify and explain the variety of Islamist movements and ideas. For the character of Islamist movement varies according to the political and social context in which these trends arise.[10] Broadly speaking, there are three such contexts. The first is Islamic popular revolt.[11] This is where a popular movement within an Islamic country challenges a secular state, or one that is regarded as insufficiently Islamic, for political power: this was classically the case in Iran in 1978–9, and it also applies in Algeria, Tunisia, Egypt, Turkey and, in very different circumstances, Afghanistan. It involves a popular revolt against the modernizing, centralizing, state. The second form of Islamic politics is where Islam is used by a state itself to legitimate and consolidate its position. Here there exists a spectrum, from the very token invocation of Islamic identity by what are in effect secular rulers (Nasser's Egypt, Morocco, the FLN in Algeria, the Ba'th in Syria and Iraq) through to the use of Islam as a more central part of the state's authority and power. Even this category permits of no simple definition, since regimes that proclaim themselves as legitimated by Islam range across the gamut of political options: military dictatorships (Libya, Pakistan, and now Sudan); tribal oligarchies (Saudi Arabia); clerical dictatorship (Iran). Nothing could make clearer the extent to which Islamic politics is dependent on the pre-existing context and serves as the instrument of state power.

The last variant of Islamic politics is in contexts of confessional or ethnic conflict. Here Islamism serves to articulate the interests and identity of groups that form part of a broader political community that is heterogeneous on religious grounds, i.e. includes Muslims and non-Muslims, or, even where all are Muslims, includes divergent sects of Islam or different linguistic and ethnic groups. This has received less attention on the international level, but it is a major part of the picture of Islamic politics in the contemporary world. Long-established variants of this are the Lebanon and the Caucasus, and the Islamic–Coptic conflict in Egypt. But modern developments have created new contexts in which such tendencies can develop as part of conflicts within specific states. This is, after all, the context in which Islamism is spreading in Western Europe, as part of a self-definition of new communities within a secular, post-Christian, society. It is equally so in the Balkans: for all the talk, mainly from Orthodox Christians in Serbia and Greece of a 'Muslim' challenge to the Balkans, it is the non-Muslims who have accentuated the situation there, and in so doing led some Muslims, in Bosnia and in Albania, to adopt more fundamentalist positions. This communal context is part, too, of the explanation for the role of Islamist ideas amongst the Palestinians, since they are, in effect, a subordinated part of a broader non-Muslim, in this case Israeli, society. Equally a part of the Islamist movement in Algeria can be seen in this light, as the expression of Arab hostility to the Kabyle minority for whom the French language, and a more secular order, provide an alternative to domination by the Arab majority. The issue of Arabic within Algeria has, therefore, several layers of significance: as a cultural assertion against French, as an Islamic assertion against non-Islamic values, and as an Arab assertion against the Kabyles. The close association of the Arabic language with Islamic identity enables this campaign for Arabic to bear these multiple, ethnic-religious, meanings. To take an example from the non-Arab world, that of Malaysia: in a society divided between Muslim Malays and non-Muslim Chinese, and growing resentment by the former of the latter, Islamism serves amongst the Malays to express an ethnic and confessional interest.

3   Contingent interpretations

This picture of the variant roles of Islam in politics can illumine the degree to which 'Islam' itself is open to differing interpretations, how the particular use made of its traditions and texts is variable, contingent on contemporary, rather more material and political concerns. In the hypostatization of doctrine this is a point that is too often obscured in discussions, by Muslims and non-Muslims alike, of the role of 'Islam' itself in these processes. The presupposition upon which much discussion of the question rests is that there exists one, unified and clear, tradition to which contemporary believers and political forces may relate. Many of the discussions that have taken place in the Islamic world have rested on this assumption, of an essential Islam. This was the case in the 1960s in the debate about whether Islam favoured capitalism or socialism. It recurred in the 1970s and 1980s in discussions of the place of women, in analysis of the proper role of the clergy in an Islamic society, in the debate on Islamic teaching on tolerance after the Rushdie affair and so forth. These all involve an assumption that there is one 'true' interpretation. Opponents of Islamist movements tend to reproduce this essentialist assumption in discussing such questions as whether Islamic societies can ever be democratic, or whether there is some special link between the 'Islamic mind' and terrorism. The reality is that no such essential Islam exists: as one Iranian thinker put it, Islam is a sea in which it is possible to catch almost any fish one wants. It is, like all the great religions, a reserve of values, symbols, and ideas from which it is possible to derive a contemporary politics and social code: the answer as to why this or that interpretation was put upon Islam resides therefore, not in the religion and its texts itself, but in the contemporary needs of those articulating an Islamic politics. These needs are evident, and secular, enough: the desire to challenge or retain state power; the need to mobilize dominated, usually urban, populations for political action; the articulation of a nationalist ideology against foreign domination and those within the society associated with it; the 'need' to control women; the carrying out of social and political reforms designed to strengthen post-revolutionary states.

4 Criteria of 'success'

Once 'Islam' and 'Islamism' are disaggregated in this way, the movements that proclaim their adherence to Islam can be seen both within their own specific contexts and as part of a loose, variegated, and unco-ordinated international system. Moreover, it may become easier to arrive at a yardstick for assessing the impact and success of this phenomenon. The criterion often raised after the Iranian revolution was whether or not there would be a repetition of what happened in Iran: on this criterion, the Iranian revolution has not spread and fundamentalism has been contained. But this criterion is in two major respects an inadequate one. First, it adopts too small a timescale. Revolutionaries themselves, whether Islamic or other, are impatient, and expect other peoples to imitate them immediately: in this sense they become disappointed just as quickly as their opponents become relieved. But in historical perspective it would seem that the timescale for assessing the international impact of revolution is not a few years but several decades: the impact of the French revolution was felt throughout the nineteenth century; it was in the late 1940s, thirty years after 1917, that the USSR enjoyed its greatest external expansion; it took Castro twenty years to secure a revolutionary ally on the Latin American mainland, in Nicaragua. In the case of the Iranian revolution, however, there is a further reason why the criterion of state power is inadequate, namely that the impact of the Islamic upheaval there has been substantial even though no other state has become an Islamic republic. It is only necessary to see the rise in Islamist political consciousness in a range of countries to see how far the Iranian model has influenced political behaviour, or to recognize the increased interest amongst young people in Islamic clothing, Islamic literature, mosque attendance, and so forth. It is commonly asserted that Iran lost its following in the Arab world after it became embroiled in the war with Iraq in 1980: but while it was often presented by Arab states as just another example of Persian expansionism and Shi'ite heterodoxy, a general identification with the Iranian revolution was evident in many countries, and, in some, such as Lebanon, took organized form. Whether or not Islamist forces of the Iranian variety do come to power in the following years or decades, the impact of the revolution and of the broader trend with which it is associated is undeniable.

As was noted earlier, each of the three forms of Islamic interaction with politics has evident relevance to the contemporary international situation, and to the Mediterranean in particular. Thus the movements in Algeria, Tunisia, Egypt, Israel, Lebanon, and Turkey are all variants of the first category, that of populist revolts, from below, against the State: indeed 'Islam' has become the dominant idiom in which such resistance is expressed. Within this category there are also major differences – some are led by clerics, others by lay personnel; some are Sunni, others Shiite. The use of 'Islam' by established regimes to promote their own legitimacy is also widespread: thus in their attempt to pre-empt Islamist revolt from below, Egyptian rulers since Nasser, Sadat, and Mubarak, have presented themselves in Islamic garb. In a more militant form, Qaddafi has also done the same thing: yet Qaddafi's espousal of the Islamic cause can be seen as much as a radical extension of the Nasserite Arab nationalist use of Islam as something involving a clear primacy for Islam. His territorial claims are Arab nationalist – on a par with the Iraqi claim on part of Iran, the Syrian on part of Turkey, the belief that Eritrea and the Canary Islands are 'Arab', or occasional evocations of *malta arabiyya*. Qaddafi has clashed with the clerical and Islamist opposition within his own country, and is widely believed to be responsible for the death of the Lebanese Shiite leader Musa Sadr in 1978. In recent years he has taken to stressing the primary role of the Arabs within Islam and has attacked non-Arab Islamic forces, such as the Jamaat-i-Islami of Pakistan and the *tabligh* movement prevalent amongst Muslims of western Europe. The role of Islam in confessional conflicts, the third broad category, is evident on both sides of the Mediterranean – in Egypt and Lebanon, but also in Yugoslavia and in those western European countries with a larger Islamic population.

In the analysis below I focus on two of the most prominent cases of Islamist revival, those of Iran and of Tunisia. The one has been the most striking success of Islamism, with consequences that still remain to be worked through. The second represents the rise of an Islamist movement in a North African context that was, Qaddafi aside, considered until the early 1980s to be relatively immune to the appeals of political Islam.

ISLAMISM IN POWER: THE RECORD OF THE KHOMEINI DECADE

The death of Ayatollah Khomeini on 3 June 1989 brought to an end the first decade of the Islamic Republic of Iran and provides one point from which to assess the character and consequences of Iran's revolution. The consolidation of the regime after 1979 and its continuation after Khomeini's death provide much material for analysis of what Islamism means in practice as far as political and social control are concerned. It also illustrates the greatest failing of these movements, which is their lack of an economic programme.

There is not space here to review the revolution itself and the analytic questions it raised: suffice it to say, in line with what has been written above, that the Iranian revolution involved a mass revolution from below against an authoritarian modernizing state, and that its success was made possible by the political leadership it received from Khomeini and his associated clerics. They provided not just the organizational framework, but also the ideology with which the mobilization became possible. Central to this ideology were three tenets, oft repeated in Khomeini's speeches and sermons.[12] The first was the belief, supposedly 'traditional' and 'fundamental', but actually a novel interpretation of Islamic doctrine, according to which it was possible to have an Islamic State in the contemporary world, even in the absence (the *gheiba* or occultation) of the Prophet's successor the Imam, and that this could be implemented through the role of the 'jurisconsult' or *faqih*, the position held by Khomeini during his lifetime. The second core ideological element was the division of the world into two categories, the oppressed or *mostazafin* and the oppressors or *mostakbarin*, two Qur'anic terms turned to modern, populist, usage. Khomeini appealed to the poorer, excluded, elements of society, in the name of a revolutionary ideal. Third there was the appropriation in Islamic terms of what was in essence a third world nationalist appeal: against the twin Satans, of East and West, against the world-devouring (*jahan-khor*) forces that had long oppressed Iran. Khomeini's appeal to Muslims was not so much the offensive, aggressive one of converting the world to Islam, the earlier meaning of *jihad*, but rather that of defending the Islamic world against occupation and corruption from outside. *Jihad* in this context acquired an inward-looking, defensive character, but one that served to divide the world clearly into the camp of the struggling oppressed third-world peoples and their enemies, the non-Islamic powers. Many aspects of the revolution were peculiar to Iran, not least the specific organizational and ideological autonomy of the clergy from state control, a feature not present in Sunni societies. But the impact of the revolution, carried out in the name of Islam and under the leadership of the clergy, had enormous effect across the Muslim world.

Khomeini's achievement was considerable – in making the revolution, in remaining in power, and not least, in ensuring a smooth transition after his death. Two factors were important here. One was that his regime had been run by a group of clergy that had been his students years before and who constituted a loose but effective revolutionary cadre around him. It was these people who maintained sufficient unity after 3 June to ensure that Rafsanjani, already the most influential Government personality after Khomeini, was able to assume power and be elected to the new, chief executive position of president. The other factor, evident in the popular response to Khomeini's death, was the immense authority which the revolution and the Ayatollah in particular retained within the population, despite all the difficulties of the post-revolutionary period. The revolution and eight-year war with Iraq had brought immense privations to Iran, and sections of the population had been alienated by repression. But there can be no doubt that, ten years after Khomeini came to power, the Islamic Republic enjoys considerable legitimacy within Iran: it was this support that made it more possible for Khomeini's associates to organize a smooth transition.

Khomeini's last years were, however, marked by great difficulties for Iran: these followed, to a considerable extent, from uncertainty within the ideology of the revolution itself. The first uncertainty was that of the role of the state in the new post-revolutionary situation, and the relationship between Government and Islam itself. In the early period of the Islamic Republic, greatest emphasis was laid on the question of how Islamic thinking could influence the policy of the state: thus the constitution was rewritten to include the concept of the *velayat-i-faqhi* the vice-regency of the jurisconsult; economic policy was altered to preclude the taking or granting of interest-bearing loans; education was transformed to reflect Islamic thinking, as was the law; women were forced to wear Islamic clothing. However, this Islamization of the state went together with another debate, the degree to which the precepts of Islam could act as a constraint upon the actions of Government. This was an argument put forward in the first instance by opponents of the Khomeini regime, who argued for an Islamic limitation of the new republican regime; but it soon came to be prevalent within the state itself, in the argument on such issues as Government control of trade and finance, and intervention in the economy in the name of planning. Those within the Government who adopted a more conservative attitude to economic policy, opposing state intervention, used this Islamic argument to block reform measures.

It was in this context that Khomeini, in January 1988, made one of his most important political pronouncements, in the form of a letter to the then president Khamene'i. Khamene'i had apparently argued that the Government could exercise power only within the bounds of divine statutes. But Khomeini disagreed, stating that government was 'a supreme vice-regency bestowed by God upon the Holy Prophet and that it is among the most important of divine laws and has priority over all peripheral divine orders'. He itemized a set of issues on which, if his view was not valid, the Government would not be able to take action:[13]

> Conscription, compulsory despatch to the fronts, prevention of the entry or exodus of any commodity, the ban on hoarding except in two or three cases, customs duty, taxes, prevention of profiteering, price-fixing, prevention of the distribution of narcotics, ban on addiction of any kind except in the case of alcoholic drinks, the carrying of all kinds of weapons.

Khomeini continued:

> I should state that the government which is part of the absolute vice-regency of the Prophet of God is one of the primary injunctions of Islam and has priority over all other secondary injunctions, even prayers, fasting, and *hajj*. The ruler is authorized to demolish a mosque or a house which is in the path of a road and to compensate the owner for his house. The ruler can close down mosques if needs be, or can even demolish a mosque which is a source of harm . . . The government is empowered to unilaterally revoke any Shari'ah (Islamic law) agreements which it has concluded with the people when those agreements are contrary to the interest of the country or to Islam. It can also prevent any devotional or non-devotional affair if it is opposed to the interests of Islam and for as long as it is so.

This explicit statement was not just a legitimation of what already existed in Iran, namely a clerical dictatorship. The concept of the 'absolute vice-regency' (*velayat-i mutlaq*) was a major new formulation of Islamist politics in the context where an Islamic state had already been created. Yet like all such legitimations, such as the dictatorship of the proletariat, it contained its contradiction: for the legitimation of the state and of the *faqih* lay in its fidelity to Islamic perceptions, and yet this authority, derived from Islam, was now being used to justify overriding whatever Islam enjoined. The key to this new legitimation was given by the concept, invoked in the quotation above of *maslahat* or 'interest' of the Muslim people: it was in the name of this interest, which the *faqih* alone could identify, that the specific injunctions of Islam could be overridden. Conservative opposition had been based in the Council of Guardians, a clerical body designed to see whether parliamentary decisions contradicted Islamic precepts: Khomeini broke this deadlock by creating a new committee, for the 'Discernment of the Interest of the Islamic Order' (*Tashkhis-i Maslahat-i Nizam-i Islami*), which now had overall power. Never were the underlying political priorities of Islamism clearer: the tactical concern of Khomeini was to use the concept of 'interest' and of the absolute authority of the jurisconsult to override conservative opposition within the regime; the overall goal was to invert Islamic authority so as to remove any Islamic restrictions, particularly with regard to property, from the actions of the state.

A similar political determination could be seen in the manner in which Khomeini handled another difficult area of state policy, namely the export of revolution. In common with all revolutions, that of Iran presented itself as a model for other peoples and sought to promote this process elsewhere. The concept 'export of revolution', *sudur-i inqilab*, was commonly used by Iranian officials: it included the conventional means of exporting political radicalism – arms, financial support, training, international congresses, propaganda, radio programmes. Islamic tradition also provided specific elements to this process: thus at the ideological level, Khomeini could claim that the Islamic peoples were all one, and that in Islam there were no frontiers. In organizational terms, the already established links between different religious communities across the Muslim world provided a network for building revolutionary links. Until the clashes of 1987 when around 400 Iranians were killed, the *hajj*, the annual pilgrimage to Mecca, acted as a means for propagating Iran's revolutionary ideas.[14]

The most important component of this policy was the attempt to export Islamic revolution to Iraq: Iran had called for this before the Iraqi invasion of September 1980, and this became Khomeini's rationale for continuing the war after July 1982 when the Iraqis were driven out of Iranian territory. In the end, of course, it failed: the Iraqi population did not rise up, and the regime did not collapse. In August 1988 Iran was forced to accept a ceasefire. In his speech calling for a ceasefire, Khomeini stated that, for him, this was worse than drinking poison: but political and strategic necessity forced him to do it. This enormous setback in the promotion of revolution abroad did not, however, lead to an acceptance that promotion of Islamic radicalism abroad was impossible. Iran continued to play a role in arming and guiding Shiite guerillas in two countries, Lebanon and Afghanistan, and in the bitter aftermath of the war it maintained a steady criticism of Saudi Arabia, whose corrupt rulers it saw as enemies of Islam.

The proclamation of Iran's continued role as leader of the oppressed across the world was important not just for external reasons, promoting the image and prestige of Iran, but also internally, as a means of sustaining the morale of the population and preventing 'liberalism', a spirit of compromise or accommodation with the outside world, from coming to the fore. After the August 1988 ceasefire, Khomeini felt there was a danger that the Iranian revolution would falter and that it would lose its revolutionary orientation. It was in this context that he reasserted his view that Iran should remain independent of international economic forces, even at the cost of austerity.[15] But he also used an issue that gave him the opportunity to provoke a major crisis with the non-Islamic world and at the same time to present Iran as the leader of the Islamic cause, namely the Salman Rushdie affair. Iran's position on this, calling for the death of the author of *The Satanic Verses*, was a means for Khomeini to meet both of his main policy goals – mobilization at home, confrontation internationally.

Both of these policies reflected the political thinking of Khomeini, and the way in which priorities of power and maintenance of state control determined his use of Islamic concepts and interpretation of 'tradition'. Ultimately, the political assessment of Khomeini's legacy will depend on whether the Islamic Republic can endure beyond his death and whether the new regime can resolve the most pressing problem it faces, namely that of revitalizing the economy. Whether or not it succeeds, however, the measure of Khomeini's achievement should not be understated: the regime survived for a decade and was able to effect a quick and smooth transition to the successor leadership. It retains considerable support from its own population and its impact upon Muslims the world over continues.

ISLAMISM IN THE CENTRAL MEDITERRANEAN: THE CASE OF TUNISIA

Tunisia is, historically, the most open and Mediterranean of the Arab countries, an improbable site for a fundamentalist upsurge: but the Islamic and Arab worlds have produced enough surprises in recent years for it to be most uncertain what the future holds, not least because it is in urban areas like greater Tunis that Islamic challenges have grown the most. During the 1950s and 1960s the initiative in Tunisia was held by secular parties, loyal to some variant of socialism. Since the 1970s there has been a growing challenge from the Islamist opposition, and it was this threat to the regime which, in part, accounted for the coup of 7 November 1987 in which Habib Bourguiba, leader of the country since 1956, was deposed. In a break with the autocratic practices of Bourguiba's reign, greater freedom of expression was allowed, and elections for the presidency and for parliament were held in April 1989. Yet this opening of Tunisia, designed to reduce polarization and reintegrate the Islamist forces into political life, soon ran into difficulty. By the end of 1989 it was clear that the regime was not prepared to make serious concessions to the opposition and in 1990, taking advantage of the Kuwait crisis to strike a nationalist pose, Ben Ali cracked down heavily on his challengers.[16]

These changes left open the question that divided Tunisia before and after the coup of 7 November 1987. Ben Ali had ended the rule of President Habib Bourguiba, because his regime was increasingly associated with brutality and corruption. Earlier challenged by the socialist and secular opposition, Bourguiba had in his later years faced opposition from the Islamic forces, the Islamic Tendency Movement (MTI). They had led nation-wide protests in 1984 against price rises, and Bourguiba had staged show trials of their leaders in 1986. It was widely believed that had Ben Ali not staged his coup on 7 November radical Islamist elements in the armed forces would have tried to do so themselves.

In the months after Bourguiba's departure Tunisia lived through an ambiguous honeymoon. Bourguiba himself was under a form of house arrest in his native town of Monastir. Squares named after his birthday, 3 August 1903, were now called after 7 November 1987. Some of his statues were pulled down. But streets were still named after him, his grand mausoleum and mosque remained well tended in Monastir. Ben Ali, who worked as minister of the interior and Prime Minister under Bourguiba, presented himself as the man of 'renewal' and called for political pluralism and respect for human rights. He opened a dialogue with the opposition forces, socialist and Islamic. An amnesty released hundreds of political prisoners and allowed thousands to return home. The press was much freer. But the state over which Ben Ali presided was still that inherited from the French and shaped by Bourguiba: Government policy was, in effect, 'Bourguibism without Bourguiba'.

During the election period of 1989, the uncertainty of Tunisia, caught between a secular state and a religious opposition, was graphically evident at the entrance to the walled old city, the *medina* of Kairouan, the holy city of North African Islam. There stood a vast portrait of Tunisian President Ben Ali, installed for the elections: the President gazed confidently at the centre of traditional religious opposition to the state, while the hoarding proclaimed him to be 'Protector of the Sanctuary and of Religion'. In the *medina* itself the walls were covered with the electoral programmes of the competing parties: red for the ruling Democratic Constitutional Rally (RCD), mauve for the opposition 'independents', the rubric under which the Islamic forces, whose party had not been legalized, ran in the elections. But the main candidate of the RCD was himself a cleric: Sheikh Abdulrahman Khlif, famous throughout Tunisia for leading a protest in the 1960s against the filming of *The Thief of Baghdad* in the Kairouan shrine.

As the example of Kairouan shows, the regime has gone some way to presenting itself in Islamic garb, much as in Egypt Sadat and Mubarak sought to appropriate some Islamic legitimacy. Posters of Ben Ali during the election campaign showed him in the white robes of the *hajji*. Soon after 7 November he went on the *'umrah*, the individual pilgrimage to Mecca. Election posters for the ruling party showed a set of hands with the slogan 'The Hand of God is with the Assembly'. Government speeches now begin with an invocation of Allah and end with quotes from the Qur'an. Religious programmes feature on television, something forbidden under Bourguiba.

Nowhere was this shift more evident than in the attitude to the Muslim month of fasting, Ramadan. Bourguiba, intent on modernizing the country, ordered restaurants to stay open and told people to eat: *'Il faut manger'*, he declared. On one occasion he took the symbolic step of drinking a glass of orange juice during a public rally held in Ramadan. Yet even at the height of the secularizing drive, in the 1960s, there was widespread observance of fasting. During the Ramadan of 1989, which began in early April, observance was over 90 per cent. In an excess of zeal, brought on in part because there had been no religious education in Tunisia under Bourguiba, many believers fasted even when Islamic codes say they should not – pregnant women, children under the age of puberty, people such as diabetics or kidney patients who should eat or take medicines regularly. The press published widely on the significance and rituals of Ramadan.

In the parliamentary elections on 2 April, the government list triumphed in Kairouan, as it did everywhere else in Tunisia. There was not a single opposition candidate in the 141-seat assembly. The most delicate issue facing the regime therefore remained that of the Islamic opposition. In the elections the Islamist 'independents' won around 17 per cent of the vote, displacing the secular left, who won around 3 per cent, as the main opposition. Given that around 1.2 million of those of voting age were not registered, and given the almost complete control which the ruling party has in the rural areas, it can be assumed that the Islamist strength is considerably greater than that 17 per cent: in the Tunis area, the figure was around 30 per cent. Until the latter part of 1989 the Islamists themselves played their cards carefully and seemed intent to maintain their dialogue with the regime in the hope that their party would be legalized.

Rachid Ghannoushi, the leader of the Islamic Tendency, now 'independents', laid greatest stress on those issues that he saw as challenging the Bourguibist legacy; the need to lessen the power of the State, and to make the economy more egalitarian and independent. In an interview immediately after the elections Ghannoushi declared:

Our social objective is to contribute to laying the cultural and social bases of a civil society which assumes its most important functions and which the state serves and which constitutes the only source of legitimacy. There is no place for dominating society in the name of any legitimacy – neither historic, religious, proletarian, nor pseudo-democratic. Bourguiba put forward the slogan of the state's prestige, but its real content was the monopoly of the party and of the capitalist interests within which power in the country was located as was the monopoly which Bourguiba exercised over this state. The time has come to raise the slogan of the prestige of society, of the citizen, and of the power which serves both.[17]

Proclamations stressed the need for Tunisia to return to its 'Islamic and Arab traditions': but it was not spelt out what these were. Ghannoushi demanded that the day of rest be moved from Sunday to Friday, but he was cautious on the question of women: while many Islamists called for the repeal or revision of the Personal Statute introduced by Bourguiba in 1956, Ghannoushi claimed this would not be necessary. He made much of Ben Ali's electoral use of Islam, arguing that this showed the state rejects European ideas of secularism. There is a world of difference between the calculations of a Ghannoushi and that of more traditional leaders like Sheikh Mohamed Lakhoua from Tunis, who was reported to have called for the return of polygamy and of slavery.

During and after the elections, the Islamists therefore requested that their Party of the Renaissance, *Hizb al-Nahda*, be legalized, but after a long period of uncertainty this was finally refused in June 1989. The truce that had lasted for some time between Government and opposition began to break down. The Islamists denounced Government authoritarianism, and Ben Ali in a major speech on 27 June warned against a proliferation of parties and the dangers of instability. By late 1989 the honeymoon was over: Ben Ali denounced those who mixed religion with politics and refused permission for the Islamists to form a legal party, allowing them only to publish a newspaper, *Al-Fajr* (Dawn). For their part, the Islamists began to denounce the 'secular left' in more violent terms and mobilized students in support of an Islamization of the curriculum. Spokesmen for *al-Nahda* also went further than hitherto in their calls for an Islamization of society: their demands now included the compulsory veiling of women, the basing of all law on *shari'ah*, the allocation of constitutional and legal authority to *ulema*, and the gradual ending of tourism. If part of the explanation for this radicalization of the political scene was simply the ending of caution on both sides following November 1987, another was the increasing polarization in neighbouring Algeria, where the FIS was taking a more aggressive stand against the FLN and what it saw as alien and secular social practices. By the end of the year there was therefore no longer any hope of compromise, and the Gulf War provided the opportunity for a government crackdown, leading in 1991 to the arrest of large numbers of army personnel accused of complicity in a coup attempt by the Islamic Tendency Movement.[18] While the regime resorted to repression, it was helped both by international support and by the improvement in the economic situation which it had been able to engineer.

The hope of the French-educated secular élite who run Tunisia is that, with a combination of concessions and firmness, the opposition threat will recede. After November 1987, hopes were indeed high that Ben Ali could resolve the country's economic problems – high unemployment and regional imbalances. He improved Tunisia's relations with its neighbours, Algeria and Libya, and his standing in the West was high: President Mitterand visited Tunis in June 1989 and there was firm, if discrete, American backing – Ben Ali was known to have worked closely with the CIA during his earlier career. Yet despite all the initial respect for dialogue on both sides, it did not take long for a more antagonistic relationship to develop. The post-Bourguibist regime remained as committed to a monopoly of power and to its secular programme as did *le combattant sûpreme* himself. On their side, the Islamists were at first biding their time, presenting a moderate face and consolidating their support, in the hope of an opening in the future.

The broader implications of this uncertainty in Tunisia are evident enough. Tunisia has long been regarded as one of the west's more sympathetic interlocutors in the Arab world, and, together with Morocco, is regarded as exerting a stabilizing influence on its neighbours Algeria and Libya. Western military and economic aid to Tunisia serves evident strategic purposes. The Tunisian government itself is keen to maintain these links, and also to strengthen its ties to the European Community. But the rise of the Islamist movements during the 1980s has raised other possibilities which the transition to Ben Ali has done only a limited amount to assuage. On the one hand, the Islamist forces in Tunisia have attracted the support of a variety of external forces – in Libya, Saudi Arabia, and Iran. Much of this support may take a uniquely rhetorical form, but it is certainly the case that these states, rivals amongst each other within the Islamic world, would like to encourage a change of orientation, internal and external, in Tunisia. Tunisia has, therefore, become the site of conflicts within the Arab and Islamic worlds as a whole, the outcome of which is by no means certain.

THE REVOLT AGAINST THE MODERNIZING STATE

In the context of Islamism itself, the Tunisian movement has certain characteristics that enable it to be compared with, and distinguished from, those in other societies. First, it represents a revolt against the secular modernizing state. As with other movements, including that of Iran, it has been the product of a growing opposition between state and society, reflecting the loss of mobilizatory power and legitimacy of a modernizing state. In the 1950s and 1960s the Bourguibist regime had considerable success in generating support from the population, through its nationalist policies, its social interventions, and its organization of much of the population into the Neo-Destour Party and its mass affiliates. Gradually, during the 1970s, this strength began to erode, and, with considerable social change, especially urbanization and education, the power of the ruling party eroded. With Bourguiba's growing authoritarianism and the corruption of the ruling party, this alienation of the population increased.

What the Tunisian movement therefore represents, as did the Iranian upsurge of a decade before, is the crisis of the post-independence regimes. Broadly speaking, it can be stated that in the first decades after independence, the initiative was held by parties and regimes that espoused a 'modernizing' programme: strengthening the state, spreading modern and secular values, seeking to transform their countries in order to bring them closer to some model or ideal of what a modern society should be. The reforms of Bourguiba, like those of Ataturk in Turkey, the Shahs in Iran and Nasser in Egypt, fell into that category. So too, in a different context and with a distinctive ideology, did those of post-revolutionary communist and other third-world revolutionary regimes.

The record of these regimes was, however, contradictory. On the one hand, there was much that was not changed or transformed, despite official appearances. Religious beliefs, pre-nationalist loyalties, family and clan ties persisted. The drive by such modernizing states to intervene also served to antagonize social groups who felt their interests, values, and status threatened. Equally important, however, the very success of these regimes acted against them: for it was on the basis of changes which these modernizing regimes introduced that much of the opposition arose. One such change was education: in Iran, as much as in Tunisia, the support for the Islamist movements draws on educated young people, and often ones with a degree of scientific education. Another was urbanization: this brought large numbers of people into cities, an environment where they were more easily organized and mobilized by opposition forces and where the tensions and problems of social change, including corruption and government inefficiency, were more evident.

Equally important is the manner in which these Islamist currents have challenged and to a large extent displaced the more traditional leaders of opposition, the parties of the secular left. This reflects several factors: in Iran, Turkey, Egypt, Tunisia, and Algeria the opposition of the immediate post-independence period tended to take a left form, with communist and radical socialist forces playing a significant role. Their main criticism of the government was that it was not going far enough in its social reforms, but they also tended to criticize the modernizing regimes for their foreign policies, especially, as was the case with Iran, Turkey, and Tunisia, for their links to the West. Left parties therefore sought to present themselves as radical social critics and as bearers of nationalist legitimacy. What has happened in the 1970s and 1980s is that these left-wing forces have been displaced by the Islamist ones. Left parties have been marginalized – as is evident in Iran, Egypt, and Tunisia – and have often adopted a defensive ideological posture *vis-à-vis* Islamism. They now claim to respect Islamic values and seek compromise with the Islamists which the latter, often confident of their greater appeal, may not want to reciprocate.[19]

This displacement has come about through several mechanisms. First, the left parties with their own secular and modernizing ideologies came to be associated with the culture and ideology of the ruling parties. They were seen more and more as just another representative of that state-centred and alien modernization that the Islamists rejected. Secondly, the social groups amongst whom the left had been based were often the secular intelligentsia and parts of the working class. Few had any following amongst the peasantry or the urban poor who were not in modern industrial employment. In the new social conditions this has meant that other social bases for opposition, ones to whom the left was unable to appeal, had developed. Equally important, however, has been the success of the Islamists in acting as an organized and ideologically coherent opposition, i.e. in rivalling the traditional left opposition in its own terms. Much as Islamist movements use traditional forms of religious organization – mosques, *madreses* or religious schools, Sufi and other underground religious sects – they have also developed modern techniques and forms of organization normally associated with secular parties: welfare programmes, including educational and health centres, cassettes and videos of sermons and speeches by opposition leaders, nation-wide political organizations, and fund-raising machineries. One of the greatest surprises of the Iranian revolution was the extent to which the apparently unworldly Islamist forces were able to bring millions of people onto the streets and run what was, by any standards, a very successful nation-wide opposition political campaign.

This success in the field of organization is matched by a success in the field of ideology. Here much emphasis has been placed, by Islamists and their rivals alike, on their appeal to 'traditional' values. They are represented as speaking for a set of values that are more in accord with the traditions of the country and hence with its people. There is no doubt that this image corresponds in some measure to the truth: that the decades of secular leaders and dirigiste states talking at their peoples in the language of modernization and development did not correspond to the world-view of these peoples, was often not understood or misunderstood, and left far less ideological impact than appeared to be the case at the time. This is as true of the relevant Islamic countries as it is of the USSR and other communist states. 'Traditional' values did survive, with greater hold on the populations than the new, state-down, modernizing programmes. But this apparently straightforward articulation of tradition also conceals 'contemporary' choices as to which parts of tradition to articulate – the more democratic or authoritarian parts, those relating to collective or individual values, not to mention varying views on the place of women, slaves, foreigners and so forth within the Islamic society. The Islamists of Iran and Tunisia have made choices as to which parts of their tradition to emphasize, and that choice is given not by the weight of tradition itself, but by modern, secular and political, concerns. Khomeini's views on the power of the state to override the *shari'ah* are a clear example of this, as are Ghannoushi's calculated views of women's role in society.

There is a second important element of the ideological success of the Islamists, namely their appropriation of the values and claims of the left. There is no need to believe that Khomeini actually read any Marxist writings or that any other Islamists have done so to see the influence of Marxist and radical ideas of the 1950s and 1960s on these third-world thinkers. Anti-imperialism, dependency, cultural nationalism, hostility to monopolies, solidarity of the oppressed peoples of the world – all these standard themes of the earlier nationalisms of the third world recur in the statements of these Islamic leaders. The economic programme pursued by Iran in the 1980s reflects many of the ideas on 'de-linking' and self-sufficiency propagated by dependency theorists such as Samir Amin, Andre Gunder Frank, and Franz Fanon.

Two central ideas are populism and nationalism: the assertion of a common popular interest against the oppressors, and not least against the intrusive authoritarian state, and, at the same time an assertion of national legitimacy against external enemies.[20] The existence of an external enemy that is rejected on both national and religious grounds, namely Israel, has of course fuelled this Islamist appropriation of nationalism, leading the left in Egypt, for example, to vie with the Islamist right in anti-Israeli, and often chauvinist, criticisms of the Camp David accords. For all the differences, the analogy with Fascism is evident: just as 'national socialism' took over some of the ideas of its left-wing competitor and provided a rival, equally well organized and ideologically more successful force than the communist and socialist parties, so the Islamists have both challenged and appropriated the ideologies of the more traditional opposition parties. The ideological success of Islamist movements *vis-à-vis* the left has therefore involved a dual process, of ideological and political displacement combined with appropriation of the latter's ideas and appeal.

CONCLUSION: ISLAMISM AND THE FUTURE

In the immediate aftermath of the Iranian revolution, it was believed by many that the Islamic world would be swept by mass revolts. This did not occur, and in August 1988 the Iranian regime faced its greatest setback by accepting the ceasefire with Iraq. However, the causes of Islamist militancy are deeper and more enduring than the particular influence of Iran and in this sense there is every likelihood that movements of this kind, and states more or less influenced by Islamism, will continue to articulate such ideas and policies for a long time to come. The advance of populist Islamism in Tunisia and Algeria is indication enough of the long-run appeal of such ideas. So too is the growing tendency of ethnic and communal movements involving Muslim interaction with non-Muslims to take an Islamist form (for example, in western Europe, Caucasus, Lebanon, Egypt). It would seem to be likely that those living on the frontiers of the Islamic and non-Islamic worlds, where these run within rather than along state boundaries, will face many difficulties in the years ahead and as much on the non-Christian (Hindu, Confucian) frontiers as on the Christian.

Much external discussion has focused on how the Islamist upsurge constitutes a 'threat' or challenge to other states, particularly the West. The issues of oil and terrorism are particularly prominent here. Analysis of the last ten years suggests, however, that these international consequences are overstated. The oil market was remarkably little affected by the Iran–Iraq war and all states need to sell their oil. Terrorism is an issue, but, compared to other global problems, a subsidiary one and not one confined to the Middle East. Indeed, for all the rhetoric and occasional spectacular act involved it could be argued that the Islamic states are if anything weakened by these new ideologies, since they create internal tension and conflict that reduces their ability to play an effective international role.[21] The greatest challenge to Islamism is, therefore, not to the non-Islamic world, but to the Muslim peoples themselves: the ability to find and implement a viable economic development strategy, the creation of co-existence and tolerance between different ethnic and confessional groups, the promotion of democracy and political tolerance. These are all goals which the heightened militancy of Islamism makes it more difficult for these states to attain.

NOTES

An earlier version of this chapter was given at the conference on the contemporary Mediterranean held at the University of Malta, December 1989, and published in Stanley Fiorini and Victor Mallia-Milanes (eds) (1991) *Malta: A Case Study in International Cross-currents*, Valetta: Malta University Publications.

1 Clare Hollingsworth, 'Another Despotic Creed Seeks to Infiltrate the West', *International Herald Tribune*, 9 September 1993; Samuel Huntingdon, 'The Clash of Civilisations', *Foreign Affairs*, summer 1993. For analysis of this issue see Esposito (1992), Salame (1993) and Halliday (1993). I have tried to produce my own, non-essentialist, analysis of hostility to 'Islam' in Halliday (1994).
2 Perhaps the most commonly invoked symbol of all for western intrusion into the Muslim world is that of 'crusader' (*salibi*). It is, however, worthy of note that

during the 1991 war between Iraq and the UN over Kuwait the term used in Iraqi propaganda was 'Hulagu', the Mongol conqueror of Baghdad in 1258. In the Iran–Iraq war of 1980–88, the Iraqis frequently denounced the Iranians as 'Magus', the word for an ancient Persian king; the Iranians tended to refer to Saddam as Yazid. In the Yemeni war of the 1960s, the royalists often attacked the Egyptians as 'Pharaohs', leading on some occasions to reports of attacks by 'Pharaonic aircraft' on tribal positions.

3 For an excellent discussion see Roy (1992) and Schulze (1993).
4 As Nikkie Keddie (1988) has pointed out, the terms 'fundamentalism', 'Islamism', 'integrism' are used almost interchangeably in current writings on movements that apply Islamic concepts to politics. All have their problems: fundamentalism presupposes a return to first principles but the question of what constitutes those first principles may be disputed. The key issue is that movements of this kind seek to mould society and the state according to what they claim to be Islamic principles.
5 On North Africa see Roy (1992), Esposito (1992) and Burgat (1988; 1991).
6 Piscatori (1991).
7 On Islamic communities in western Europe see Kepel (1988), Gerholm and Georg (1988), and Nielsen (1992). See also my review article, 'The Struggle for the Migrant Soul', in the *Times Literary Supplement*, 14–20 April 1989 in which I discuss the Rushdie affair and political uses made of it. On the ramifications of the Rushdie affair, see Appignanesi and Maitland (1989), and Ruthven (1990).
8 For further analysis of the Iranian case, and comparisons with Pakistan, Israel and the Arab states, see Halliday and Alavi (1988). In my chapter on Iran in this book I have developed an account of the causes of the Iranian revolution (Halliday 1988). For my earlier study of the Shah's regime and its internal contradictions see Halliday (1978).
9 For comparative studies see Marty and Appleby (1991) and Landau (1993).
10 For one of the most lucid expositions of this contingency see Zubeida (1988).
11 Islamist movements from below are covered in Burke and Lapidus (1988) and in Halliday and Alavi (1988).
12 For analysis see Zubeida (1988), Abrahmanian (1993); Vieille and Khosrokhavar (1990).
13 The text of Khomeini's letter to Khamene'i is in *BBC Summary of World Broadcasts* Part 4, 8 January 1988. For analysis see Reissner (1988). Khomeini's theorization of how an Islamic state can, for reasons of state interest, override religious precepts has an ironic relevance to the Rushdie affair: Iranian and other defenders of the death sentence on Rushdie claim that Khomeini's condemnation of Rushdie to death cannot be overriden because it is necessitated by religious principle. Application of Khomeini's *maslahat* principle would suggest that, if Iranian political leaders thought it was in their interests to do so, they could cancel the death sentence. That they do not is not because of some religious compulsion but because, within the politics of the Islamic world, it is still profitable for them to maintain their stance.
14 On Iranian foreign policy since 1979 and the place within it of Islamic themes, see Halliday (1986).
15 The concept of *zuhd* or austerity, often associated with forms of mysticism, was important in Khomeini's rhetoric and melded conveniently with the anti-consumerism of third-world populist and revolutionary ideology. In some ways Khomeini's use of anti-imperialist *zuhd* was analogous to the usage of the concept by the Imam of Yemen who in the 1950s declared that Yemen would prefer to be poor and independent than rich and dependent. How far the

Iranian, or Yemeni, people were committed to such austerity was, and is, another matter.

16 For the Tunisian background, see Esposito (1992), Burgat (1988; 1991), Keddie (1986), Moore (1965) and Salem (1984).

17 Interview with Ghannoushi in the Tunisian weekly *Realities*, 192, 21–7 April 1989. Further Islamist critiques of the Ben Ali regime reported in *Le Monde*, 9 June, 5 September, 10 November, 6 December 1989.

18 The trial of those arrested, held a year later, seemed to indicate that the coup attempt had not been as serious as claimed at the time: some of the defendants were released, whilst others received unexpectedly light sentences (*Le Monde* 19 January 1994).

19 This was classically the case in the Iranian revolution: the Islamists allowed the left to ally with them in the initial revolutionary period and then isolated and destroyed them one by one.

20 On the 'modernity' of Khomeini's theories and the contemporary preconditions for the emergence of his movement see the very perceptive study by Zubeida (1988).

21 For a critique of contemporary Islamism from within the Muslim world, and the weakening of Islamic society and culture it entails, see Ahmed (1988).

REFERENCES

Abrahmanian, E. (1993) *Khomeinism: essays on the Islamic Republic*, London: I.B. Tauris.

Ahmed, A. S. (1988) *Discovering Islam: Making sense of Muslim history and society*, London: Routledge and Kegan Paul.

Appignanesi, L. and Maitland, S. (1989) *The Rushdie file*, London: Fourth Estate.

Burgat, F. (1988) *L'islamisme au Maghreb: La voix du Sud*, Paris: Karthala.

—— (1991) *L'Algèrie par ses islamistes*, Paris: Karthala.

Burke, E. and Lapidus, I. (eds) (1988) *Islam, politics and social movements*, London: I. B. Tauris.

Esposito, J. (1992) *The Islamic threat: Myth or reality?*, Oxford: Oxford University Press.

Gerholm, T. and Georg, Y. (eds) (1988) *The new Islamic presence in western Europe*, London: Mansell.

Halliday, F. (1978) *Iran: Dictatorship and development*, Harmondsworth: Penguin Books.

—— (1986) 'Iranian foreign policy since 1979: Internationalism and nationalism in the Islamic revolution', in J. Cole and N. R. Keddie (eds) *Shi'ism and social protest*, New Haven: Yale University Press.

—— (1988) 'The Iranian revolution: Uneven development and religious populism', in F. Halliday and H. Alavi (eds) *State and ideology in the Middle East and Pakistan*, London: Macmillan.

—— (1993) 'Western Europe and the Middle East: The myth of the Islamic challenge', in B. Crawford and P. Schulze (eds) *European dilemmas after Maastricht*, Berkeley: Center for German and European Studies, University of California.

—— (1994) 'Anti-Muslimism in contemporary politics: One ideology or several?', in A. Gresh (ed.) *Un péril Islamiste?* Paris: Le Monde Diplomatiques.

Halliday, F. and Alavi, H. (eds) (1988) *State and ideology in the Middle East and Pakistan*, London: Macmillan.

Keddie, N. R. (1986) 'The Islamist movement in Tunisia', *The Maghreb Review* 11 (1).

—— (1988) 'Ideology, society and the state in post-colonial Muslim societies', in F. Halliday and H. Alavi (eds) *State and ideology in the Middle East and Pakistan*, London: Macmillan.

Kepel, G. (1988) *Les Banlieues de l'Islam*, Paris: Seuil.

Landau, D. (1993) *Piety and power: The world of Jewish fundamentalism*, London: Secker.

Marty, M. and Appleby, R. S. (1991) *Fundamentalisms observed*, Chicago: American Academy of Arts and Sciences, The Fundamentalism Project.

Moore, C. (1965) *Tunisia since independence*, Berkeley: University of California Press.

Nielsen, J. (1992) *Muslims in western Europe*, Edinburgh: Edinburgh University Press.

Piscatori, J. (ed.) (1991) *Islamic fundamentalisms and the Gulf crisis*, Chicago: American Academy of Arts and Sciences, The Fundamentalism Project.

Reissner, J. (1988) Der Imam und die Verfassung, *Orient* 29 (2).

Roy, O (1992) *L'échec de l'Islam politique*, Paris: Seuil.

Ruthven, M. (1990) *A satanic affair: Salman Rushdie and the rage of Islam*, London: Chatto.

Salame, G. (1993) 'Islam and the West', *Foreign Policy* No. 90.

Salem, N. (1984) *Habib Bourguiba: Islam and the creation of Tunisia*, London.

Schulze, R. (1993) 'Muslimische Intellektuelle und die moderne', in J. Hippler and A. Lueg (eds) *Feinbild Islam*, Hamburg: Konkret Lieteratur Verlag.

Vieille, P. and Khosrokhavar, F. (1990) *Le discourse populaire de la révolution iranienne*, Paris: Contemporaneité.

Zubeida, S. (1988) *Islam, the people and the state*, London: Routledge.

Chapter 6

Contemporary Islamic movements in the Arab world

Abubaker A. Bagader

This chapter shows how the so-called 'Islamic resurgence' or 'Islamic revival' is deeply rooted in the history of Islam and is not the new phenomenon sometimes supposed. Moreover, it suggests that no single Islamic group or movement is the sole representative of this trend, which is rather made up of many different groups. Finally, it outlines the internal critique which currently characterizes Muslim society, and which questions from the inside some of Islam's most fundamental premises.

THE ISLAMIC IDEAL

Islam presents itself as the blueprint of a social order, as a way of life based on a set of rules and principles that are eternal, divinely ordained and independent of the will of its followers. Thus it has played and continues to play an important role in the life of Muslims. Unlike Christianity, which renders onto Caesar that which is Caesar's, Islam does not separate or distinguish between the spheres of the secular and the sacred, but retains both within its control. Thus, ideally, it does not have different institutions for church and state but sees the two as inseparable. In addition, Islam is equally accessible to all believers; it does not have a formal church or priesthood. All believers have the right to speak for Islam provided that they are learned and have followers (Gellner 1981: 1–2; Lewis 1988: 3–4).

This is the ideal, though it has never yet been fully realized. Nevertheless, it was never challenged openly. There have been several sects in the history of Islam, like the Qaramites, Druzes, and the Sufi orders, which have expressed heretical views, but all such groups either became separate religious societies, or presented their views in such esoteric language that they were incomprehensible to the majority of believers. Their views therefore never constituted a direct challenge to the whole society. In fact, most political powers tried to assert their legitimacy not only by stressing that they submitted to the Islamic ideal but also by working to protect and embody it. Thus the constitutions of most Muslim states mention that the state religion is Islam and that the Shariah laws are the major source of the legal system. Similarly, some leaders have adopted titles which suggest religious authority, such as commander of the faithful or Imam. Any deviation from the ideal has usually been interpreted as coming from within the tradition, not as a challenge to it, and is still criticized, opposed and rejected from within the tradition, as a religious issue rather than a distinctively political or civic one.[1]

THE ISLAMIC IDEAL IN HISTORICAL CONTEXT

During some periods of political decline and turmoil, the ideals of Islam have been stressed in order to combat the threat of change, irrespective of whether this came from inside or outside. In some cases, the ideal was used as a means of holding on to political power. The *ulema* and the institutions under their power and authority, in particular the educational, legal and *wakf* systems, exercised a strong influence over the masses. They were to mobilize and to direct the masses to profess strongly and clearly the Islamic ideal, especially in times of crisis.

Just such a crisis occurred in the later medieval period when the Muslim world was invaded by the Mongols, who destroyed Baghdad, abolished the caliphate, and established their own government over the Muslims. However, their rule was brief and they soon converted to Islam, clear testimony to the power of the Islamic ideal. The Mongols did not represent the challenge of a competing doctrine so that it was mainly their military power that had to be dealt with. The Muslims were confident that they were superior to the enemy and felt sure that they had been defeated only because they lacked political unity and had deviated from the teachings of Islam. Such confidence ultimately enabled them to become the teachers of their enemy (cf. Krawulsky 1993: 196–8).[2] They looked on the crusaders with the same view (cf. Maalouf 1989; Ibn Munqid 1988: 121–5). Eventually, Muslim lands were cleared of the foreign aggressors and it was thought that the old order would be restored.

Later encounters between Islam and the Western powers, beginning with the French expedition to Egypt under Napoleon at the turn of the eighteenth century, were very different from previous encounters.[3] For the first time the Muslim world, from within its traditional leadership, admitted defeat not only on the military but also on the socio-cultural level. Some Muslim thinkers even exhorted the community of Islam (the *umma*) to try to learn from the West's scientific and other achievements.[4] Muslims were now governed by non-Muslims under a regime that lasted nearly two centuries. During this colonial rule, which covered most of the Muslim world, Muslim societies encountered multi-dimensional challenges, not just the military challenge. In the process, they underwent some fundamental changes, which deeply shaped them (Al-e-Ahmed 1980).

This Western challenge led some Muslim thinkers – for the first time in the history of Islam – to ask questions such as, what is the secret of Western superiority? Why are we defeated? What is wrong with us? How could the community of Islam regain its leadership role and status? These questions became the basis of an ongoing auto-critique in the Muslim world. This auto-critique led the *ulema* to play a major role in co-ordinating the struggle against the colonial powers, a struggle which eventually led to independence (Keddie 1972; Bagader 1980).

However, during the long period of colonial rule the traditional *ulema* who, until then, had represented the intellectual leadership of Muslim society, lost much of their control over basic social institutions such as the educational system and the legal system (Thorpe 1965). During its modern renaissance, the Muslim world has been faced with two types of education, the traditional and the civil. Civil (and to some extent secular) education is patterned on the Western model. Traditional education, while it maintained the old style at first, has gradually lost its influence over the job market for its graduates. Now many governments find themselves forced to remodel it, in order to make it better fit the new roles expected of religious functionaries. Even modern Turkey, with its strong secularist ideology, retains religious schools for mosque preachers and prayer leaders.

As for the legal system, the picture is not very different. In most Muslim countries the Shari'ah laws were limited to matters of personal law, and to the administration of religious foundations (*wakf*). All other aspects of law – criminal law, common law, commercial law – had therefore to be reformed; for example, by codifying and incorporating new legal procedures which are based on, or at least not in conflict with, the Islamic legal heritage. In some instances, modern Turkey being a good example, certain Western laws were adopted or even copied.

Furthermore, with the end of the 'nominal' office of the caliphate in Ottoman Turkey, Muslim societies had to accommodate themselves to new political systems.[5] Islamic political unity (for example, the idea of pan-Islamism) was replaced by the nation-state, and this created many resounding changes in the definitions of identity and in the political and cultural visions of Muslims.

The changes in these areas, and in many others, were actually first encouraged during colonial rule, when they established roots in the social, economic, political and cultural order and had a certain amount of local support (from, for example, Taha Hussein, Lutfi Al-Sayyid, and most of the modern Egyptian thinkers). The *ulema* and the traditional leadership tried to resist these changes, but it seems they were not very successful. Their priority during the colonial period was the struggle for independence, and they did not initially realize that they were in danger of becoming marginalized in the emergent socio-political order. They were confident that, once the colonial powers were forced to leave, the traditional Islamic order would be restored, as would their own authority and status. In the event, their expectations were not fulfilled. Much of the colonial legacy was retained. The only difference was that now it was administered by local people. Some Muslim intellectuals even dared to publish books which seemed either to challenge various Islamic doctrines or at least to question them. The writings of Taha Hussein, Ali Abdul Razik and others have become classics and are good examples of this new trend. But the *ulema's* prompt reaction in mobilizing public opinion against such writing forced these authors to change their views or withdraw them altogether. If they did not, they were publicly condemned.[6] The *ulema's* success in this confrontation went part way to restoring their traditional authority.

The new educational system made the spread of mass education possible, facilitated upward mobility, and created new opportunities for wide sectors of the population. In addition, most of the Muslim nation-states adopted new political and philosophical ideals such as nationalism and socialism (Hanna and Gardner 1969). These changes dominated political thought and social planning in most Arab Muslim societies, which added to the marginalization of the traditional Islamic leadership and limited the scope of its activities. New institutions of Islamic learning were established to compete with the traditional ones.[7] The graduates of these new institutions combined traditional learning with a touch of the reality of the contemporary world. These changes were to lay the foundation for the emergence of many of the new Islamic movements.

THE NEW ISLAMIC MOVEMENTS

One of the most powerful of the new movements, the Muslim Brothers in Egypt, was founded by Hassan Al-Banna, a graduate of the new Islamic institution of Dar Al-Ulum. Al-Banna's vision of the message of Islam and its role in contemporary society was radically different from that of the traditional *ulema*. He believed that Islam could offer the alternative social order needed for the welfare and progress of Muslim society, an interpretation that clearly resonated with many of his peers since he was to establish one of the leading Muslim organizations in modern times. The growth of its membership, the spread of its message and the wide support it has received have made it the model for many subsequent Islamic movements. Al-Banna presented a new vision of the role and function of Islam in the modern nation-state without losing sight of the dream of pan-Islamism (Mitchell 1969).

Abu'l Alla Al-Mawdudi was also a product of the new educational system. An Indian Muslim initially trained as a journalist, he established one of the most influential Islamic movements on the Indian subcontinent. Although his political views were somewhat different from those of Al-Banna, he shared the latter's vision of a new role for Islam in contemporary society. He stressed the notion of Allah's sovereignty over the state, a notion that was to have a major influence on the most radical of the contemporary Islamic movements. The notion of Allah's sovereignty meant that, through his teachings to the Prophet, Allah is the only legitimate source of law-making. Any other laws are considered unlawful. This notion thus entails the complete rejection of the legal and political claims of the nation-state.

Mawdudi's ideas influenced Sayid Qutab, one of the most influential thinkers among the young members of the new Islamic movements. Qutab began as a literary critic, with a lucid and powerful style. Later in his career, as a writer, he published several books that guaranteed him a wide readership in Islamic circles. He became the inspiring force for many young people, largely because of his radical and uncompromising positions on modern society and its political systems (cf. Ahmed 1991a; 1991b). He was executed for his views (Diab 1988). The legacy and example of Sayid Qutab, as a martyr for his beliefs, have attracted the attention of many of the leaders of the radical Islamic movements.

Although the spread and intensity of Islamic movements were very much influenced and shaped by political and economic factors in the region, other factors must also be taken into account. Four factors in particular help to explain the increase in activities of Islamic movements in the 1980s and 1990s. First, the success of the Muslim Brothers and their struggle, and of the Islamic Revolution in Iran, bequeathed a legacy of new ideas and ideals with which Muslims everywhere could respond to the challenges of the modern world. Second, the decline of Arab nationalism after the Arab–Israeli War of 1967, the continuous economic and social crisis since the mid-1970s, and the diminishing legitimacy of most of the ruling élites were the major factors encouraging young people to search for meaningful alternatives to the old order. Third, the modernization process in the Arab world, which was encouraged by many of the Muslim governments, facilitated the emergence of new social classes and the marginalization of some traditional groups and structures. This in turn stimulated the growth of an urban middle class, more able to challenge the ruling class when it felt betrayed. And finally, the spread of westernization and secularization among the élites in most of the Arab Muslim societies exacerbated the tensions and increased the gap between the educated and the masses. This led the latter to reject the intellectual leadership of the former.

It is possible to discern a range of responses to the changes taking place in Arab society. Responses differ in their objectives, means, philosophies, number of adherents, significance, and ideological articulation. While not elaborating on the details of these responses, it is possible to sketch them in general terms; though it should be emphasized that the categories indicated are not mutually exclusive.

1 Spiritualist groups: The followers of such groups usually disregard this-worldly matters and emphasize instead spiritual or other-worldly concerns. Some members of this group emphasize chanting and dancing as a means to express religious experience. This 'sufi' orientation is tolerated, and even encouraged, by some states as a manifestation of peaceful and traditional Islam. It is usually spread among the urban poor and the peasantry. Most of these spiritualist groups today adopt a folkloristic stance, as preservers of cultural traditions which are otherwise likely to disappear, and sufi orders in the classical sense of movements for change are vanishing.

2 Ritualistic groups: The followers of this trend emphasise 'Islamic appearances' or what is called the *sunnah*, such as having a beard, dressing modestly, using the *souak* (a traditional tooth brush) and, in the case of women, wearing a complete veil. They stress moral issues and social conduct. Much of the time they are relatively unconcerned with political and economic issues. Some of these groups stress the need to teach only the basic doctrines of *tawheed*; the best example of this perhaps being the traditional understanding of Islam found among the older Islamic groups in Saudi Arabia (cf. Nouah 1990). The followers of ritualistic groups share their appearance with most other Islamic groups, especially radical ones, a fact which accounts for their sometimes being mistaken for revolutionaries.

3 Revolutionary or radical groups: These groups demand an immediate and fundamental change in contemporary Muslim society. They do not believe in peaceful and gradual religious reform and they feel that it is only through violent and extreme confrontation that a truly Islamic order will be established. They believe that, since Muslim societies have abandoned Islam, it is acceptable in Islamic terms to fight against them. Islamic groups that have actually used violent means to change society are representatives of this trend.

4 Muslim Brothers' groups: This category includes many different groups, but all of them in one way or another take the teachings and aspirations of Al-Banna as their starting point. One such group succeeded in holding political power in Sudan, another in winning general elections in Algeria, yet another in presenting a 'balanced' political opposition in Tunis, and another in representing moral and political authority in Egypt for a wide spectrum of Islamic groups.

5 Intellectual groups: The members of these groups are mainly intellectuals from outside the traditional Islamic leadership. Although some of them are nationalists or leftists, they also write and campaign on Islamic issues. Adel Hussein Abdelaziz, Al-Bishri and Munir Shafeeq are well-known representatives of this category. The members of these groups are not usually accepted by the traditional groups, who either consider them to be opportunists wishing to take advantage of the

popularity of Islam among the masses, or who disbelieve them when they claim to have relinquished their former ideological positions. In addition, there are some thinkers who claim to represent the Islamic left, such as Hassan Hanfi, or to represent Islamic liberals and revisionists, such as Abid Al-Jabri. These groups have a wide following among university students, but their influence on the religious movement more generally is negligible.

6 Traditional leadership groups: This group includes a number of Islamic 'personalities' such as the late Shaikh Mohamed AbuZahra, Shaikh Mustafa Zarka, and the late Shaikh Sobhi Al-Salah, as well as muftis, jurists and professors of Islamic studies at Muslim universities. Usually such individuals present themselves as specialists on Islamic matters. The category also includes those religious preachers with mass influence, such as Shaikh Ben Baz in Saudi Arabia and Shaikh Sharrawi in Egypt, even though these two men see themselves as part of the established order rather than as leaders of religious movements. It also includes many others who exert moral leadership over their followers.

Most of these groups agree that there is a need for change in Muslim society, but they differ on what these changes should be, on how fast they should take place, and on how they should be brought about. Some choose peaceful means: persuasion, public lectures, social activities and education. They believe in gradual change. They recognize the power and authority of the nation-state, appreciate its function in keeping law and order, and believe that confrontations with it will lead to failure. They try to maintain some independence and they work through the system to bring about change in society.

But other groups believe in confrontation with, or disaffection from, the state as well as from contemporary Muslim society more generally. Such groups do not exclude the use of violence as a means for change. They believe that most of the political regimes currently ruling Muslim states are not ruling in accordance with the teachings of Islam; that, in fact, these rulers are *against* Islam and should therefore be replaced.

It is these latter groups that have received so much attention and media coverage. Ahmed has summarized the basic literature on these groups in Egypt (Ahmed 1991a; 1991b). It is clear from this literature that these groups follow the teachings of Ibn Tayyamiah, Al-Mawdudi and Sayid Qutab. They reject the political status quo and seek to change it, even if this means using violence. They justify their position and their actions by recourse to religious interpretations, rather than by political or social analysis.[8] Dharif presents a review of the political discourse of the Islamic movements in the Arab world. He identifies a number of social, economic, psychological and political factors that led to the emergence of these movements (Dharif 1992b: 5–15). He also presents a panoramic review of the main Islamic movements in North Africa and some other Muslim countries, which complements Ahmed's earlier coverage of the Egyptian material (Dharif 1992a). By analysing both the underground and the published literature of these movements, Dharif is able to identify some basic differences in style, approaches to change, and political views, especially on the relationship to the state.

CONTESTED MEANINGS

Recent literature on Islamic movements indicates that some Muslim thinkers (e.g. Shaikh Qaradawi and Shaikh Gazali),[9] while stessing the need for an Islamic solution to the problems of Muslim societies, nevertheless seek dialogue with and an openness towards other views in society. At the same time, they express their disagreement with the violent style of the more radical groups popular among young people (Qaradawi 1988; Huwadi 1988). In Tunis, for example, Ghannoushi actually recognized the right of non-Islamic groups to participate fully in the political process of an Islamic state.[10] However, this should not be understood to mean that these thinkers condemn the extremist groups, or deny their legitimacy. Nor should it be understood as some sort of alliance with the state against them. They are merely restating their position regarding the need for a return to the Islamic ideal, and pointing out that this return need not be violent.

In addition to this internal critique, there have been several other voices and points of view participating in the on-going ideological debate about Islam's relationship to contemporary society. Some critics of the Islamic movements nevertheless support them and try to understand their struggle against and opposition to today's society (e.g. Ahmed 1989). Others are less critical and see the Islamic movements, even the extremists and the radical groups, as a necessary and justifiable instrument of social and political change. Yet others have no more in common with these groups than their shared rejection of Western thought, values, and influence in the Arab world. Some of those who hold such views are journalists who have assumed the role of spokesperson for particular Islamic groups. However, despite their efforts, such individuals are rarely recognized or accepted by the Islamic groups as part of their movement.

If the Islamic groups have their supporters from outside their rank and file, they have their critics too. The late 1980s witnessed a new phenomenon, the appearance of individuals who not only criticized the style and methods of many of the Islamic movements, but who publicly announced their opposition to the rule of the laws of Islam over society. Faraj Foudah, for example, advanced a secularist view and rejected the application of Shariah laws.[11] He accused the Islamic movements of corruption, of catering to vested interests, and of being agents of destruction against the civil society (Foudah 1986; 1988; 1992). Hussein Amin is another example.

His critique stressed that the Islamic movements, especially the violent and extremist groups, should not be allowed the privilege of monopolizing the representation of Islam. Instead, he presents his own vision of a liberal, westernized Islam, mocking the notion of putting Shariah laws into practice and giving them a different meaning. He condemns the style of Islamic groups, which he describes as blood-thirsty, barbaric, violent, and un-Islamic (Amin 1987; 1988: 287–307). Though not alone, Foudah and Amin are perhaps the best examples of this trend (for other examples, see Flores 1992).

It seems that the success of, and the attention given to, the Islamic movements led many Arab thinkers to try to present their own visions of the Islamic perspective. Hassan Hanfi is such an intellectual. Of the Islamic left, Hanfi offers a complex mixture of philosophical, theological and revolutionary writing intended to update and upgrade the ideas of Sayid Qutab (Hanfi 1987; 1990). Although his views are not taken seriously by the members of the different Islamic movements, he is widely read in intellectual circles, where his works have been welcomed as offering a novel Islamic alternative (Abou Zaid 1993; Tarabichi 1991).

Hanfi has tried to introduce an Islamic version of liberation theology into Muslim society (Hanfi 1990). His ideas were not well received in traditional circles, but found acceptance among the former Marxist and leftist writers (Ali 1993; Dammishiqia 1990), who had also tried to present to Arab readers the theological experience of Latin American Catholics and to suggest that similar efforts should be undertaken in Islam. Such views are still very marginal and are not widely known.

Others have engaged the Qur'anic texts themselves. Shahrour's work on the Qur'an, for example, represents a radically different challenge to received wisdoms than Hanfi's attempts to introduce liberation theology. Shahrour's ideas are not only in conflict with the traditional views of the Qur'an but constitute a serious departure in Qur'anic studies as these are taught in the Arab world (Shahrour 1990). Abou Zaid's (1990) treatment of traditional Qur'anic scholarship, which applies the new methods and theories of literary criticism to the Qur'anic text, also constitutes a radical break with the past. Yet these writers have criticized the position of the Islamic movements on the question of women (Lutfi 1988; Yassin 1992; Al-Missri 1986), and on banking and economics (Al-Ashmaoui 1991; 1992a; 1992b; Shuhaib 1992). Such works took positions so radical that they could be considered to be in opposition not only to the views of the Islamic movements, but even to Islam itself. Although such views are very unorthodox, and are entirely new interpretations in the Arab world, they are already becoming increasingly common particularly in Egypt and Tunis.

CONCLUSION

These divergent views from inside and outside the Islamic movements indicate how complex the issues are. Moreover, they suggest that Muslim society is undergoing a basic and fundamental change, a change towards pluralism. While it is true that many parties try to impose their views by different means, it is nevertheless clear that different perspectives are at work, even if they do not yet genuinely recognise one another's right to co-exist. They are not yet ready to respect one another or to grant other groups the rights which they claim for themselves (Talibi 1992: 65–8). Gellner (1992: 2–22) stresses that the dominant voice in Muslim societies is that of fundamentalism. Perhaps he is right. But close observation of the changes that are taking place in the Middle East indicate that we should ask what sort of fundamentalism we are talking about. There are many types. And Gellner's classification is too static to take into account how these can change in response to changes in the wider society. Society is undergoing many changes, which are shaping its future direction. Whatever the outcome, provision must be made for these divergent and different perspectives to continue and to flourish. Otherwise there will be continuous violence and conflict. In this chapter, I hope to have shown that Islamic movements are an integral part of the historical and cultural make-up of Arab society; as such, they should not become a marginalized trend. Such a fate can be avoided only if their discourse takes modern social and cultural changes into consideration (Talibi 1992: 64–121).

NOTES

1 It should be noted that religious thought in the sense used here encompasses the social, the economic and the political, a usage which stems from the discursive tradition of the Qur'an and Sunnah.

2 Krawulsky's (1993: 199–202) account of Ibn Tayyamiah's position towards the Mongols is of particular interest here, since the same position was later adopted by Faraj Foudah in modern Egypt (see 'The Absent Duty', [Al-Faridha Al-Ghaiba], cited in Ahmed 1991b). In 'The Absent Duty' Foudah equates Saddat's regime with the Mongols and his own opposition to Saddat with Ibn Tayyamiah's opposition to the Mongols (Ahmed 1991b: 127–47; see also Saunders 1977).

3 Most Arab historians regard this date as the beginning of the modern Arab liberal age, which they consider Muhammad Ali of Egypt to have initiated.

4 Cf. Al-Jabarti (n.d., vol. 2: 100–94 and 433–40). Jabarti's position became a model for most writers who have followed him in their assessments of the sciences of the west. Al-Afghani, Abdo and Rida were preceded by reformers and thinkers such as Al-Tahtawi, Ali Mubarak, Khir al-din al-Tunisi and many others, all of whom suggested borrowing from the West.

5 The absence of the institution of the Caliphate gave the new political orders, especially the notion of a republic, a kind of legitimacy.

6 Taha Hussein had to withdraw his views in his book *Fi Al-Adab Al-Jahili*

(1958), and to revise them in *Mustakabal Al-Thakafa fi Misr* (1965). Abdul Razik lost his degree, his title and his position as a Qadi and was publicly condemned as the result of the publication of his *Al-Islam wa Usul Al-Hukum* (1978 [1925]).

7 For example, Dar Al-Ulum was established as an alternative to Al-Azhar in Cairo. It is said that Taha Hussein was behind the idea, in order to educate a new breed of Islamic scholars.

8 See the documents cited in Ahmed (1991a; 1991b), particularly those which give the views of Shukri Ahmed Mustafa (Ahmed 1991b: 53–103).

9 Al-Gazali and Qaradawi enjoy recognition and respect from both the Islamic movements and the nation-state. This gave them the role of mediator, especially in Egypt, on several occasions. It enabled them to negotiate with non-Islamic groups (cf. Abdullah 1987).

10 Ghannoushi's view sounds very liberal, but Tunisian intellectuals do not trust him (cf. Omami 1992). The issues of *Outrouhat*, a university journal, use strong and harsh language against the Islamic movements in general and Ghannoushi's group in particular.

11 Foudah was assassinated by unidentified assailants, allegedly belonging to one of the new Islamic groups; they are said to have killed him for his heretical ideas. Shaikh Gazali issued a *fatwa* proclaiming that whoever killed Foudah should not be held responsible, since Foudah was a heretic.

REFERENCES

Abdullah, Ismail Sabri (ed.) (1987) *Al-Harkat Al-Islamiyya Al-Moʿassira fi Al-Watin Al-Arabi* (Contemporary Islamic Movements in the Arab World), Beirut: Center for Arab Unity Studies.

Abou Zaid, Nasr H. (1990) *Mafhoum Al-Nass: Dirsosa fi Aloum Al-Quran* (The Concept of Text: a Study in the Sciences of the Quran), Cairo: Al-Hiaʿa Al-Aamma li Al-Kitab.

—— (1993) *Al-Khitab Al-Dini* (The Religious Discourse), Beirut: Dar Al-Muntakhab Al-Arabi.

Ahmed, R. S. (1989) *Al-Harkat Al-Islamiyya fi Misr wa Iran* (Islamic Movements in Egypt and Iran), Cairo: Sina Publications.

—— (1991a) *Al-Nabi Al-Musslah, Al-Thairoon* (The Militant Prophet; the Revolutionaries), London: Riad El-Rayyes Books Ltd.

—— (1991b) *Al-Nabi Al-Musslah, Al-Rafidoon* (The Militant Prophet: the Rejectionists), London: Riad El-Rayyes Books Ltd.

Al-Ashmaoui, M. S. (1991) *Al-Khalaf Al-Isslamiyya* (The Islamic Caliphate), Cairo: Sina Publications.

—— (1992a) *Al-Islam Al-Siyyasi* (Political Islam), Cairo: Sina Publications.

—— (1992b) *Al-Riba wa Al-Faida fi Al-Islam* (Usury and Interest in Islam), Cairo: Sina Publications.

Al-e-Ahmed, J. (1980) *Occidentosis: The Plague of the West*, Chicago: Mizan Publications.

Ali, Haider Ibrahim, (1993) *Lahoot Al-Tahrir: Al-Din Wa al-Tawrra fi Al-Alam Al-Thalit* (Liberation Theology: Religion and Revolution in the Third World), Cairo: Center for Sudanese Studies.

Al-Jabarti, Abdel Rahman (n.d.) *Tarik Aja-ib Al-Attar fi Atrajim wa Al-Akhbar* (History of the Wonderful Events: Biographies and News), Beirut: Dar Al-Jeel, (4 vols).

Amin, Hussein (1987) *Dalil al-Muslim Al-Hazin* (The Sad Muslim's Guide), and

Dawa Tatbik al-Shariah (The Call for the Application of Shariah Laws), Cairo: Madbooli Bookshop.

— (1988) *Al-Islam fi Alam Mutaghir* (Islam in a Changing World), Cairo: Madbooli Bookshop.

Al-Missri, S. (1986) *Khalf Al-Hijab* (Behind the Veil), Cairo: Sina Publications.

Bagader, Abubaker (1980) *The Ulema and the Modern Nation-state*, Kuala Lumpur: ABIM.

Dammishiqia, G. (1990) *Lahoot al-Tahrir* (Liberation Theology), Damascus: Dar Al-Ahali.

Dharif, M. (1992a) 'Al-Islam Assiyassi fi Al-Maghrab' (Islamism in Morocco), *Journal of Moroccan Political Sociology*, Casablanca.

— (1992b) 'Al-Islam Assiyassi fi Al-Watin Al-Arabi' (Islamism in the Arab World), *Journal of Moroccan Political Sociology*, Casablanca.

Diab, M. H. (1988) *Sayid Qutab: Al-Khitab wa Al-Idiolojia* (Sayid Qutab: the Discourse and Ideology), Beirut: Dar Al-Taliaa.

Flores, A. (1992) 'Al-Mothkafun Al-Misruin Wa Al-Islam As Siyassi Wa Al-Dawala' (The Egyptian Intellectuals and Islamism and the State), *Il-Ijthihad*, 4 (4): 189–99.

Foudah, Faraj (1986) *Al-Hakika Al-Kaiba* (The Absent Reality), Cairo: Dar Al-Fikir.

— (1988) *Al-Maloub: Qissat Sharikat Tawdif Al-Amwal* (The Trick: the Story of Finance Investment Companies), Cairo: Dar Misr Al-Jadida.

— (1992) *Nakoun wa La Nakoun* (To Be Or Not To Be), Cairo: Al-Hiaʿa Al-Missriah Al-Amma li Al-kitab.

Gellner, E. (1981) *Muslim Society*, Cambridge: Cambridge University Press.

— (1992) *Postmodernism, Reason and Religion*, London: Routledge.

Hanfi, H. (1987) *Min Al-Akida ila Al-Tawrra* (From the Revolution), Cairo: Madbooli Bookshop (5 volumes).

— (1990) *Al-Din Waa Al-Tawrra* (Religion and Revolution), Cairo: Madbooli Bookshop (8 volumes).

Hanna, S. and Gardner, G. (1969) *Arab Socialism*, Leiden: E. J. Brill.

Hussein, T. (1958) *Fi Al-Adab Al-Jahili* (On Jahili Literature), Cairo: Dar Al-Maaref.

— (1965) *Mustakabal Al-Thakafa fi Misr* (The Future of Culture in Egypt), Cairo: Dar Al-Maaref.

Huwadi, F. (1988), *Izmat al-Waʿai Al-Dini* (The Crisis of Religious Consciousness), Saʿnna: Dar Al-Hikma Al-Yamaniyyah.

Ibn Munqid, O. (1988) *Kitab Al-Itibar* (The Book of Reflections), Beirut: Dar Al-Fikir Al-Haddith.

Keddie, N. R. (ed.) (1972) *Scholars, Saints, and Sufis*, Berkeley: University of California Press.

Krawulsky, D. (1993) *Al-Arab, Wa Iran* (The Arabs and Iran), Beirut: Dar Al-Muntakhab Al-Arabi.

Lewis, B. (1988), *The Political Language of Islam*, Chicago: Chicago University Press.

Lutfi, S. (1988) *Al-Islamyoun wa Al-Marra: Mishrou Ettihad* (The Islamics and Woman: A Project of Oppression), Tunis: Bairam Publications.

Maalouf, A. (1989) *The Crusades as seen by the Arabs*, Beirut: Dar Al-Farabi.

Mitchell, R. (1969) *The Society of Muslim Brothers*, Oxford: Oxford University Press.

Nouah, O. A. (1990) *Al-Tarik il Al-Jamaa Al-um* (The Path to the Mother Group), no publisher given.

Omami, A. (1992) *Tanizmat al-Irhab fi Al-Alam Al-Islami, Inmozaj Al-Nahadh* (Terrorist Orders in the Islamic World: Al-Nahda case study), Tunis: Al-Dar Al-Tunissia Linashar.

Qaradawi, Y. (1988) *Al-Sahwa Al-Islamiyya wa Humoum al-Watin Al-Arabi wa Al-Islami* (The Islamic Resurgence and the Worries of the Arabic and Islamic Countries), Cairo: Dar Al-Sahwa.

Razik, Abdul (1978 [1925]) *Al-Islam wa Usul Al-Hukum* (Islam and the Essentials of Government), Beirut [Cairo]: Dar Makttbat Al-Hayat.

Saunders, J.J. (1977) *Muslims and Mongols: Essays on Medieval Asia*, Christchurch: Whitcoulls for the University of Canterbury, University of Canterbury Publication No 24.

Shahrour, M. (1990) *Al-Kitabu wa Al-Quran* (The Book and the Quran), Damascus: Dar Al-Ahali.

Shuhaib, A. Q. (1992) *Al-Ikitraaghi Kadiat Sharikat Tawdif al-Amwal* (The Penetration: The Case of Investments Companies), Cairo: Sina Publications.

Talibi, M. (1992) *Aial Allah* (Children of Allah: New Ideas for the Muslim's Relations with Himself and Others), Tunis: Dar Siras.

Tarabichi, G. (1991) *Al-Motakafun Al-Arab wa Al-Torath* (Arab Intellectuals and their Heritage), London: Riad El-Rayyes Books Ltd.

Thorpe, C. L. (1965) *Education and the Development of Muslim Nationalism in Pre-partition India*, Karachi: Pakistan Historical Society.

Yassin, B. A. (1992) *Izamatal-Mirfi Al-Mojthaia Al-Dthokouria Al-Arabia* (The Crisis of Women in the Patriarchal Arab Society), Damascus: Dar Al-Hiwar.

Chapter 7

Challenges for Muslim women in a postmodern world

Anita M. Weiss

The contemporary Muslim world is facing unprecedented internal and external challenges. Entering the twenty-first century, Muslim societies are struggling in their confrontations with enormous cultural dilemmas as they are rethinking, renegotiating and in some instances re-inventing traditional society but with unique, modern tones. Where women fit into this process is critical, since Muslim social order revolves around the concepts and values associated with *izzat* (respect) and *sharafat* (honour), in which women's actions are pivotal. Kandiyoti (1991) argues that the social construction of women is a communal symbol within Muslim society. Therefore, conflicting notions regarding the place of women in the new social order is resulting in profound social, economic and political consequences.

The restrictions which Muslim society has placed historically on women's mobility and activities – the *purdah* or curtain separating the worlds of men and women – have been as practical as they have been symbolic. That curtain is slowly yet perceptibly opening throughout the Muslim world: in some places and among some classes women are ripping it down, in others it is a gradual process brought about both by the necessities of survival and the easy intrusion of external cultural influences.

Western European and Muslim social organization have traditionally had fundamentally different starting points. For example, reasons cited for the necessity of the existence of a state in western social thought range from it having a monopoly on coercive force to maintaining economic stability. Feminists argue that the state has also been an important sustainer of patriarchy. Alternatively, in Muslim social thought, the state is widely understood to have one singular purpose: to create an environment where Muslims can practise their religion unhindered. Enabling this, the state is legitimate; hindering this, the state is not.

This chapter seeks to understand the conflicting roles women are encountering and the ways in which women and men think of accommodating them in contemporary Muslim societies. I focus on how a reallocation of obligations is occurring, resulting in a redistribution of gender-based rights and obligations. Inherent within this is the perceptible way in which external cultural norms are encroaching upon Muslim values, and while not shaping them, certainly seem to be influential in framing them.

MUSLIM SOCIETY AND GLOBAL INCORPORATION

The combination of the new international division of labour and the global telecommunications revolution is having a more penetrating effect on social norms within Muslim society than any external force ever had. Earlier political and economic upheavals such as the Crusades and the dawn of imperialism and colonialism had greater effects on *men* in Muslim societies with little reverberations on women and the domestic sphere. As a rare example, Ahmed (1992: 120) cites the response of some Muslim theologians in medieval times to new innovations such as women attending public baths (*hamams*) – they decreed that such actions were unislamic. But the wider social implications of this decree were insignificant.

The uniqueness of this contemporary external force is how it is rapidly integrating areas once considered far outposts of the western world into having a sense of being a part of a global community. International donor agencies, non-government organizations, transnational corporations and their advertising firms, along with infrastructural changes in airline travel, facsimile transmissions and global television networks all contribute to a growing sense that the world shares many social values.

This resultant global 'superculture' is something regarded by many people throughout the world as desirable: dancing in discos while listening to loud rock music or sitting in an auditorium listening to tranquil classical music, travelling to destinations once prohibited by cost or political restrictions, reading small-town newspapers which give coverage to events in Bosnia, Jamaica and Vietnam on the same page, and eating a burger or pizza virtually anywhere in the world.[1] While initially there were a handful of élite universities in the United States and western Europe which were mainstays of this superculture, now the core curriculum at most universities anywhere in the world corresponds to its norms.

Ali Mazrui (1990) observes a hidden cultural agenda in the conflicts which appear to exist between cultures, such as that of the West and the Muslim world. In delineating the American value system as the most powerful in the world, Mazrui (1990: 119) describes its relationship with other cultures as a 'dialogue of the deaf' leading to the 'coca-colonization' of the world. He argues that this is symbolic of a much wider on-going process of the transformation of cultural norms and values into what Boulding (1985: 75) argues is a twentieth-century phenomenon of the world finally having a 'single social system'.

In contemporary Muslim society, such cultural conflicts often manifest in demands for western forms of education, participatory democracy and social justice co-existing with traditional Muslim notions of gender relations, social production and jurisprudence. In most instances, these two worldviews are complicated further by the underlying values and assumptions of local, indigenous culture. While the perpetuation of these local cultures has pre-empted the emergence of a monolithic 'Muslim society', they also limit what we can say about the existence – or coming into existence – of a monolithic *postmodern* Muslim society.[2] As local culture is often more influential in domestic domains, this is particularly true when addressing changing gender roles and perceptions.

NEGOTIATING GENDER

There are some common issues that are being grappled with in most Muslim areas. There is a growing necessity in most areas (e.g., Morocco, Egypt, Pakistan, Bangladesh) for more women to earn a cash income, and for those who had traditionally worked for cash in the informal and domestic sectors to increase what they have earned in the past and to be recognized for their efforts.[3] Associated with this is the marked expansion in women-oriented and women-run social and political movements throughout the Muslim world.[4] Some of these have emerged in response to the growing use of *shari'ah* (Islamic jurisprudence) in the formal legal structure of states, which has often resulted in limiting women's rights.[5]

Another critical social issue is the rise in demand for heightened male and female literacy levels (based on western notions of education). This is evidenced in the expanding numbers of women receiving primary and secondary education in a cross-section of Muslim countries, as shown in Table 7.1. In a quarter of a century, these figures have increased dramatically. When greater numbers of men and women are receiving such education, there are bound to be new demands on a system to enfranchise the recipients. Greater numbers of people in a society – particularly when this includes women – who can read, write and comment on events opens social discourse to entirely new segments of a population.

A fourth issue concerns population planning and an awareness of the effects of high fertility rates on compromising national economic goals. Nearly every country in the Muslim world has a national population policy, but the implications of this are enormous. Public discussions of sexual practices and promotion of family planning techniques has become prevalent from Morocco to Bangladesh to Indonesia. But in societies reticent even to *reveal* its women, especially when they are pregnant, such programmes contrast greatly with traditionally prevailing social norms. However, research has shown that a successful population planning programme is also based on a concomitant rise in the status of women, which subsequently results in changing images of women in society.[6]

Table 7.1 Percentage of women (in age group) enrolled in primary and secondary schools in various Muslim countries, 1965–89

Country	Primary		Secondary	
	1965	*1989*	*1965*	*1989*
Bangladesh	31	64	3	11
Egypt	60	89	15	71
Indonesia	65	115	7	43
Iraq	45	87	14	37
Malaysia	84	96	22	59
Morocco	35	55	5	30
Pakistan	20	27	5	12
Saudi Arabia	11	70	1	39
Tunisia	65	107	9	39

Note: Figures exceeding 100 per cent include adult recipients of primary education

Source: Based on World Bank (1992: 274–5)

The expansion of global media networks, such as CNN and BBC's World Service, to virtually all parts of the world has enabled women to have immediate access to news that most had been dependent on men to inform them of previously. This is particularly true in areas with low female literacy levels. However, as Hijab (1988) argues, opening up women's access to information increases women's social power. This also has serious social repercussions.

A final issue being grappled with in a range of Muslim countries is the effects of initiatives undertaken on the part of donor agencies (e.g., World Bank, UNICEF, USAID, UKODA) to incorporate women into ongoing development projects. While such projects may well increase women's access to resources or participation in the larger society, this may well be in contradiction to patriarchal norms of the traditional society.[7]

An important demarcation unique to contemporary Muslim society *vis à vis* women is the sense that most men have regarding their social obligations to their family. While this is not necessarily waning, women are asserting themselves more to take over some of these obligations. Naturally, issues associated with this concern gendered empowerment, veiling or not veiling, and consequent changes in female mobility.

A common result of the above is the resultant changes in gendered perceptions which is occurring throughout contemporary Muslim societies. Residents of the old, walled city of Lahore, Pakistan, anchored in centuries-old traditions while being forced to confront the challenges of contemporary life, provide cogent examples of changing gender attitudes among men and women in a poor working class area. We must bear in mind that while details may change from one Muslim area to another, there are common results which are changing people's perceptions, and ultimately these are contributing to substantive social change throughout the Muslim world.

WOMEN IN THE WALLED CITY OF LAHORE

Life in the old, walled city of Lahore – the *andarun shehr*, the inner city – appears to the outsider to exist in the public space of the male world. This one square mile of land is home to over a quarter of a million people, housing the largest concentration of urban poor in the country. This is a vibrant centre of economic, social and political activity for both Lahore and the greater Punjab, and is widely considered the cultural heart of the province. What happens in Lahore – be it in the realm of industrial development or changing social relations – is often replicated in smaller cities in Pakistan.

On the surface, we see men active in all spheres of economic activities: they hawk fruits, vegetables and *samosas* from small carts; run sewing machines in their tailoring shops; sell dry goods to a largely male clientele; work by hand fabricating tools in workshops; and seem to congregate endlessly around tea stalls. The city was laid out hundreds of years ago with thin streets and *galis* (alleyways) lined by high buildings providing cooling relief to the inhabitants below while seemingly eternally hiding the pavements in shadows. Minimum space exists for movement along the narrow walkways, and buildings are occupied usually by a shop or workshop on the ground level, with two or three levels of family living quarters above, and topped with a latrine and a flat roof. It is difficult to recognize people in the darkness of the alleyways, in the inner sanctum of some *kuchas*, the walled-city term for neighbourhoods. The high buildings enable social exchanges to be carried out on rooftops, where people sleep in the summer and from which they greet each other year-round.

The walled city is overwhelmingly working class. Most families live in one or two room homes in neighbourhoods with densities often seven times higher than that found in other parts of metropolitan Lahore. Such high densities, however, are not a new feature in the walled city. An early twentieth-century account describes the city as being overcrowded and already in a decrepit state and that 'the streets of the Old City are narrow and tortuous, and are best seen from the back of an elephant'.[8]

Most women spend the bulk of their lives physically within their homes; they go outside only when there is a substantive purpose. While some women aspire to move out of the walled city – to escape the dirt and crowds and raise their status – most feel that life there is so convenient that they do not want to leave.

Underneath this public face lies a significant amount of social confusion, particularly regarding changing gender roles, expectations and possibilities. Characterizing traditional society as patriarchal, patrilineal and patrilocal tells us little about the actual relations between men and women in this poor urban area. Importantly, there has been a separation between most aspects of men's lives and women's lives as *purdah* has been an essential element of everyday life. Of course, women would interact with closely related men often throughout the day. Their relationship, however, was one of servitude: women were to ensure a clean home, tasty cooked food, obedient children, and maintain social relations. Maintenance of social relations included attending the many functions associated with marriage, birth, death, and performing certain rites identified with Islam expected of a woman in that particular family.[9] Men would never discuss any issue of a personal nature associated with their mother, sister, wife or daughter even with their closest friends.

The institution of the family plays an essential role in the walled city. The gendered division of labour within the family is due to a unique combination of economics and status concerns. Men do not necessarily have complete authority over household economics; in a sizeable minority of families, women have traditionally been responsible for daily decision making and often have input in determining major purchases. Men's power within the family, however, is absolute in its control over women's actions and mobility, as women are considered the repository of their family's respectability.

Access to many opportunities is often contingent on the connections which one's family has with others. Family traditions are perhaps the greatest factor in whether or not daughters are sent to school, parallel cousin marriages are preferred, or women must wear a veil. Families provide a virtually complete package of economic and social support, provided that members abide by its norms. If a man should violate a social norm, it may raise some concern, but if a woman violates virtually any social norm, it becomes a calamitous event for her family with disastrous results for the woman's future.

Gender roles and expectations, however, are undergoing substantive change with the introduction of new kinds of technology which free up women's time (e.g. running water from taps, gas connections for cooking, covered drains creating more hygienic conditions, easy availability of low-cost transportation), the availability of waged labour for women (albeit in the informal sector), women's increased exposure to higher education, and their growing attentiveness to mass media. For example, Laila's mother was born in the Walled City, was married just after her first menstrual cycle, and has never earned any income on her own despite the severe financial need of her family.[10] When I would meet with her, she was invariably washing dishes or clothes using a neighbourhood hand-pump, and only spoke her regional language, Punjabi. In our last meetings, she was very apprehensive about her family's future as they were faced with the imminent destruction of their home as developers sought to expand a nearby wholesale bazaar. The opinions she voiced regarding local political matters were those of her husband or sons.

In contrast, her daughter Laila has grown up with other expectations about her life. She has been a recipient of the Pakistan government's success over the past two decades in providing basic medical care in urban areas and knows that she had her first inoculations when she was a year old, followed by injections against measles and smallpox a few years later. Her life also reflects changing views on *purdah*, as she wears a loose-fitting *chador* instead of the fitted *burqa* worn by her mother. Laila had been a student in the Anjuman Khudamuddin Banaat Girls Public School, a small school with ten rooms for some three hundred girls inside Sheranwala Gate. Most of the girls studying there are young and from poor families. As they are able, families transfer their daughters to English medium schools as this gains greater status.

Her goals and values are very different from her mother's, as she expects to take initiatives to affect some aspects of her future which women rarely did in the past. When asked about what was the best day in her life, she replied it 'was the day that I passed my matric [tenth class] exam'. She chose not to continue in a secondary school but rather to attend a government-run sewing and embroidery centre. During this time, she and her sister began to do intricate *salma sitara* embroidery on a piece rate basis for a local shopkeeper. Some of this money went towards her dowry, the remainder went towards her family's daily expenses.

She is an avid supporter of Benazir Bhutto. Laila feels that Bhutto is an important role model for women in Pakistan. The confidence Laila has gained from her independent experiences is reflected in her other attitudes, such as desiring to have a say in whom she will marry, where she will be living after marriage, whether she will have to earn an income, and the size of her family after her marriage. Laila, as is increasingly becoming the norm in Lahore, desires to have a small family consisting of only four children.[11]

However, Laila does not necessarily see herself as in a *better* position than that of her mother when young. While their lives are very different, she considers that her mother was freer, because she did not contribute to the family's income as Laila does by doing embroidery. The expectation was not there, as women in the past did not do such work in their homes. Indeed, both out of necessity and by choice, what women are doing today is different from what they did in the past, resulting in the renegotiation of traditional norms, values and power relationships.

BEHIND THE WALLS

We can see that the multi-faceted system of norms and controls which has served to constrain female activities and mobility in traditional Muslim society does not exist mainly out of concerns regarding female promiscuity. Instead, as a form of social control, it is the notion of what is accepted as *respectable* and what is not – perhaps initially tied to matters of sexuality but no longer – which is the fear which drives most people to suppress their women's freedoms. This results in a general consensus that any activity in which a woman engages outside the home needs to be monitored. This explains why conditions of high density in the walled city – as in other poor urban areas in Pakistan – have become factors in strengthening the power held by families over their members, particularly by males over females.

When young, a girl was placed into seclusion before the onset of puberty. This decision was usually made by some close male relative who decided that her interactions with other males should now become limited. One older woman in the walled city recounted to me how one day her grandfather decreed that she was no longer to go outside and play with the other children in the neighbourhood. From age nine onwards, she was only to observe social life on the streets from the roof of her home, but not to partake of it.

During my field research in the old walled city of Lahore, I observed that while both boys and girls needed to be obedient in front of their elders (particularly older men), mobility restrictions were imposed only on girls, boys being allowed to wander as they wished. Social pressure was instead applied to boys in three arenas: school attendance, choice of career and marriage selection. Even then, it seems that parents and other elders were rather relaxed about enforcing the first two: I heard many accounts that a boy stopped going to school because he 'wasn't interested in studying' or he 'didn't like to study'. Career options became available through informal networks which often did not require a decision to be made. It was only in the latter kind of pressure – to marry a spouse of one's family's choice – that it seems men and women both generally submitted to the will of their family. While it was possible for a boy to suggest a potential spouse, this was unheard of in the case of a girl who would have disgraced herself and her family just to have voiced a choice. However, once the decision was made as to who would be married, both sons and daughters were generally unable to break the engagement without severe discord and antagonism within the family.

The partition of the Indian subcontinent in 1947 forced some dramatic changes upon families in the walled city. Many parts of the walled city ended up in flames, especially those neighbourhoods historically inhabited by Hindus and Sikhs. Popular lore estimates that about half of the walled city's residents abandoned their homes and fled to India during Partition;

new Muslim occupants replaced them. It is assumed that many of the *muhajirs* (immigrants) who settled in the walled city were poor as it was here that the 'evacuee property' was in the least demand (PEPAC 1987: 19). Some *muhajirs* came with kin, others created 'kin' through fictive ties, and a renewed culture was built upon the rubble of the old.[12] The effect of this on gender relations, in practical terms, was that the close knit communities which had once existed were disrupted as more social outsiders moved into old neighbourhoods. From the life stories told to me by women who lived through this period – either who had migrated to Lahore from India or who were born in the walled city – it appears that restrictions on women's mobility intensified in an attempt to retain a sense of moral order within families.

BEYOND THE WALLS

The renegotiation of gender images and expectations appears to fall into three categories: first, women being allowed – and in some cases, encouraged – to study beyond the stage of simple literacy; second, expanding labour opportunities for women resulting in changes in the perception of gendered work; and third, the renegotiation of personal power and mobility within the family. The first two of these areas are direct outcomes of what it is that women are doing differently from the past, resulting in men relinquishing some of the powerful control they have held over women and also expecting women to hold different roles. The last category, the renegotiation of personal power and mobility within the family, is a direct result of the first two. Because of women's increased competencies, men are also realizing that women do not need them as much as in the past, and that it is possible for women to now be self-reliant. Needless to say, this creates ample confusion in a society where social norms still revolve around honour and respect as there is a discernible increase in men's fears of what *uncontrolled*, qualified women might do.

Increasingly, parents are allowing their daughters to acquire a higher education, even though such mobility for a post-pubescent girl is antithetical to traditional mores. That girls from this working class area are completing secondary education is, therefore, no small event. Indeed, men's diminishing ability to control the mobility and activities of women within the family is due in large part to the increase in female education and related access to mass media and information. It may not be what is actually learned in school but the experience of *leaving one's home after puberty and attending classes* that exposes a woman to other students and teachers and, in effect, to the larger society from which she was once hidden and uninformed.

The lifestyles and status of élite women – those who have received such a higher education – have changed as most have been able to break away from traditional social controls. The majority of élite women in Lahore hail from Kinnaird College or Lahore College, and it has become fairly common to find a woman in this group who has pursued a university degree, entered a non-female domain profession, joined a women's political movement, or even selected her own husband. Their lives have changed in a pattern similar to many women worldwide.

This is not true for most poor women, though there are some similarities. Based on interviews I have conducted, I would venture to state that most adults resident in the walled city would heatedly argue that the above four activities are outside the bounds of female respectability, and that élites have become too westernized for their own good. Yet these same working class parents aspire for their daughters to attend Islamia Girls College (Cooper Road) or the new Government College for Women in Bilal Ganj, both of which are in the vicinity of the walled city.[13] Idealized norms have not yet caught up with the pragmatics of daily life which often require college degrees to arrange a good marriage or for poor girls to earn an income.

In my research at the latter two girls' colleges, I found that the kinds of changes in perception once associated with élite areas are gradually making their way into these college-going girls' perceptions as well.[14] I was once virtually accosted by some fifty girls at Islamia College, all of whom were from the walled city and had heard of my earlier research there on women's lives. They expressed to me a dilemma they were facing that I had not observed. On the one hand, they had been exposed in their college to a lot of nationalist ideology and propaganda: the increased emphasis on Islamic and Pakistan Studies in the curriculum, campaigns to help flood victims in rural areas, support of autonomy in Indian Kashmir and the defence of Pakistan near the Siachen glacier, and other issues to make them strive to do something for the larger society. Given their new level of educational attainment, they also expected that they would eventually experience a significant rise in class and status. However, on the other hand, they expressed a real frustration in not knowing what they could actually do with their newfound knowledge, awareness and sense of nationalism. When I formally questioned the female students (in a written questionnaire format) about their occupational aspirations, the vast majority wrote that they wanted to become teachers. However, in our informal discussions, more creative professions surfaced (e.g., journalist, shop owner, banker) which are culturally in the male domain, as well as confusion regarding what other avenues they could take. One girl from the walled city even told me she wanted to become a freedom fighter for the Muslims in Kashmir, this despite the fact that the Pakistan military does not accept women into combat positions nor is it actively engaged in skirmishes at the Kashmir border.

I found two different kinds of responses regarding the merit of educating women among men studying at colleges in Lahore. The majority from upper class families found it to be a good thing and would prefer a highly educated wife, but most men from working class families (similar to those found in the walled city) stated that there was no reason why women should occupy places in colleges that men could take or jobs that men need. Despite their studying with women in their classes, they would not approve of their own sister or wife studying in their college. Clearly, the latter felt more threatened by the prospects of educated women than the former.

This loss of will to maintain the extended family also seems to have repercussions for women regarding domestic violence. The system of arranged marriages fits well with the structure of the extended family. While the desire by men to control their wives has a long-standing basis, domestic violence was contained by the intervention of other family members in resolving conflict. While extended family members continue to intervene despite the shift to nuclear families, the lack of others physically present within the household leaves open the possibility of increased domestic violence.

In the case of many women, such as the shoemaker and the *samosa* maker, when a woman's work is combined with that of her family, the gendered division of labour within the family changes due to the woman's enhanced economic contribution, but that has a minimal effect on increasing her decision-making power. When a woman becomes the primary economic support of her household – such as a woman who makes artificial jewelry inside Bhati Gate whose husband's used goods shop never makes a profit, or a woman inside Delhi Gate who has become a hairdresser because of her husband's drug addiction – she gains a stronger voice in influencing important family events, but she by no means becomes an independent agent. Even a widow who strings flowers to support her son and daughter must ultimately defer to her late husband's brother's choice when arranging marriages for her children.

This leads us to the third category in which gender images and expectations are being renegotiated, that of personal power and mobility within the family. Men and women have very different visions of significant changes which can be discerned.

While men view women as being able to be more capable than in the past, they also feel threatened by the potential of uncontrolled educated and/or economically independent women to compromise their honour and therefore their status among other men. They do regard women as more honest than men in economic matters.

Men no longer have the same level of profound trust of other men, including biological and fictive kin, as in the past. This is due to the acute rise in corruption in recent years which has, in the eyes of many of these working class men, favoured unscrupulous actions over integrity and has promoted an unprecedented regard for crass materialism.

Many women expressed to me that they feel they can no longer rely on the men of their family as securely as they had in the past. They have seen men abandon their wives, go abroad to work leaving the wife virtually on her own, and increased drug addiction among men. One woman, an artificial jewelry maker, told me that the most viable survival strategy now for daughters is to get them a good education, as gold and property can always be taken away by someone else. She is afraid for her daughters, because she has witnessed many extended families break down and people relinquish traditional obligations.[15] She and many others feel that the education and work opportunities now available to women can help them take a tentative step towards independence.

The extent to which women have changed their images of other women is probably greater than the changes in the above three areas. They know women are now more capable, and are raising their expectations of what women can be responsible for and what they can achieve – especially what their educated daughters might achieve – to unprecedented levels.

That changes in gender relations will continue to escalate is reflected in the opinion voiced by many women to me that no women in the walled city will be wearing a *burqa*, a body veil, in ten years, although it remains common today. However, while the physical restrictions on women's mobility by her own family may be lifting, this is being replaced by a new threat to her mobility: the rise in violence against women by unknown assailants, especially when women venture outside the walled city. In the past, rape was comparatively rare and generally effected as retribution against the property of an enemy. This has changed given the current level of frustration (political and economic) that many men experience in the larger society. The materialism which has pervaded most sensibilities stresses status, the assertion that one is powerful. Does the rise in violent crimes against women indicate that men perceive this as a way of being powerful, or that they are punishing women who are acting outside of traditional norms which emphasize limited mobility?

An important outcome is that the nature of restrictions on women's actions is being modified in this rapidly changing urban context. The stereotyped view of women's place in the family and other traditional notions of family dominion which people will continue to *articulate* in speech is perpetuated by a number of factors, especially repressive images of women being promoted and perpetuated by the state. The government of Zia ul-Haq had idealized the image of women faithful to '*chador aur char diwari*', remaining veiled and within the confines of the four walls of their home, while ignoring the reality that women's lives were becoming increasingly integrated into the public realm.

In conclusion, how can we understand the implications of changing gender images regarding social well-being? We cannot separate this from the results of other events that are happening globally. The breakdown in a social contract which, Gellner (1981) argues, was once ensconced in the Qur'an and which now has a difficult time in acquiescing to the norms of a changing civil society, is resulting in social confusion spreading over into gender relations. Confronting these challenges and recognizing the empowerment of women as both welcome and inevitable will ultimately strengthen a rejuvenated Muslim social order.

NOTES

1 Boulding elaborates on his notion of a global superculture in Boulding (1985: 75–83).
2 I am using the term in the sense employed by Gellner (1992).
3 This issue is not unique to Muslim societies but is common in many parts of the world. For an excellent discussion, refer to Waring (1988).
4 For further discussion, refer to Macleod (1991), Moghadam (1993), Mumtaz and Shaheed (1987), and Zuhur (1992).
5 Mernissi (1991a) has investigated the historical roots of dominant Muslim views towards women, and argues that they have more to do with existing patriarchal norms than with theological foundations. She argues that the way women's rights have been interpreted through the *hadith* has cultural as opposed to religious doctrinal roots (Mernissi 1991b).
6 The United Nations Development Programme's annual *Human Development Report* has played an important role in making this connection every year since 1990 (UNDP 1990–3).
7 An excellent discussion of this in the context of Pakistan is found in Shaheed and Mumtaz (1992).
8 *Encyclopaedia Britannica* (1929) vol. 13, 14th edn, London.
9 These obligations differ both by sect and family tradition. Some women, for example, feel it important to visit saints' shrines such as Data Ganj Baksh or Bibian Pak Daman periodically, while others will visit other women's homes to help them in a rite – a *khutum* – during which time the Qur'an is consulted.
10 This example is based on fieldwork conducted in 1987. See Weiss (1992) for further elaboration.
11 Pakistan's fertility rate (the number of children a woman is likely to have) of 5.8 in 1990 was among the highest in the world, about a third higher than the average for lower income and lower middle-income countries (World Bank 1992: 270). A family with only four children is indeed smaller than average.
12 Fictive kinship relationships based on a common region of origin, the shared experience of a refugee camp, or residential proximity in a common neighbourhood have often been cemented through marriages.
13 This is based on research conducted in 1987, and followed up in the ensuing five years (see Weiss 1992) .
14 This research was conducted in 1992 at eight colleges in Lahore on a CIES Fulbright Lecturing/Research grant.
15 For further discussion of women's views on how family obligations are changing refer to Weiss (1992: 121–2).

REFERENCES

Ahmed, Leila (1992) *Women and Gender in Islam: Historical Roots of a Modern Debate*, New Haven: Yale University Press.

Boulding, Kenneth E. (1985) *The World as a Total System*, Beverly Hills: Sage Publications.

Gellner, E. (1981) *Muslim Society*, Cambridge: Cambridge University Press.

— (1992) *Postmodernism, Reason and Religion*, London: Routledge.

Hijab, Nadia (1988) *Womanpower: the Arab Debate on Women at Work*, Cambridge: Cambridge University Press.

Kandiyoti, Deniz (ed.) (1991) *Women, Islam and the State*, Philadelphia: Temple University Press.

Macleod, Arlene Elowe (1991) *Accommodating Protest: Working Women, the New Veiling and Change in Cairo*, New York: Columbia University Press.

Mazrui, Ali (1990) *Cultural Forces in World Politics*, London: James Currey Ltd.

Mernissi, Fatima (1991a) *Women and Islam: an Historical and Theological Enquiry*, (translated by Mary Jo Lakeland), Oxford: Basil Blackwell.

— (1991b) *The Veil and the Male Elite: a Feminist Interpretation of Women's Rights in Islam*, (translated by Mary Jo Lakeland), Reading MA: Addison-Wesley Publishing Co., Inc.

Moghadam, Valentine M. (1993) *Modernizing Women: Gender and Social Change in the Middle East*, Boulder CO and London: Lynne Rienner Publishers.

Mumtaz, Khawar and Farida Shaheed (1987) *Women of Pakistan: Two Steps Forward, One Step Back?*, Lahore: Vanguard Books.

Pakistan Environmental Planning and Architectural Consultants, Ltd. (PEPAC) (1987) *Conservation Issues and Intervention Alternatives: a Strategic Framework*, prepared for the Lahore Development Authority, Conservation Plan for the Walled City of Lahore, April.

Shaheed, Farida and Khawar Mumtaz (1992) *Women's Economic Participation in Pakistan: a Status Report*, Islamabad: UNICEF Pakistan.

United Nations Development Programme (1990–3) *Human Development Report*, New York: Oxford University Press.

Waring, Marilyn (1988) *If Women Counted: a New Feminist Economics*, San Francisco: Harper.

Weiss, Anita M. (1992) *Walls within Walls: Life Histories of Working Women in the Old City of Lahore*, Boulder CO: Westview Press.

World Bank (1992) *World Development Report 1992: Development and the Environment*, New York: Oxford University Press.

Zuhur, Sherifa (1992) *Revealing, Reveiling, Islamist Gender Ideology in Contemporary Egypt*, Albany: State University of New York Press.

Chapter 8

Women and the veil
Personal responses to global process

Helen Watson

To speak of the 'veil' is an exercise in misleading reductionism given the diverse styles of female dress both within and across classes in Muslim societies. However, the familiar motif of 'unity and diversity', which allows commentators to address local variations of Islam within the overarching framework of universal principles and practices, can also be used to approach the question of *hijab* (religious modesty) and veiling. There is a wide range of 'styles of veil' from the uniform black cloaks worn by women in post-revolution Iran, to the exclusive 'designer' scarves of women of the 'new aristocracy' in Egypt. Along this continuum of veiling, which runs from state-regulated attire to individual fashion accessory, there is ample room for the many local varieties, including the brightly coloured scarves of Turkish peasant girls, the 'Tie Rack' wraps of European Muslims, the white *haik* of Algerian women and the *burja* of women in Oman. The universal aspect of each of these different styles of dress stems from the formal symbolic and practical aims of *hijab*; to preserve modesty and conceal the shame of nakedness.

From the viewpoints of western commentators there are few forms of dress which are so often the object of controversy and intellectualized kneejerk reactions as the veil. The plethora of books about women behind, beyond or beneath the veil may give the impression that Muslim women's main activity and contribution to society is being in a 'state of veil'. For non-Muslim writers, the veil is variously depicted as a tangible symbol of women's oppression, a constraining and constricting form of dress, and a form of social control, religiously sanctioning women's invisibility and subordinate socio-political status. Unni Wikan suggests that the typical western view of *hijab* and seclusion implies that with its 'constraints on movement and self-actualization, seclusion must be inherently suppressive, therefore oppressive' (1982:105).[1] Indigenous writers, Muslims, and others with a more positive view of *hijab* stress the liberating potential of veiling and the personal, strategic advantages of public anonymity. Fadwa El Guindi suggests that young women who adopt the veil in Egypt are concerned with retaining 'repectability' and 'untouchability', given their increased presence in public spaces (1981:465–85). The dialectical relationship between the 'constraining' and 'liberating' potentials of the veil is therefore more complex than might be suggested by its appearance. Farah Azari argues that for veiled women in Iran, 'the restriction imposed on them by an Islamic order was therefore a small price that had to be paid in exchange for the security, stability and presumed respect this order promised them' (1983:71). From this brief outline of the various, often conflicting interpretations of the significance of *hijab*, it is clear that the veil has both a practical and a symbolic dimension.

A discussion of veiling and *hijab* has a place in contemporary debates about processes of globalization and postmodernity. There is a multiplicity of arguments about the meaning and significance of the veil in past and present societies. *Hijab* as a topic of popular controversy seems to be of equal interest to theorists and commentators, transcending the cultural boundaries between East and West, Muslim and non-Muslim. Debates about the veil involve contested theories, polemic and rhetoric which invoke such postmodern themes as style, iconography, consumerism, and issues of power, representation and Otherness. Salman Rushdie provided a clear indication of the potent symbolism associated with Western images of *hijab* when he called the brothel in *The Satanic Verses* 'The Veil'.

At the beginning of the nineteenth century Goethe predicted that the Orient and Occident 'can no more be severed', implying the dissolution of ancient East-West divisions and the 'New Enlightenment's' concern with the universality of humankind. By the end of the same century Goethe's vision of the integration of East and West was fading fast, the gulf had widened, and the pervasive voice was that of Kipling: 'East was East and West was West' (see Hourani 1991:ch 5). Towards the end of the present century, in typical postmodern fashion, it seems both positions remain vital and coexist with curious effect. Many markers of cultural distinctiveness have become blurred, yet in many parts of the world there are signs of vigorous commitment to ethnic boundaries and recreations of tradition. This point is particularly pertinent with respect to veiling. The global spread of migration and cross-cultural mobility has resulted in the presence of veiled women in the streets of Western cities, yet that is not to imply that a sensitive, pluralist concept of the veil has developed in popular Western imagination. The veil still remains an icon of the Otherness of Islam and is denounced as a symbol of Muslim women's oppression. There is evidence to suggest that contemporary anti-Islamic sentiment in Europe reflects a variant on Kipling's theme, the fear that 'West is becoming East' as the public presence of other cultures becomes more evident.

My aim in this chapter is to address veiling (understood here as *hijab*) as a global process in the light of subjective personal responses to the veil. On a general level it is important to recognize the cultural meanings of clothing, and the role of fashion as an index of social status and individual identity. The gendered meanings of European fashion have been the object of feminist analysis, which has revealed the personal and political significance of dress.[2] Less attention has been given to the personal and political dimensions of *hijab* as both a 'required' form of dress and a personally chosen article of clothing. This commentary on 'meanings' of the veil approaches the question from two interrelated angles, the religious/scriptural and the socio-cultural. The aim is to address universal principles of *hijab* and the fundamental basis of debates about the nature of *hijab* by examining some of the concepts of modest dress established in the Qur'an. In order to examine how *hijab* is perceived and experienced at local level, the personal significance of veiling is related through the words of three women: a British-born student, an Algerian factory worker in France and an Egyptian vegetable seller.[3] The range of attitudes represented in the women's accounts of the significance of veiling suggests that there is no single 'Islamic attitude' towards *hijab*. Rather, it is perceived to be a matter of personal choice, a way of making a statement about one's social position, and at the same time, a religious duty and a traditional style of dress.

UNIVERSAL PRINCIPLES

Many issues central to a discussion of veiling revolve around the Qur'anic concept of modesty. The concept of modesty, *sitr al-'aura* (literally 'covering one's nakedness'), provides the basis for regulation of behaviour, the segregation of the sexes and proper dress. The Qur'an speaks of being 'modest in thy bearing' (verse 31;19) and mentions Allah's reward for men and women 'who guard their modesty'. In other translations into English the Qur'anic notion of modesty is clearly associated with sexuality; Arberry (1964) translates the phrase rendered by Pickthall (1976) as 'guard their modesty' by the words 'guard their sexual parts', and Dawood (1956) prefers 'chaste'. Specific instructions for women are set out in verses 24;30–1: 'Tell the believing women to lower their gaze and be modest, and to display of their ornaments only that which is apparent, and to draw their veils over their bosoms and not to reveal their adornments save to their own husbands and fathers.'[4]

In Islam, interaction between men and women not related by blood or marriage is permissible only in carefully controlled circumstances and conditions. The desirable state of *nikah* (narrowly translated as marriage) and the prohibited state of *zina* (unlawful intercourse) are the two fundamental categories of interaction between men and women. As Sanders has argued, these categories define and reinforce the boundary between the sexes, which is 'deeply embedded both in views of the cosmos and in social structures':

The most visible expression of this boundary, the social segregation of men and women, was only a particularly concrete demonstration of the notion that male and female were opposites, and that an orderly human society depended on maintaining boundaries that had been ordained by God.

(1991:74)

The Qur'anic concept of modesty and its implication for licit and illicit sexual relations applies equally to male and female behaviour (verses 24;58 and 33;13). However, interpretation has tended to give primary focus to the dangers that women's sexuality pose to social order. Muslim jurists considered that women were a major source of *fitna* (social disorder) because of the illicit sexual relations which might result from men's suscep- tibility to innate female seductiveness.[5]

There is general consensus that there are certain parts of the body which must be concealed in order to avoid shame and preserve modesty. For women, these have been variously interpreted as encompassing the entire body, with the exception of the face, palms of the hands and soles of the feet.[6] If *hijab* is to have the virtue of covering shame and nakedness, then it is helpful to consider what is to be concealed from public gaze. In the most basic terms, how does the concept of the shame of nakedness shift towards a perception that the hair, face or entire female form must be covered?

The Qur'anic references to dress, modesty and nakedness need to be examined in chronological and textual context. In the seventh chapter (Sura *al-a'raf* 7;22), the loss of innocence of Adam and Eve leads to a recognition of the shame of their nakedness: 'And when they had eaten of the tree, their shameful nakedness became visible to them and they both covered themselves with the leaves of the garden'. This Sura is from the early era of Meccan Islam when religious beliefs and practices were being communicated to new converts. Sura *al-a'raf* distinguishes between the concept of shame and nakedness, and the concept of a state of piety achieved through faith. A key point is that the covering of nakedness *per se* does not necessarily entail piety. References to dress are gender-neutral and the shame of nakedness refers to a basic human state of universal significance.

In Sura *an-nur*, the Qur'an begins to make references to shame and nakedness in the context of social relationships. Men and women are equally enjoined to preserve modesty, but there is particular reference to proper female dress (24;31). There are examples of permissible forms of modest dress for specific categories of women. For instance, an acceptable form of dress for old unmarried women is mentioned: 'It shall be no offence for old spinsters who have no hope of marriage to discard their cloaks' (24;60).

In Sura *al-ahzab*, there are references to the seclusion of the Prophet's wives: 'If you ask his wives for anything, speak to them from behind a curtain. This is more chaste for you and their hearts' (33;53). The veil is also represented as a public sign of Islamic identity and a safeguard against women being molested: 'Enjoin your wives, your daughters and the wives of true believers to draw their veils close round them. That is more proper, so that they may be recognised and not molested' (33;59).

It is important to note that Sura *an-nur* and Sura *al-ahzab* were part of the Qur'anic revelation during the fifth and sixth year of the *hijra* when the Muslim community was becoming established at Medina. In this context, there are grounds for viewing the more specific prescriptions on dress as part of the process of establishing personal and social codes of conduct in the nascent Muslim society. Leila Ahmed notes:

> The vision of society developed by men of this period, and their understanding of the relations that should pertain between men and women, was established as the ultimate and infallible articulation of the Islamic notion of justice which has, ever since been imposed as finally binding on Muslims.
>
> (1991:61)[7]

The close association between veiling and licit sexuality or marriage is implicit in 24;31, which lists those individuals who may see an unveiled woman. In addition to a woman's husband, these exceptions to the rule comprise relatives forbidden in marriage (*muhrim*), her father, father-in-law, sons and sisters' sons, as well as others who pose no sexual threat including women-servants, eunuchs and young children. The Qur'anic references to dress and modesty in the two later Suras also emphasize female attire in relation to both public and private domains. A distinction is made between indoor and outdoor dress which has important implications for women and the pattern of gender roles and relations in Muslim society. In 24;31, the Qur'an instructs women to draw their veil (*khumur*) over their bosom in the presence of strangers in what can be assumed to be the domestic sphere. A public environment is referred to in 33;59, when women are enjoined to cover themselves with their cloak (*jalabib*) when they leave the house. Two obviously interrelated points are contained in the pronouncements on modest dress in Sura *an-nur* and Sura *al-azhab*; the social requirement of female modesty given the dangers of female sexuality, and the strict controls on female attire required in the public more than in the private or domestic context.

To approach Qur'anic concepts of dress from another angle, it is important to consider the pronouncement concerning all forms of clothing which cover human nakedness. A verse of Sura *al-a'raf* raises questions about dress which relate to *hijab*, piety and modesty: 'Children of Adam. We have given you clothing with which to cover your shame, and garments pleasing to the eye, but the finest of all these is the robe of piety' (7:26). A literal reading suggests that the verse refers to three distinct forms of dress. First, there are basic garments which cover nakedness, setting 'civilised human society' apart from an 'animal state of nature'. Second, there are 'fine clothes' which may indicate individual status, wealth and personal taste. Third, there are the more symbolically suggestive 'robes of piety' (*libasut taqwa*). On one level, this might refer to a style of dress which signals the wearer's piety, modesty or religious inclination, but a more metaphorical interpretation might lead to the 'robes of piety' being interpreted in terms of a 'state of being pious' which is not simply achieved by a specific form of dress. In other words, the latter reading of 7;26 implies that dress *per se* cannot be regarded as a reliable index of modesty. There is the instruction to 'dress well when you attend your mosques', but this is qualified by a warning against 'excess' (7;31). The Sura makes clear that Allah esteems piety above all else and that the quality of a believer's clothing is irrelevant to their spiritual worth.

With these arguments in mind, *hijab*, in the sense of a covering for shameful nakedness, may be viewed as a robe of piety which signals the wearer's modesty and religiosity. However, from a theological Islamic perspective, the wearing of the veil does not provide an automatic guarantee of piety. In order to return to the basic theme of veiling as it is practised, understood and experienced in any socio-cultural and political context, it is necessary to try to relate Islamic ideals and Qur'anic prescriptions to indigenous views of *hijab* and veiling. In particular, there is the question of multiple interpretations of dress on a personal and socio-cultural level, the interplay between socially ascribed attitudes and female appearance in the public domain, and the meanings of *hijab* to women who adopt the veil. The underlying problems of formulating any generalized view of the global phenomenon of *hijab* are encapsulated in the comment of a woman from a poor district of Cairo:

> When I was a girl you could tell the difference between fashion and proper dress . . . Modesty is an attribute of the person not her clothes. A lot of the young girls who are returning to the veil these days seem to think that a length of cloth is all they'll need to be considered good Muslims.

PROBLEMS OF INTERPRETATION

Beyond the scriptural references to the absolute requirement of modesty, a central problem is the relationship between *hijab* and the social process of veiling. Commentators have debated whether the wearing of the veil is demanded as an absolute religious obligation; there is, at best, a questionable basis for the practice in the Qur'an. Debates within Islam emphasize the lack of consensus on the precise form of dress stipulated by the requirement of modest conduct.[8] Akbar Ahmed makes the useful general point that 'Islam is specific about modesty in both men and women. A dress that looks best when skin-tight and intended to indicate the contours of the torso violates this injunction' (1992:192–3). However, apart from the problem of distinguishing intention or motive from style of dress, modesty remains a complex cultural concept in that it refers both to an internal state and to a repertoire of behaviours indicative of that state. In this regard, it can be argued that the veil makes both dimensions of modesty literal.

A further complicating factor is the observation that the veil as a status symbol, rooted in pre-Islamic Arab traditions, is at odds with the reforming egalitarian inspiration and ethos of Islam. Commentators who identify themselves as both Muslim and feminist focus on the potential emancipation of women represented by Islam, stressing that the 'true message' of the Qur'an was distorted by interpretation which sought to preserve patriarchial pre-Islamic traditions. Mernissi has argued that manipulation of the scriptures 'is a structural characteristic of the practice of power in Muslim societies. Since all power from the seventh century on was legitimated by religion, political forces and economic interests pushed for the fabrication of false (pre-Islamic) traditions' (1991:9).[9] The fundamental point is that:

> Islam does not advance the thesis of women's inherent inferiority . . . On the contrary, the whole system is based on the assumption that women are powerful and dangerous beings. All sexual institutions (polygamy, repudiation, sexual segregation etc.) can be perceived as a strategy for containing power.
>
> (Mernissi 1985:19)[10]

In so far as they are not explicitly mentioned, these concerns and reservations do not seem to touch the women whose individual accounts of *hijab* and veiling are presented below. Nevertheless, they form the backdrop to these accounts and constitute an undercurrent of contested meanings which continually threaten those these women hold. What the cases do show quite explicitly, however, is how subjective meanings of the veil emerge from religious conviction and draw on religious imagery. Moreover, the experience of veiling has a political and symbolic significance for each of the women which extends into the secular domain. The different voices of Nadia, Maryam and Fatima express the view that choice of dress is both a personal and political issue for women who in various ways are 'caught between worlds'. In this sense individual views of the importance of *hijab* cannot be divorced from an understanding of personal perceptions of Islamic modesty in its wider socio-cultural context.

PERSONAL RESPONSES

Nadia is proud of her academic achievements studying medicine at university. She is the eldest daughter of a second generation British-Asian family, the first girl to have an education beyond secondary school. She adopted the veil at the age of sixteen.

My choice of the veil is one of the most important personal decisions of my life. I was at school thinking about applying to university. I was attending a small school and felt quite at home there because all the pupils knew each other. But I had the idea that university would be very different – huge classes and lots of people you would never get to know. In that kind of world I felt that it was important to dress so that people would know that I was a Muslim. At that time I was also thinking about my religion, and feeling that it was the most important thing in my personal life. I had all the other usual interests of most girls my age – music and cinema, and my dream was to get high enough grades to get a place to study medicine like several friends of mine, but Islam makes me different. . . . My cultural background and my family's roots are in another part of the world. These things are very important to me and make me feel special. It is important to me not to lose these parts of my life. My decision to wear the veil also ties into my feeling of coming from this different kind of background.We are a British family but because of Islam and our links with Pakistan we have different values and traditions from the families of my non-Muslim friends . . . I would feel completely exposed without my veil. It is liberating to have the freedom of movement and to be able to communicate with people without being on show. It's what you say that's important not what you look like. My non-Muslim friends are curious about what it feels like to wear the veil. They ask what it's like to be invisible. But in my experience it can be just the opposite if you are the only person in a room full of students wearing western dress. The point is that it's what wearing a veil feels like for the girl that is important, not what kind of veil it is, or what she looks like. For me it's important to have a kind of uniform appearance which means that I don't draw attention to myself or my figure. At the same time wearing the veil makes me feel special, it's a kind of badge of identity and a sign that my religion is important to me. Some of my friends at first had the impression that my father or family had a kind of rule that forced girls to dress like this at a certain age. But it was my decision and my choice for those reasons I've tried to explain. In some ways it's also a custom and I feel that it's a necessary part of becoming an adult woman. It's not so very different from deciding to wear a bra at a certain age or a wedding ring to show that you are married. Most girls I know wouldn't question either of those things . . . I would feel uncomfortable in tight-fitting clothes which show off every curve and angle. It would simply feel wrong to wear something like that, I would feel ashamed and embarrassed. Not to wear clothes like this is also a matter of taste I suppose, just like non-Muslim women who wouldn't dream of wearing a mini-skirt or sun-bathing topless . . . There are also a lot of other kinds of advantages to wearing the veil . . . I find it easier to mix and get around in public and not be bothered by lecherous stares or worse. But these are just advantages of a certain style of dress which doesn't draw attention to the body or fit the Western stereotypes of sexy clothes. They don't have anything specific to do with Islam, they have more to do with being female in a sexist and male dominated society where women are judged by how they look.

Maryam is a lower-class, middle-aged woman who has lived in France with her husband and children for ten years. She lives in an Arab migrant district and works in a textile factory. She adopted the veil shortly after her first year in France when she started to work.

I did not think to wear the veil as a younger woman at home in Algiers, it was not important then. At that time my mother, aunts and sisters wore a western style of clothes and did not cover their hair or face. Most women did not think about *hijab* twenty years ago. Times have changed a lot of things in my life, and all Muslim women have had to face numerous changes, especially women like me who end up living in a Western country. In earlier days it was as if the Muslim people were living in a dream. They were blind and deaf, not realizing how dangerous the world was becoming, how politicians and the wealthy classes were becoming greedy for money, corrupt and westernized . . . Immorality and corruption had a serious impact on poorer families like my own and on the health of the whole society. But thankfully we woke up after we saw what happened in Egypt and experienced the aftermath of the war with Israel and other conflicts with the West. Then there was the big example of Iran and the people's struggle to throw out their corrupt ruler, rid the country of the ill effects of Western influences and make a better society.These things all had the result of making me more aware of the importance of Islam and my conduct and duty as a mother and wife for the future of the next generation . . . When my husband and I came to France we faced a lot of hardship. When money was short because things did not turn out as we had expected I had to find employment . . . there was no question that I would not wear a veil. It is difficult enough to live in a big foreign city without having the extra burden of being molested in the street because you are a woman. It is important to me to keep my appearance private and not to be stared at by strange men and foreigners. My husband was happy with my decision to take the veil. Once I am dressed in this way it makes it easier for him.

He doesn't have to worry about my journey to and from work and being outside without him. There is nothing for him to be concerned about when I am veiled and it allows me more freedom and shows that I am a woman concerned about her modesty. The experience of being in a foreign place is unpleasant and difficult, and wearing the veil eases some of the problems. It is not so frightening to walk through the streets for one thing. Being *hijab* also makes it clear that the person is Muslim and that is also important to me. We cannot forget that we have a different way of life, one which has different concerns and priorities with regard to morality from those of the French people. Sometimes wearing the veil means that you attract the attention of the French people who hate Islam, but experiences like this make me more proud of being an Arab and a Muslim . . . you also feel safe when wearing the veil in any kind of situation – it is a protection as well as a sign of love of Islam.

Fatima is a a widow in her late seventies who sells vegetables in Cairo. She was born in the city shortly after her parents moved there from a small village in Upper Egypt.

Why have young girls started to cover themselves in this new type of veil and dress like old women? I think that it is just a trend, a fashion like any other. Times change and new fashions come to the fore . . . but this one is quite different from the kind of fashions which attracted girls when I was young. Fifty years ago girls were most interested in the fabrics, colours and designs which would attract a possible husband's interest . . . we only thought about clothes in this sense. It wasn't that *hijab* and modesty were unimportant, it was just that girls were not so serious about it, meaning that we took modesty for granted and did not associate a certain style of dress with the actual modesty of the person underneath the clothes. Of course, the world was a less dangerous place then and girls faced fewer risks to honour and reputation because they spent more time at home. . . . So many other things have changed in the ways that people live and the values they cherish which make wearing the veil attractive – young men in particular have become addicted to foreign ways and place less importance on morals and modest behaviour . . . it's not just girls who have to be honourable, but I can understand that girls are worried about facing the dangers of city streets without covering themselves as much as possible. . . . However, I do not think that this new veiling is a religious duty. A woman's modest conduct is more important than what she wears. The new veils are expensive. I could not afford to buy them for my daughters, they have to be satisfied with the peasant women's scarves which just cover the hair. Does this endanger their modesty? 'Rubbish', I tell them when they raise the issue of the new veil, '*hijab* is not about any one type of dress, it's about your behaviour and what's in your mind, so give that your greatest attention'.

Although I have this opinion about the new veil being a trend which is not an essential part of Islam, I am not against what it stands for if it means that society is becoming more concerned with morality and turning against some of the modern ways and western values which started to take hold. . . . It is important for the Arab people to rediscover their own traditions and take pride in themselves. Our ways of dressing can even be part of this . . . it seems very important when you see how the world has changed for the worse. . . . we have become used to seeing Western women almost naked in our streets, and if because of this, our women want to cover themselves in the new veil, then it is a welcome protest against indecency and our overwhelming past interest in all things foreign. The women who adopt the new veil do so for a number of reasons, but it should not be a matter of law but one of personal choice . . . for instance now it is important to think about how you appear to strangers and to know why you have chosen to safeguard modesty by an extreme measure. I have made my own decision and my personal views may explain why I have started to wear the new style of veil, even if I am an old woman.

CONFLICTING IMAGES AND POLARIZED PERSPECTIVES

The narratives force us to rethink women's roles and responses to *hijab* in broader terms than is permitted by debates solely about the veil's 'constraining' or 'liberating' potential. Each woman is 'caught between worlds' in the sense of facing conflicting pressures and managing competing cultural values, traditions and personal aspirations. From a global historical perspective, changes in style of dress and notions of 'appropriate female attire' are driven as much by the market as by changing social mores and the political climate. The West has had an impact on style of dress and fashion in the Arab Muslim world in previous centuries. Mahmud II made formal frock coats *de rigueur* at court. Upper class Egyptian ladies commissioned copies of the latest French and Italian fashions from issues of the *Ladies Illustrated Periodical*.[11] It is possible to see the 'new veiling' as part of a reversal of this process. Akbar Ahmed (1992) has observed that a critical element in the late twentieth century resurgence of Islam has been the emphasis on traditional female dress. Male attire has undergone a similar 'dewesternisation' with the tie being shunned as a symbol of western dress. In this respect, the adoption of an identifiable Islamic form of dress can be regarded as 'a sign of the times' which entails the assertion of independence, separate identity and a rejection of Western cultural imperialism. Rezig (1983) describes how European attempts to discourage the wearing of the *haik* in Algeria led to it becoming a symbol of national resistance for women. Wikan (1982) mentions how Reza Shah Palavi's prohibition of the veil in the 1930s provoked a wave of migration from Iran among affluent families for whom the wearing of the *burja* signified prestige and wealth.

It has been argued that it is vital to regard the return to the veil not as an imposed constraint on women's freedom of movement and self-actualization, but as a deliberate act of choice, influenced by the Iranian Revolution, which springs from a certain view of what an Islamic society should be. Mernissi makes an important general claim about young women's return to the veil in contempory Arab-Muslim societies:

> In the streets and places of work, and particularly in schools and universities, an increasing proportion of young women were covering their hair if not their faces and avoiding social and professional mixing with men. By what might seem a paradox, this was more a sign of their assertion of their own identity than of the power of the male.
>
> (Mernissi cited in Hourani 1991a: 442)

From a similar perspective, Kandiyoti has noted:

> The response of some women who have to work for wages . . . may be an intensification of traditional modesty markers, such as veiling. Often, through no choice of their own, they are working outside the home and are thus 'exposed'; they must now use every symbolic means at their disposal to signify that they continue to be worthy of protection.
>
> (1991a:36)

Thus the apparent paradox of a return to the *hijab* among women in the public worlds of employment and education is not 'anti-feminist', but is a kind of 'feminism in reverse' with a moral connotation as well as a political one. The interweaving of secular and sacred concerns represented by the adoption of the veil also can be seen as a reaction against the secular feminism of the West, and as part of the search for an indigenous Islamic form of protest against male power and dominance in public society.

Minces argues that 'the veil is a clear symbol of demarcation from the corrupt morals of the ruling classes' (1982:100). For the economically exploited and socially disadvantaged the return to *hijab* is both a protest against the consumerism of the élite classes and against westernization, which is seen as the root cause of socio-economic and political problems. In these respects the veil represents a way of visibly preserving cherished values and signalling the need to restore former systems of morality in a rapidly deteriorating world. It is possible to interpret the new, late twentieth-century political dimensions of the return to *hijab* as part of an ongoing public politicization of women, albeit by a mirror image of the strategic actions of Hoda Sha'rawi and the 'Arab feminists' who removed their veils as a sign of their participation in the Egyptian nationalist struggle in the 1920s (see Philipp 1978; Khater and Nelson 1988).

MacLeod has illustrated how the return to the veil among lower middle-class working women in Cairo does not represent a simple retrogressive and reactionary reproduction of power relations. A key argument is that the women are 'enmeshed in the confusing choice of modernizing Cairo, caught between conflicting worlds and wishing neither to reject the practices and values of their own culture nor to embrace or aspire to a westernized lifestyle' (1991:45). In this respect, veiling is both a symbolic expression and a resolution of the double dilemma faced by working women. The power of the veil lies in 'the ambiguous message' it communicates; expressing on the one hand, protest against the erosion of valued identities and statuses, and on the other, acceptance of the cultural ideal of women's primary roles as wife and mother. Women resolve the everyday conflicts they face in maintaining a balance between the competing ideologies of 'woman as worker' and 'woman as wife/mother' via the 'contradictory intentions' signalled by adopting the veil. This 'style of struggle' involves both resistance and acquiescence. In the title of MacLeod's study, the new veiling is an 'accommodating protest' in that it provides a useful synthesis of the personal and political dimensions of *hijab*.

Akbar Ahmed has commented that the 'wholly incorrect, negative media stereotype of (Muslim) women as inanimate objects . . . (reflects) the poor opinion, bordering on misogyny, that Western society, inspired by the Greeks, holds of women' (1992:43). The image of a veiled Muslim woman seems to be one of the most popular Western ways of representing the 'problems of Islam'. As already mentioned, a commonplace observation within Western discourse on the veil has been that it is an overt sign of Islam's oppression of women. In Abu Lughod's terms, the submissive veiled shadows suggest the nadir of women's status and autonomy (1986). From the briefest of glances at descriptions of Muslim women we find metaphors and similes for the veil such as 'shroud', 'disguise' and 'black modesty'.[12] In general terms, Western reactions to veiling have tended to fall into one or other of two broad categories: an outraged interpretation of the veil as an overt symbol of the oppression of women under Islam, or a romanticized view of the veil as part and parcel of the exotic, sensual Otherness of Oriental traditions. However, as historical studies have shown, the adoption of the veil was as subject to cross-cultural variation in the past as it is in the present. Italian travellers in seventeenth century Safavid Iran noted the 'shocking exposure' of local women.[13]

MacLeod (1991) provides a more sophisticated analysis of the new veiling than is typical of many non-Muslim Western commentators. Her study shows how difficult it is to approach an understanding of the indigenous meaning of *hijab* if commentary is grounded in notions of 'freedom' and 'constraint' which derive from a Western cultural context. In this way the veil and the question of women and Islam itself remain firmly associated, directly or indirectly, with assumptions of women's inferiority, subordination and powerlessness:

> The paradox of women seeming to support their own subordination, and even to reproduce it under new conditions, is part of the generally perplexing story of women's participation in the interactions of tradition and modernity, and the related renegotiations of power.
>
> (1991:93)

Images and ideologies of the veil remain contested and polarized as long as analysis attempts to evaluate the degree of constraint and control represented by the practice of veiling. Keddie has remarked:

> Although veiling and seclusion do not prevent women from living varied and significant lives, they are parts of a system where males are dominant and females are to be controlled. The system affects even non-secluded women who are expected to be modest and circumspect and are subject to sanctions if they transgress the rules. It is true that the overall system is more important than veiling as such.
>
> (1991:12)

In Keddie's terms, veiling is part of an institutionalized 'system' of male control and domination of women. But is this 'system' Islam? Is it possible to integrate this perspective with those of Nadia, Maryam and Fatima? The comment reminds us of the problems of Western ethnocentrism, Orientalism and the awkward relationship between feminism and Islam. In an attempt to understand contemporary Islam, it is essential to return to the question of 'unity and diversity' in relation to the meaning and interpretation of the veil. It is equally important for commentators to consider the extent to which their work repeats and reinforces negative media representations of Muslim women.

The perennial issue implicit in Western attempts to understand women's status in Islam is the compatibility of Islamic ideals and female emancipation. A central analytical problem in discussions of the veil in the context of gender and power relations in Muslim society is that generalizing theories tend to ignore what Kandiyoti calls, 'the specificity of Muslim women's subordination . . . and the influence of both Islamic ideology and practice in the reproduction of sexual inequality in Muslim society' (1991:24). At the socio-cultural level, it is important to recognize the many variations in Muslim women's roles and responsibilities across classes and cultures, and the differing degrees of women's independence within a rural, urban, tribal or 'westernized' social setting (see Beck and Keddie 1978; Fernea 1985). The concept of polyvocality has become familiar through the influence of postmodern theory via attention to multiplicities of meaning and contested narratives. It is worth remembering how the women's movement in the West challenged the bias and reductionism of a monolithic category of 'woman'. If Western feminist scholarship seeks to repeat the process in an analysis of gender and Islam, we might optimistically expect that, eventually, the diversity of Muslim women's experience and perceptions will be fully recognised in both popular and specialist discourse.

A second analytical problem lies at the ideological level. If debates about the institutions and structures of Muslim society are framed within Western notions of equality, individualism and freedom, the absence of equivalent concepts in Islam may lead to the misleading conclusion that 'democracy and Islam' are incompatible, or that 'sexual equality within Islam' is impossible. Enayat reaches the heart of the matter when he argues that 'the Western challenge to the credibility and integrity of Islam as a total ideology', represented by the global diffusion of concepts such as equality and democracy, poses one of the most important cultural and political problems facing all Muslims (1982:111).

However, a clash between Western worldviews and the politicized Islamic blueprint for a new social order may be circumvented by a focus on indigenous representations of gender and power relations. While researching into the nexus of Western and Muslim ideas of emancipation and sexual equality, I was confronted by a series of questions which forced me to rethink the standard interpretations of the 'new veiling'. Women repeatedly asked me why they should embrace Western feminism with no guarantee that it would offer them anything better than what they held to be the ideal form of gender relations promised by Islam. From their perspective, social problems were caused by flux or decay in Islamic principles of social organization. The question on their lips was why people consistently failed to work towards restoring what was perceived, within their own tradition, to be the ideal balance and division of labour between the sexes. Personal problems within marriage and the family were caused by men, equally subject to the pressures of life in a rapidly changing world. Here again the women's questions were provocative. Do feminists in the West live free from the hardships caused by men? Do the modernized husbands of working women take on household chores? In such discussions it quickly became evident that Muslim women's voices provide a vital corrective to the homogenizing tendencies of Western theoretical perspectives on Islam. The women's questions and commentary point to the need for studies which recognize critical or divergent views of Western norms and values, and attempt comparison of such contested domains. The integration of other voices and first person narratives of experience and perception also supply a narrow path which bypasses the cul-de-sac of a polarized Western feminist representation of Muslim women. Moreover, attention to individual interpretations of a global process like veiling provides a way of illustrating the commonalities of personal experiences of Islam in different social contexts.

The narratives give a local-level perspective on veiling as a personal act of resistance which relates to both individual and social conditions. The women's words provide no suggestion of an assumed inferior status or subordinate social position. An outsider might conclude that the women suffer from a classic case of 'false consciousness' and the active reproduction of the means of their own subordination. But from the women's viewpoint, the oppression and subordination of women (concepts which are relevant to actual experience in all three examples) are the result of secular social processes not associated with their ideal view of the 'true' and 'yet to be fully realized' form of Islam. Another Cairene woman's perspective is relevant here:

> Of course women suffer. But the government and the problems of poverty are to blame. Both things affect people badly, but economic troubles can have a particularly bad effect on men because they have to worry about the welfare of the family, and if men are upset they will tend to take it out on their wives. You can't blame a people's religion if women suffer in a situation like this. . . . There's only suffering and hardship for women when people don't follow the good ways expected of them by their religion, but that isn't always easy.

Returning to the question posed by Keddie's remark cited earlier, Islam is not the 'system' which controls or dominates women. The three voices which give an impression of women's personal interpretation of *hijab* reveal that the 'new veiling' involves a complex intermeshing of personal and political concerns. For Nadia, *hijab* is a public sign of personal religious faith, tinged with awareness of cultural pride and difference. For Maryam, veiling allows her to work in an alien public domain in a foreign country where she has experienced culture shock, racism and a political self-awareness. For Fatima, the new veiling is not an essential part of Muslim duty, but a new style of modest dress which represents an important way of making a statement about decaying social morality, national pride and the negative effects of Western influence. What these women who have adopted the veil in very different environments have in common is that they are making an active politicized response to forces of change, modernity and cross-cultural communication.

On a broader level, the 'new veiling' may also be seen as an Islamic example of the global trend of reaction against change experienced as chaotic or challenging, which takes the form of a renewed interest in fundamental principles of social and moral order. Marty and Appleby define contemporary fundamentalism in world religions in relation to a common word, 'fighting': 'fighting against any perceived threat to paramount fundamentals' and 'for a worldview . . . inherited or adopted' (1992:ix).[14] In a similar way, it is possible to see the return to the veil as part of women's personal and political struggle against the status quo, as well as a symbolic struggle for the improvement of existing conditions.

The issue of dress as a personal and political concern is one which has implications for gender and status in all societies and cultures. Questions about fashion, tradition, choice and force are of particular relevance for women in relation to socio-cultural representations of female sexuality. In these respects, debates about the new veiling force all women to recognize that choice of dress is both a personal and political matter. It may be one of the few forms of political protest some women have.

NOTES

1 Elsewhere Wikan's analysis shows the importance of addressing the subjective meaning of veiling. She states that far from producing feelings of oppression; 'these constraints and limitations are perceived by women as a source of pride and a confirmation of esteem' (1982:184).
2 Pioneering feminist studies of dress and gender include Wilson (1985) and Garber (1992).
3 Data from field research in Egypt 1986–8, France 1990 and England 1991–2.
4 The verse goes on to specify other categories of individual to whom women may 'reveal their adornment'. All quotations from the Qur'an are from Pickthall's (1976) translation.
5 The Prophetic tradition; ' I have not left any *fitna* more damaging to men than women' has often been cited to express this attitude. See references on female sexuality and *fitna* compiled by Bouhdiba (1985: 118ff).
6 Abu Daud (817–89) records the Prophet's instructions that 'A girl who has attained puberty cannot show her body with the exception of her face and the palm of her hand' (see Bouhdiba 1985; Musallam 1983).
7 Also see Moghadam (1993).
8 Khalaf Allah argues that the Qur'an does not prescribe a particular form of 'Islamic dress' for women since clothing styles: 'change with the times and with social conditions, just as do the rules of etiquette and the norms of public behaviour' (cited in Freyer Stowasser 1987:263). In contrast to this interpretation, Freyer Stowasser quotes a conservative theologian on the necessity of full Islamic dress for 'the truly Muslim woman': 'failure to do so means that the woman's faith has been shattered and that she will surely be punished by God . . . firstly, because she transgresses when she fails to veil and, secondly, because she becomes guilty of corrupting all the males who come in contact with her and whose unbridled lust she incites' (Freyer Stowasser 1987:273).
9 Also see Al-Hibri (1982; 1992) and L. Ahmed (1991; 1992).
10 Also see El Saadawi (1980; 1982).
11 Hourani (1991) provides an interesting description of the impact of European contact on Arab fashions; see also A.S. Ahmed (1990; 1992).
12 See El Saadawi (1980) and Rugh (1985) for examples. Abou Saif's fascinating memoir (1986) places an account of her personal struggle in the context of the anti-veiling protests, language and debates of international feminism.
13 See Waddy (1980) and Keddie and Baron (1991). An interesting example is provided in the memoir of Lady Mary, the wife of the British consul to Istanbul in the early 1700s:

> 'Tis very easy to see that they have more liberty than we have, no women of what rank so ever being permitted to go in the street without two muslins, one

that covers her face all but her eyes and another that hides the whole dress of her head and hangs halfway down her back. You may guess how effectively this disguises them . . . This perpetual masquerade gives them the entire liberty of following their inclinations without danger of discovery (cited in Waddy 1980: 128–9).

14 For a brief commentary, see Watson (1993).

REFERENCES

Abou Saif, L. (1986) *A Bridge Through Time: A Memoir*, London: Quartet Books.
Abu Lughod, L. (1986) *Veiled Sentiments*, Berkeley: University of California Press.
Ahmed, A.S. (1990) 'Jeans for You, Robes for Me', in *The Guardian*, 5 July.
—— (1992) *Postmodernism and Islam: Predicament and Promise*, London: Routledge.
Ahmed, L. (1991) 'Early Islam and the position of women: The problem of interpretation', in N. Keddie and B. Baron (eds) *Women in Middle Eastern History: Shifting Boundaries in Sex and Gender*, New Haven and London: Yale University Press.
—— (1992) *Women and Gender in Islam: Historical Roots of a Modern Debate*. New Haven and London: Yale University Press.
Al-Hibri, A. (1982) *Women and Islam*, Oxford: Pergamon.
—— (1992) *Women and Gender in Islam*, New Haven and London: Yale University Press.
Arberry, A. J. (1964) *The Qur'an* (translated with introduction), Oxford: Oxford University Press.
Beck, L. and Keddie, N. (eds) (1978) *Women in the Muslim World*, Cambridge MA: Harvard University Press.
Bouhdiba, A. (1985) *Sexuality in Islam*, London: Routledge and Kegan Paul.
Dawood, N. J. (1956) *The Qur'an* (translated with notes), London: Penguin Books.
El Guindi, F. (1981) 'Veiling Infitah with Muslim Ethic; Egypt's Contemporary Islamic Movement', *Social Problems* 8: 465–85.
El Saadawi, N. (1980) *The Hidden Face of Eve: Women in the Arab World*, London: Zed Press.
—— (1982) 'Women and Islam' in A. Al-Hibri (ed.) *Women and Islam*, Oxford: Pergamon.
Enayat, H. (1982) *Modern Islamic Political Thought*, London: Macmillan.
Fernea, E. W. (ed.) (1985) *Women and Family in the Middle East*, Austin: University of Texas Press.
Freyer Stowasser, B. (1987) 'Liberated Equal or protected dependent? Contemporary Religious Paradigms on Women's Status in Islam', *Arab Studies Quarterly* 9 (3) pp 77–89.
Garber, M. (1992) *Vested Interests: Cross-dressing and Cultural Anxiety*, London: Routledge.
Hourani, A. (1991) *A History of the Arab Peoples*, London: Faber and Faber.
Kandiyoti, D. (1991a) 'Islam and Patriarchy: A Comparative Perspective', in N. Keddie and B. Baron (eds) *Women in Middle Eastern History*, New Haven and London: Yale University Press.
—— (ed.) (1991b) *Women, Islam and the State*, London: Macmillan.
Keddie, N. (1991) 'Deciphering Middle Eastern women's history', in N. Keddie

and B. Baron (eds), *Women in Middle Eastern history: Shifting Boundaries in Sex and Gender*. New Haven and London: Yale University Press.

Keddie, N. and Baron, B. (eds) (1991) *Women in Middle Eastern History: Shifting Boundaries in Sex and Gender*, New Haven and London: Yale University Press.

Khater, A. and Nelson C., (1988) 'Al-Harakah al-nissa'iyah: the Women's Movement and Political Participation in Modern Egypt', *Women's Studies International Forum* 2(5) pp 465–83.

MacLeod, A. (1991) *Accommodating Protest: Working Women, the New Veiling and Change in Cairo*, New York: Columbia University Press.

Marty M. E. and Appleby R. S., (eds) (1992) *The Fundamentalism Project*, vol 1, Chicago: University of Chicago Press.

Mernissi, F. (1985) *Beyond the Veil: Male–female Dynamics in Muslim Society*, London: Al Saqi Books.

—— (1991) *Women and Islam: An Historical and Theological Enquiry*, Oxford: Blackwell.

Minces, J. (1982) *The House of Obedience*, London: Zed Press.

Moghadam, V. (1993) *Modernising Women: Gender and Social Change in the Middle East*, Boulder CO and London: Rienner Publishers.

Musallam, B. F. (1983) *Sex and Society in Islam*, Cambridge: Cambridge University Press.

Philipp, T. (1978) 'Feminism and National Politics in Egypt', in L. Beck and N. Keddie (eds), *Women in the Muslim World*, Cambridge MA: Harvard University Press.

Pickthall, M. M. (1976) *The Meaning of the Glorious Qur'an* (translated with notes), London: Nadim and Co.

Rezig, I. (1983) 'Women's Roles in contemporary Algeria: Tradition and Modernism', in B. Utas (ed.) *Women in Islamic Society: Social Attitudes and Historical Perspectives*, London: Curzon Press.

Rugh, A. B. (1985) *Family in Contemporary Egypt*, Cairo: American Univeristy of Cairo Press.

Sanders, P. (1991) 'Gendering the Ungendered Body', in N. Keddie and B. Baron (eds) *Women in Middle Eastern History*, New Haven and London: Yale University Press.

Waddy, C. (1980) *Women in Muslim History*, London and New York: Longmans.

Watson, H. E. (1993) 'Why Fundamentalism?', *Government and Opposition*, 28(4).

Wikan, U. (1982) *Behind the Veil in Arabia*, Baltimore: Johns Hopkins University Press.

Wilson, E. (1985) *Adorned in Dreams: Fashion and Modernity*, London: Virago.

Chapter 9

Sojourners abroad

Migration for higher education in a post-peasant Muslim society

Richard T. Antoun

A vast literature on international migration exists. Most of it is focused on labour migration and on the economic, demographic, and social implications of that migration on the economies and polities of sending and receiving countries.[1] Little attention has been paid to the interpersonal aspects of migration and the reactions of migrants to prolonged exposure to alien cultures and political systems and to radically different living circumstances. Even less attention has been paid to international migration for education. One of the few books to focus on the more personal aspects of migration and, peripherally, on education, Eickelman and Piscatori's (1990) *Muslim Travellers: Pilgrimage, Migration, and the Religious Imagination* discusses migration mainly in terms of the quest for and realization of religious identity. It points out (see, for example, the chapter by Masud) that the institutions of *hajj* (annual pilgrimage to Mecca) and *hijra* (the religious obligation of Muslims to migrate and simultaneously break ties, distance oneself from evil, and form new bonds of religious brotherhood) have over the centuries institutionalized migration. In addition, the Qur'an and the Traditions of the Prophet have urged the quest for knowledge abroad, and Muslim scholars widely pursued knowledge peripatetically in the medieval Islamic world (see Gellens 1990).

However, in the modern Middle East the 1973 oil-pricing revolution triggered a quantum leap of international migration in which the pursuit of higher education played an important role, albeit in a completely different context: the pursuit of secular education to gain professional skills in a postmodern world in which national borders were being breached and multicultural societies established, willy-nilly, within national borders.

The three case studies of Jordanian migrants described below begin to fill this gap in the literature, first and foremost, by focusing on the experiences of migrants and the humanistic implications of their quest for higher education abroad; and second, by exploring the degree to which, counterintuitively, the quest for secular education continues to have important religious dimensions. In addition, the chapter calls attention to the specific multicultural contexts in which migrants abroad seek to, alternatively or simultaneously, engage in the important processes of accommodation, acculturation, assimilation, reinterpretation or rejection of particular aspects of the host societies and cultures into which they are plunged. Finally, it briefly evaluates the usefulness of concepts such as acculturation by refining them, and suggests the usefulness of other concepts such as compartmentalization, preadaptation, encapsulation, the vicarious quest for identity, exclusionary closure, 'living on the border', and 'the constantly shifting centre'.

MIGRATION FROM KUFR AL-MA

In January 1986 I returned to the village of Kufr al-Ma, Jordan where I have been conducting research since 1959.[2] One day that winter I was sitting in the men's guest room (*madafa*) of a large extended family along with their relatives and neighbours, when a middle-aged man engaged me in conversation, indicating that he had just returned from Saudi Arabia where he was a travelling sales supervisor for Winston cigarettes.

My previous visit to the village in 1979 had alerted me to the growing importance of international migration, an importance confirmed by the occupations and place of work of the seventeen men in the guest room: six were serving in the Jordanian army, two were teachers, two students, one a postal clerk, one a designer and interior decorator, and one a retired cultivator. Of the seventeen men only one, the postal clerk, worked in the village. The two teachers taught at junior colleges elsewhere in Jordan. One of the men serving his compulsory military service had just finished a B.Sc. degree in agronomy from Peshawar University in Pakistan. The designer had a B.A. degree in fine arts from Cairo University. This was certainly a post-peasant society with a vengeance: not a single man worked the land and only one man ever had.

The Al-Kura subdistrict of northwestern Jordan in which the village lies is a badly eroded area, and in modern times its climate and low rainfall have precluded a majority of villagers from tilling the land, though in 1960 dry cereal farming was still an important activity in Kufr al-Ma and, together with shepherding, occupied about 40 per cent of the population.

By June 1986, 72 individuals from the village (67 males and 5 females from a total population of 4,500) had worked on the Arabian Peninsula with 63 currently working there in occupations that included the following: teachers, soldiers, health specialists, business managers, accountants, engineers, clerks, surveyors, translators, telephone operators, automobile mechanics, masons, construction workers, and drivers.

More interesting perhaps, was the fact that 36 men had returned from studying abroad and 35 were currently pursuing higher education abroad in 14 different countries including the following: Pakistan, Egypt, Greece, Lebanon, Syria, Turkey, Romania, Yugoslavia, Russia, Germany,

England and the United States. Their studies ranged from engineering, medicine, agriculture, journalism and law to English language and literature, Arabic language and literature, and Islamic studies, and from political science to psychology, naval science, veterinary medicine and linguistics. The time they spent abroad, whether for education or for work, was usually five or more years and sometimes significantly longer. One third of those working on the Arabian Peninsula in 1986 had spent from 7–9 years there, another 12 per cent, 10–12 years and another 12 per cent, 12–18 years. Of the five men from Kufr al-Ma pursuing higher education and/or work in the United States interviewed by me in 1991, one had spent 13 years and three 11 years in that country.

Although women have not yet left the country to pursue higher education abroad, in 1986, 36 women from the village had pursued or were pursuing tertiary education elsewhere in Jordan, 28 in junior colleges and 8 in four-year colleges. Twelve of these women were currently employed as teachers and two as head mistresses in junior high schools. In terms of marital status eleven were single and still studying, eight were married with children and working (teaching) and six were married and teaching.

To appreciate the significance of these facts one must understand the material, social, and cultural circumstances of the village in 1960, twenty-five years before. At that time all houses were built of clay and stone (as opposed to cement today); the village roads were narrow lanes with numerous rock outcrops; refuse (the mark of civilization) was non-existent, since no one could afford to purchase food in glass or plastic containers, and the only canned goods available in the meagre village stores were tuna fish and sardines. Only one man in the village purchased a newspaper – so there was no paper. The winter rains were collected in cisterns which usually ran dry in July, after which time water had to be purchased from the next village which had a spring; (today all houses have piped water); there was no electricity, and on moonless nights one stumbled along the narrow paths (now paved) with a flashlight or a Coleman lamp; (today all homes are electrified and every family has a television, and some have two).

In 1967, there was one automobile and one telephone – in the village post office. In 1986, there were 30 telephones, (and a long waiting-list for installation), and 123 automobiles and trucks. In 1960, one bus a day went to Irbid, the nearest market town, early in the morning and returned late in the afternoon. In 1986, buses and taxis began running at 6 a.m. and continued throughout the day and early evening. In 1960, approximately two thirds of the working male population worked in and around the village. In 1986, more than three quarters worked outside it. In 1960, eleven tiny grocery shops existed, stocking sugar, tea, one brand of plain packaged biscuits, matches, native Nablus soap, pencils, canned sardines and tuna fish, kerosene wicks, rock candy, and rubber plough shoes, among other things; peasants often paid the shopkeeper in kind with sacks of grain harvested in June. In 1960, no fresh vegetables or fruits or plastic goods of any kind were sold in the shops.

In 1986, there were 52 commercial establishments in the village, which had now achieved the official status of municipality (*baladiyya*), including 20 grocery shops, eight green-grocers, six chicken-sellers, four building-block workshops, four electrical supply shops, three builders' suppliers, two tile-making workshops, two petrol stations, one plate-glass seller, one aluminium seller and one auto garage. No payments in kind were accepted in these establishments. In any case little grain was grown on village lands any longer; most land had either been converted to olive growing or to housing plots for an expanding village which had begun to assume a homestead pattern in certain areas.

Most important, for our purposes, in 1960 two schools had existed in the village, one for boys through the sixth grade and one for girls through the third grade. Only one young man had left the village for higher education abroad (to Germany) in 1960, and only one other was in high school (in the nearby market town). In 1960, it would have been unimaginable for anyone to suggest that large numbers of young men would leave the village and the country for higher education abroad on four continents and even more ridiculous to suggest that any women in the village would leave it to pursue a high school education, not to speak of higher education.[3]

In the remainder of this chapter many of the interesting implications of international migration for rural communities in the Muslim world suggested above will be neglected. Rather, the description and analysis will concentrate on the implications of one type of migration, that for higher education, focusing particularly on those who have left the Arab world for education in Europe and North America. This is perhaps the most radical type of migration in its implications for cultural change and the creation of a global society.

THREE STUDENTS, THREE COUNTRIES, THREE ACCOMMODATIONS OF TRADITION[4]

The following cases document the educational careers of three students, one of whom went to Germany to study medicine, one to Egypt to study Islamic law and subsequently to England to study linguistics, and one to the United States to study engineering and subsequently data-processing and business management. These three students illustrate the possibilities of 'acculturation,' 'assimilation,' and 'living on the border', three processes of socio-cultural transformation to be explored below.[5] All three young men, hence referred to as Ali, Yusuf and Zayd, spent considerable periods abroad: Ali, 15 years in Germany, Yusuf, five years in Egypt and nine years in England, and Zayd, eleven years in the United States.[6] They will be discussed in the order in which they left Jordan, Ali in 1963, Yusuf in 1967 and Zayd in 1979.

Assimilation and the preservation of religious identity in Germany

Ali arrived at the University of Erlangen in West Germany in 1963. He spent his first year studying German and his second taking a pre-medical curriculum. He passed his medical exams in 1971, and thereafter specialized in surgery. From 1972–80 he practised medicine in West Germany while pursuing his specialized studies.

In 1970, at the urging of a Lebanese fellow-student who had just married a Lebanese girl from Beirut, he went to Lebanon to visit the latter's family – she had an eligible unmarried sister. He went from Beirut to Jordan and returned with his father who went with him to make the formal request of marriage. In 1970, he returned to Germany with his wife. Four of his five children were born there.

In 1980, he received a certificate of advanced medical learning from the head of hospital (*chef arzt*) and returned to Jordan, opening a medical practice in the regional capital of Irbid. The German head of hospital where he had practised medicine invited him to stay on permanently, telling him that he would deal with any bureaucracy involved: 'You can do it all [practise all aspects of medicine] whether you're Arab or not.' Ali turned down the offer.

He said in interview that he had never contemplated marrying a German woman: 'If I marry a German woman, I must stay (in Germany); if I brought her to Jordan it would be difficult for her.' To understand his decisions to marry an Arab Muslim and to return to Jordan to practise his profession, it is necessary to note the circumstances of his early student life abroad and the views he developed of Germans and German culture. For seven years before his marriage he lived with German families as a lodger in their homes. When I asked him to describe his social relations in this period he replied that he developed close relations with these families. They brought him out of his room every day to watch television; they brought cakes and coffee to his room during his late evening study hours; they washed his clothes; on weekends they took him with them on visits. He noted that Germans were energetic: they always went on hikes and for rides in the car; they always took an annual vacation outside Germany. All of this he viewed in a positive way.

He viewed university life and his professional work in German hospitals in an even more favourable light. He said that in these hospitals the patient was cared for to an extraordinary degree; medical care was extremely efficient – time was dear for Germans and they put it to good use – all lab tests were returned within three days; the patient was always matched with the appropriate care by a qualified specialist. He was impressed by the human concern demonstrated by the medical system: all persons were treated regardless of expense; no favouritism was shown to Germans; the chief physician treated each patient like a member of his family. None of the pejorative terms commonly used in the United States to describe a system of 'socialized medicine' or a 'welfare state' were found in his vocabulary.

But he also described what he viewed as the negative aspect of German family and social life. 'After 18 the child is independent and can marry whom she wishes [without receiving a parent's consent]. Both the husband and wife work, and this leads to problems,' he said. Both men and women drank too much. I asked him, 'Did you drink?' He replied, 'You know what kind of family I have,' referring to the piety of his father. He observed that the German father returned home after work and sat down in front of the television and watched whatever he preferred without considering the wishes of the other members of the family, behaviour he considered egotistical. He noted that if two people quarrelled in the street no one interfered; if they acted at all, they called the police. For him these behaviours clearly indicated a lack of human concern.

Ali's comments about German family life were not simply that. They had significance for a general world view and way of life that was considered to be religiously appropriate, as became clear when I asked him at the end of the interview, 'What is the importance of religion in Germany?' He replied that it was of little importance there. He elaborated, 'In Germany they say, "Religion is for the church not the office".' He said that a German came to Jordan and went back to Germany and gave a lecture and said, 'If you want to see a social (collective) life go to Jordan; if you want to see religion, go to the Middle East.'

Ali was clearly a person with a drive to succeed who practised deferred gratification over a long period. He said he did not interact with Arab students in Germany (who proliferated in the 1970s) or enter into any of their organizations because it took up too much time. He said that for every grade of 'excellent' in a subject, he paid reduced fees at the university.

I asked Ali whether, while abroad, he ever visited another student from Kufr al-Ma who had also gone to West Germany to study medicine or vice-versa. He replied that he had never visited him. 'He has another mental-ity,' he said. 'He wants to drink and have his girl-friends. We have nothing in common. Every day he was with another girl. One day he came and visited me; he was with his secretary (i.e., his girl-friend)'. To understand Ali's evaluation of German life and other aspects of his world-view it is necessary to understand his relationship with his father.[7]

Ali's father had finished primary school in the adjoining sub-district centre (which then was only a village) and junior high school in the market town of Irbid before World War Two, an accomplishment that was unusual for a village boy at the time. After graduation he worked for three years as an Arabic-English translator on the oil pipe-line that linked Kirkuk in Iraq with Haifa in Palestine, before serving as a customs officer in Amman for two years. He then married, opened a village shop, and engaged in small-time grain trading between Palestine and Transjordan for ten years prior to joining the Islamic court as clerk-usher in the nearby village and sub-district centre of Deir Abu Said between 1954 and 1963. From 1963, the year his son left for Germany, until 1970, the year of his death, he managed his own orchard – which he had planted – in the Jordan Valley on land he had purchased with a bank loan. He also engaged in various entrepreneurial activities including buying a tractor and a stone-cutter, and, with his second son sometimes driving, renting them out to the area's cultivators. He used the profits to finance his son's medical education and to modernize his home, replacing its stone and adobe walls with cement and adding a colourful painted grille around each window.

Two things stand out about Ali's father and his family background. One is the aura of religious piety in which he grew up. The name of the family itself, *al-shariʿa*, literally, 'the way', meaning the Muslim way and, more specifically, the whole code of Islamic law and ethics, was attached to the family as a result of their reputation for piety and religious learning. The other is Ali's father's early contact with foreigners through his position as translator and customs officer and his commitment to material modernization and pioneering entrepreneurship (that was only moderately successful) – no one else in the sub-district had introduced tractors or stone-cutters at the time. Notable is the fact that in 1965 Ali's father borrowed money from the bank at interest to finance his investments. Five years before, securing bank loans with interest (referred to as *ribaʿ* or usury by some Muslim scholars) had been a subject of debate in the village, and the consensus, particularly among the pious village elders, was against it.

In a certain sense Ali's student life and professional training were a vicarious realization of his father's goals and feelings. His father had not been able to continue his schooling because his own father had died and his uncles could not afford to continue his education in town. Ali's father had loved his mother and suffered for many years because doctors were not able to diagnose or treat the illness which led to her early demise. In Ali's words, 'My father always had it in his mind – it was his dream – that I should be a doctor; he planted the idea in my mind.'

I asked Ali, 'What is your view of your childhood in the village?' He replied, 'What my children have I didn't have. It was a good memory because my father was good to me.' In another interview I asked him the same question and he replied, 'I didn't have everything I wanted, but I had everything I needed. My father monitored my activities, even when I became adult.' He said that his younger brothers got away with a lot more.

Ali continued, 'There was mutual love between us,' and he proceeded to give a trivial but nevertheless important example: 'I hated smoking; my father was a constant smoker; if I came in and sat down my father would throw away his cigarette.' I asked Ali, 'Did your father send letters to you in Germany?' He replied, 'Yes, the most important advice he gave me was, "I enjoin you to fear God (be pious, *ittaqa allah*)".' Ali said that his father meant by that that he should abstain from alcohol and running around with girls. He said that the result (of his father's advice) was that he finished his medical studies in a relatively short period of time. I asked Ali, as I did all migrants, what he thought of tribal law in Jordan, what he thought of Jordanian televison, and what he thought of the unemployment problem in Jordan. His answers reveal his orientation towards modernization and modernity and the relationship of that orientation to Islam, government, and the socio-economic order.[8]

He said that tribal law had both positive and negative sides. The positive side was that it helped solve problems. But it was 'backwards, a thing of the last century. The king wants it,' he said. I replied, 'The people came and asked the king for it,' (i.e., to restore tribal law after it had been abolished by government edict). He replied, 'The people, the Pasha – if the (civil) law is not here, they have no value. It is difficult now; if two pupils 12 years old, kick one another and one gets a fracture, they [the perpetrator's patrilineal relatives] must go to his family and pay. I'm not completely against tribal law, but if they have a problem they take not what we have now [i.e., civil law]. Life [today] is not the same as forty years ago.'[9]

In answer to my question, 'What is the impact of television in Jordan?' he replied:

Television in Jordan has a broad effect: [first] in science, everybody can see the civilized countries. They [Jordanians] try to say we have and others haven't. They know now how strong they [western countries] are. Second, they now see that they themselves have nothing and other countries have so much. Third, when you see how beautiful other countries are, and they [Jordanians] don't have [that beauty]. Fourth, in medicine we know now that we have not: we have no hospitals [in the district] like *madinat husayn* [the so-called king's hospital in Amman]. Not everyone can go there – only people in the army [and their families]. People became jealous of the West as a result of television. Television [also] brings out the negative side of western civilization: how to be a drunkard; for girls, sometimes we see in film what girls do with their [boy]friends; it [sexual immorality] is against our religion. Films in Germany are native [to Germany], but our films are from abroad. Too many people see what is on the television screen as real. They see the same forty people every week [on the television screen].

Finally, in answer to my question, 'What is the solution to the unemployment problem in Jordan?' he replied: 'Providing jobs for all the graduates of institutes and universities.' He said that the Germans distinguished many different occupational statuses: *hilfsarbeiter* (assistant worker), *arbeiter* (worker), specialist, master and engineer. 'Jordan,' he said, 'only had the worker on the one hand and the engineer on the other and nothing in between.' He continued, 'In Germany everything is according to certificates; the shoemaker and the barber have to have certificates.' He said that the educational institutions in Jordan only gave academic degrees. He said that there was only one trade school in Jordan. 'What is the solution to the problem of unemployment' I asked again? 'The solution,' he replied 'was the founding of trade schools in all specialities,' i.e., the country needed technical experts. I said, 'But aren't there lots of people who can fix televisions?' He replied, 'They don't really know how to fix televisions; they just fool around with them.'

Ali is perhaps the most 'modern' of the three migrants measured in terms of his commitment to science and its application to societal improvement and individual welfare, particularly in the field of medicine where he observed and clearly vouched for the superior German hospitals, personal medical care, and match of specializations with individual needs. In his evaluation of the impact of television, Ali seemed to equate progress with science and applied science, and in his earlier remarks on the German health system, with the effective use of time.

He also stipulated what he believed to be a superior German socio-economic system in his view that the unemployment problem in Jordan would be solved by the differentiation of roles and the hierarchicalization of society: differential training and distribution of knowledge and skills and formalization of hierarchy by the issuing of certificates at all levels. This commitment to the development of a necessarily differentiated and hierarchical society is interesting, because in his earlier remark on German religious attitudes he repudiated the notion that religion should be separated out from office (i.e., government and business).

In some respects Ali's views of how television represented the civilized West as opposed, by direct implication, to uncivilized Jordan, as well as his earlier story of how the German traveller found religion and collective life in the Middle East (and not in Germany) is a caricature of Western 'orientalist' discourse. In this respect Ali not only acculturated to German ways but assimilated them in the sense of identifying with their underlying values: effective use of time, material modernization, hierarchicalization, human concern for the individual, and a universalistic system of rewards that did not recognize ethnic differences – though his remarks about the German hospital director's offer indicated that his ethnic identity had not in fact been cancelled. His qualified response regarding his view of tribal law clearly relegated it low on the ladder of progress, a vestigial institution –

now that civil law and state order had emerged. All this seems to indicate that Ali went to Europe and returned as a cognitive retread.

But his remarks about television and civilization end with a return to a persistent theme in the interview: Western civilization is deeply flawed by its immorality, familial, sexual and alcoholic. This theme emerged as an explanation of his refusal to visit the other son of the village in Germany, it coloured his description of German family life, and it was dramatized in his father's admonition in his letter.

More significant than either the strictly sexual or the alcoholic dimension is the broader immorality of German familial/societal life: when both husband and wife work, and the daughter is free at age 18 (as opposed to monitored, as Ali was by his father into adulthood) to make her own decisions, then, truly, the world has been turned topsy-turvy, and an ordered and religious way of life cannot be lived. Thus Ali married within his own religion and ethnic tradition and decided to return to Jordan to practise medicine, even after he had an opportunity to do otherwise in a society that he admired for its educational system, quest for knowledge, application of science, efficiency, and fairness. How could a Muslim lead a meaningful life in a society where religion was barred from office?

The theme of the survival of the religious person in the secular society emerges again but with a very different twist and involving a different father–son relationship with Yusuf, the migrant to England.

Preadaptation and controlled acculturation in Cairo, London and Leeds

Yusuf's early peripatetic schooling was a forerunner and perhaps preadapter to his later peripatetic higher education. He attended primary school in three different locations in Jordan, only the first two years being in Kufr al-Ma; for the remainder of his early schooling he attended junior high school in the northern border town of Ramtha where his father was a customs officer; his first two years of high school were spent in Deir Abu Said, the sub-district centre adjoining Kufr al-Ma, because his father was now posted there as a clerk of civil court; while his final year of high school was spent on the West Bank in Nablus at a special school oriented towards preparing students for the religious university of Al-Azhar in Cairo, which he entered in 1967.

He received a B.A. degree in religious law and state law (*al-shari'a wa al-qanun*) from Al-Azhar in 1971. His father wanted him to return home, obtain a position in the bureaucracy (nearly all teaching positions in Jordan are government positions), start earning money – since he had two younger brothers who needed educating – and settle down. Yusuf insisted on continuing his education. His father acquiesced to another year at Al-Azhar studying educational psychology (and thereby enhancing his teaching credentials); he received his diploma (M.A. degree) in 1972 and began exploring the opportunities of continuing his studies abroad. One Egyptian professor suggested studying in England. So even though his father adamantly opposed such a move, and without his knowledge or consent, Yusuf, as he said:

> packed [his] suitcase. I had a thousand dollars in my pocket. At that time I thought I'd stay one or two years working and learning the language [before continuing Islamic studies in England]. When I went in 1972 I didn't know anybody in England, not a single person.

After his departure for England, Yusuf's's father cut off communication and correspondence with him for over two years.

I asked Yusuf about his relationship with students of other nationalities in Cairo and with Egyptians. He said that for the first three months he had lived in university dormitories together with Africans, Malaysians and Indonesians, but had eventually moved out and lived in a series of flats by himself. He found the quarters at the university very crowded with 10–15 students in one block, and the food was unsavoury. I asked whether he maintained contact with students whom he had met there. He replied that he still has contact with one Bahraini who is the director of an Islamic college, and with a Tanzanian who is a teacher in Ajman. He also has a few Egyptian friends who teach at Cairo University and with whom he stayed on a return visit in 1985. His closest ties from his student days were with the four Jordanians who went with him to Al-Azhar from the religious high school in Nablus; he still corresponds with all of them.

I asked Yusuf whether he got to know many Egyptians. He replied, 'The nature of the Egyptian is open. If any stranger comes, they say, "Hello, where are you from?" You get to know them.' They would go out together and engage in reciprocal hospitality. I asked Yusuf what he thought of Egyptian character. He replied, 'Very open. They are excellent; they laugh; they are helpful; greedy; some take you for a friend in their own interest; they like money very much; they will introduce you to the whole family; they don't feel shame (as Jordanians do) about introducing you to their women.' 'What did you feel about this contact with women?' I asked. He replied, 'I liked it. It was very nice. That was my impression when I was there.'

Yusuf's view of Egyptian (specifically Cairene) character changed somewhat in 1985 when he returned for a visit.

> They are still open. Greedy. They like you for your money. [But] morals are [now] degraded. A man gives you his word, but it isn't worth anything. If you ask him to do anything he won't do it unless for money. For instance, filling out papers – he won't do it unless it's for money. . . . When I was there in 1967 you'd go to any shop, they'd give

you the right answer [if you asked directions]; now he'll tell you, 'I don't know'.

I asked Yusuf, 'Are Jordanians discriminated against in Egypt?' He replied, 'Jordanians are all considered Arabs along with Syrians, Palestinians, Iraqis. The Egyptians don't distinguish between them unless there are political problems [i.e., government-to-government problems]. There were none at the time.'

I asked Yusuf what he thought of Egyptian women. He said that they were very poor, and 'When a foreign man came they said, "Hi" and treated him as if he were the prime minister of his country.'

I asked Yusuf how he evaluated his education at Al-Azhar. He replied, 'The only weakness is that they didn't have foreign languages – no French or English; the other aspects were excellent.' While at Al-Azhar he focused his studies on the Qur'an, the Traditions of the Prophet, Islamic law (*fiqh*), principles of Islamic law (*usul al-fiqh*), *qanun* which, he said, included study of both Islamic and civil law and their interrelationship including the operation of the mixed courts, Arabic language and literature, oratory, and Islamic history. He specialized in the Shafaʻi school of law because, he said, most Jordanians follow that school. I asked him whether memorization was an important part of his studies. He replied that he had memorized one third of the Qur'an, a few Traditions of the Prophet on each subject and verses of both pre- and post-Islamic poetry. I asked him how he evaluated his teachers at Al-Azhar. He said that the lecturers were advanced in years, and so they were good, i.e., advanced in knowledge; they were all Egyptians. He said that you could go to the professor's house, and he would help you if you had any difficulties; he did not go because he had none, but others went.

Yusuf's Islamic education at Al-Azhar had a direct impact on the pattern of relationships he formed both with other Muslims in England and with the English both in London and Leeds. When he arrived in Leeds in 1976 he found a very active Muslim religious movement dominated by Pakistanis called, *al-daʻwa*, 'The Mission [of spreading Islam]'. There Muslims centred their activities around a mosque in Leeds and engaged in periodic missionary campaigns of religious intensification. As Yusuf described it:

> They continually urged me to go on their campaigns which involved sleeping in the mosque and then going and preaching in various people's houses, saying, 'Peace be upon you. Are you a Muslim? Do you pray? Why not? Do you fast? Why not?' Then they called the person, or (if he resisted) dragged him to the mosque for prayer.

Because Yusuf did not drink and because he did not date girls, they regarded him as one of them.

More important, Yusuf quickly became well-known in the local Muslim, mainly Pakistani, community in Leeds when it was discovered that he was a graduate of Al-Azhar and that he recited the Qur'an better than they did. They made him the prayer-leader (*imam*) of the mosque, and so he assumed a position of leadership in the diaspora as the *shaykh* of the local mosque, which not only involved leading congregational worship on Friday but also giving children lessons in the Qur'an.

In Leeds he interacted mainly with Pakistanis since, he said, 'The English are very conservative and difficult to get to know.' He stopped participating actively in the *da'wa* movement, however, because he had to pursue his studies and also, by implication, because he did not particularly care for their overly-aggressive missionary style. During this time he became acquainted with the works of the leading Pakistani fundamentalist scholar, Abu A'la al-Maududi, and he mentioned that one of the Pakistani students at Leeds and a friend of his, who was one of Maududi's students, later became Minister of Education in Pakistan.

Yusuf's other arena of activity and social network at Leeds was the university. Whereas he characterized his four years in London (1972–76) as 'mixing with people from society', he characterized his life in Leeds as 'weekdays at the university and weekends at the mosque'. He said that he mixed with students at the university, and they exchanged hospitality. He elaborated, 'Student life was very good, but it was entirely different outside [the university gates]. The [English] students themselves criticized society. The man in the street, you can't get to know; only the university students; they are middle class; one was the son of a knight.'

I asked him if he got to know English girls at the university. He said that there was a common room where all the students met, but he never got to know any of the girls. When I pressed him further about his impression of English women he replied:

> You have to get to know the English girl. Arab students are influenced by films. Most of my extra time – because I was a *shaykh* (religious scholar) – I spent in the mosque or at religio-social get-togethers. I spent my extra time in the library – I had a special room at the library.

Then he returned to the previous subject of English women, commenting, 'It is not difficult to grab a girl [i.e., to get a date]. [But] she has no intention of going with you to your house – just because she went [with you] for tea or coffee.'

He established an important and satisfying relationship with his mentor at the university, the head of the Semitics department who was a Yemeni Jew with whom he still corresponds. It was he, in fact, who convinced him to switch from general Islamic and Middle Eastern studies to research in linguistics: Yusuf's Ph.D. dissertation in descriptive linguistics was on the Arabic dialects of the Jordan Valley. It was this professor who wanted him to stay as a permanent member of the linguistics department at Leeds when he graduated. He said that he still corresponded with him.

When I asked Yusuf if he had ever thought of settling in England, he mentioned the fact that the head of the department had asked him to stay and elaborated, 'No, they [the English] look on you as second class. I hated it. I had the opportunity of staying – working there as a teacher. The head of the department even now wants me to come and teach as Lecturer.' He said that he would consider going to England as a Visiting Professor [only]. His final statement on the subject was telling:

> You're not inside the academic community all the time. You have to go home and have neighbours, and if you don't have good neighbours you won't be happy.

Yusuf had nothing but praise for the English university system. He much preferred the concentration on one course the whole year with an end-of-the-year exam to the American semester and credit system, proliferating shorter courses and electives (which was the system prevailing at the university in Jordan where he taught). But in Leeds if his weekly round oscillated between the space of the university and the space of the mosque, there was a third and encompassing space – the world – which compromised both of these confined and limited spaces and made assimilation impossible.

To understand the relationships he had with the English and the attitudes he developed towards them we must return to the circumstances of his arrival in London and his four-year experience there. On his first Friday in London he asked someone at the hotel at which he was staying where the nearest mosque was, and he was directed to the Islamic Cultural Centre where he met a graduate of Al-Azhar who worked as the *imam* of the mosque. Initially, he worked at this Centre as a clerk and spent four months studying English. For the following three years he taught Arabic in various English grammar schools and also gave private lessons, all of these positions having been arranged through the Islamic Cultural Centre. During these four years in London he lived happily. He saved money for his future education (the forty pounds a week he earned was more than enough to cover his frugal living expenses) and he bought a car.

I asked him, 'How did you spend your leisure time in London?' He said that he travelled. I asked, 'Where did you go?' He replied, 'Anywhere. I would get in my car and go. I know England more than Jordan. I went everywhere. I stayed overnight in only a few places. I went by myself. I liked to go by myself.' When I asked him why he didn't go with others, he replied, 'Why would I want to do that?' He said it was a bother to take other people because then you had to take care of them if something happened to them. He clearly enjoyed the freedom of his new life. I asked him whether he attended films or plays in London. He replied that he had no time to attend films or plays: he went to work at eight in the morning and did not return to his flat till eight in the evening. It must be noted again that he was saving money in order to apply to a graduate programme at an English university; (he applied to six and Leeds was the first to admit him). During this entire period in London he lived in single-room flats where he cooked his own meals; otherwise he ate at the Islamic Centre. He said that he never got to know any of the people living in the adjoining flats. Whereas in Leeds he developed a largely Pakistani social network outside the university, in London he said, 'I mixed with people from society'; by this he meant Pakistanis and Indians as well as English Muslims at the Islamic Cultural Centre.

Just as they were to be later in Leeds, his social relations in London were highly structured and limited in part as a result of his Muslim higher education and his work, in part as a result of his economic circumstances as an aspiring and later struggling student, and in part as a result of his own staunchly independent (some would consider him a loner), goal-oriented and highly curious (with respect to foreigners and other cultures) character.

What is unusual about his relationships with the English he met in London in the course of his work is that although as a foreigner from a part of the world formerly dominated by them and presumably, therefore, inferior in status, as a teacher he was always in a superordinate position. Over a four-year period he did not get to know any of the students he taught in London or their families outside of class, although a few of the adults he tutored invited him for tea or dinner. His egalitarian relationships with English persons in Leeds and his superordinate relationships with them in London almost always took place within restricted and formal milieus: the university in Leeds and the grammar school classroom in London. The one important egalitarian relationship he had with English people 'in the world' was in a religious (also specific) context. Regularly, once a year, he attended a three-day 'Conference of Concordance' between Muslims and Christians. He much enjoyed interacting with others at these ecumenical meetings, and through them he developed a friendship with a certain vicar with whom he exchanged hospitality.

Otherwise, in the world, and his own perception must have been strengthened by his interactions with South Asians in London (whom he resembled to some degree, being short and rather dark in complexion), he viewed the English as 'conservative'. Yusuf elaborated, 'They didn't mix with foreigners, and especially blacks; they avoided anyone not from Europe. They showed jealousy to Arabs, because [they believed] they were all rich.'

When I asked Yusuf what he liked best about the English, he replied that he liked the system of government and social order:

Everyone had the right to do what he likes. Oppose what he likes. The government, talking without any opposition. I like it. The way they [the English] behave – from the social side the way they treat people. From the religious side, if anybody argues about religion, they say 'Okay, do what you like'. They forced everybody riding motor bikes to have a motor helmet. The Sikhs said they couldn't take their turbans off, so the government allowed it [i.e., to keep them on].

He liked the English countryside and the fact that 'any kind of food in the world is available, eastern and western'. He even said he liked the conservatism of the English, but then added: 'But not the way they closed themselves for themselves. If they had a bit of openness it would be better.' When I asked Yusuf what he did not like about the English he said:

Some of them are arrogant. Everyone from the Middle East is [considered] riff-raff. [They think to themselves], 'We colonized them'. From the inside you can't open up people's hearts [but] they dislike the Arabs: for one thing they are Muslims; the second thing, they are rich. But if he [the Englishman] has an interest involved [e.g., a company doing business in the Middle East], they make propaganda for the Arabs.

At the end of the interview Yusuf looked at me directly and asked, 'Why do they [Westerners] dislike Muslims?'

His life in London, then, gave him strong and favourable views of English democracy and religious pluralism, although that democracy and pluralism were flawed by racial bigotry, ethnic arrogance and a certain insularity of mind and social relations. But the life he led in London like the life he led in Leeds was encapsulated, encapsulated even at an imaginative level since he never frequented films or plays.

His relations with and attitudes toward English women and his views of relations between the sexes provide further insight into the mode of acculturation he pursued in England. His exposure to Egyptian women, in a way, preadapted him to social life in England: for the first time (unlike the rural tribal society of Jordan from which he came) in Egypt he was able to interact with unrelated women in a free and open manner within the contexts of visits to the families of his friends and classmates. He enjoyed that contact. I asked him during the interview, 'What do you think of relationships between the sexes in England?' He said that they did not strike him as extraordinary. He had gone to Germany for two months during the summer of 1970 to work – he secured a job with a shipping company numbering cartons and putting them on a truck. When I asked him whether he made much money, he replied that he had gone to Germany 'just to see the life', not to make money, so that when he came to England the (public) kissing and hugging (among couples) did not strike him as unusual. One chap below his flat was always drunk, he said, and often invited him in. While in Germany he worked along side other Arabs at the company, roomed with two Jordanians, and later toured Europe by car with them. Thus, by the time he arrived in England Yusuf already had two preadaptive experiences in Egypt and Germany.

I asked Yusuf whether he ever thought of marrying an English girl. His father had told me earlier that Yusuf had written a letter to him towards the end of his stay suggesting the possibility of marriage.[10] He replied to my question:

> I wrote to my father just proposing the idea of marrying an [English] girl. I had no one in particular in mind. I just proposed the idea. First, I never considered it seriously because I wouldn't be able to find a virgin girl, or I would have to go deep into the countryside there. A vicar told me once that [in one country district] once you get engaged to a girl you have to marry her; you couldn't go out with her privately; you could only sit around with her family.

I interjected, 'You must have been entertaining the notion of marriage or you wouldn't have written the letter.' He replied that he wrote the letter because of the possibility of his staying in England, saying 'You know how it is when you're abroad – many ideas go through your mind.'

Yusuf's actual relations with English men and women were an interesting mixture of freedom and control. He greeted girls on the university campus and spoke with them in the common room (something of which the members of the *da'wa* movement disapproved), but he never dated them. He attended mixed gatherings and even parties hosted by the ecumenical conference, but he never drank, and if drinking became blatant, he left. The vicar, knowing this, never offered alcohol to guests when Yusuf was present. He was not disturbed by husbands and wives kissing in public, regarding it as a 'custom'. However, he strictly observed the Muslim food taboos on pork and alcohol. Yusuf's behaviour was an interesting example of 'antagonistic acculturation': picking and choosing what to borrow and avoiding those acts or beliefs that undermined one's basic values.[11] Yusuf's ability to control acculturation in this fashion was facilitated by his superordinate status (as teacher and *imam*) among both Muslims and non-Muslims in specific spaces of work and study; by the varied preadaptive experiences he had; as well as by the considerable travel he undertook within England.

The latter two experiences inside and outside the country allowed him to develop some empathy, tolerance and a certain sense of cultural relativity towards many of the alien customs he witnessed, whether in Egypt, Germany or Great Britain.

Be this as it may, in the end his evaluation of English life and his own world-view was religious. Indeed, it was in England that his Muslim identity was shaped and sharpened. I have no evidence that he was particularly pious as a youth. He was sent to a religious high school in Nablus in part because the high school he attended in Transjordan had no science programme, and he could not qualify for other professions such as medicine or engineering. But he returned to Jordan in 1980 with a clipped beard, an indicator of his religious identity and commitment.

His condemnatory religious evaluation of English life emerged at the end of a conversation we had about his reaction to English ways, including public kissing and the consumption of alcohol. He said, referring to English life in general:

> They are all working for themselves [i.e., without God's plan]. Women work because they [the family] can't afford [to buy] a telephone [otherwise]. Women would like to stay home; over 60 per cent don't want to work. After 18 they leave the house. A girl, a secretary, living at home, gives £10 a week as rent to her father! She saw the cheque I received from my father for £1,000. [After Yusuf entered the university his father relented and began sending him money as did his elder brother who was a doctor in Saudi Arabia]. She was astonished [by that]. Sometimes the parents even rent the house to the son!

Despite his observation of free, public cross-sex relationships over a long period of time, including women's active participation in the work force, Yusuf regarded English women as essentially conservative. They had been profaned and family life undermined by a topsy-turvy secular world where women had to work, children paid rent to their parents, and God's plan for the family and society had been abandoned.

In Jordan I observed that Yusuf's interpersonal relationships reflected the same kind of controlled acculturation that had organized his life abroad. At the time of interview he was a professor at the university. He invited me to his house in town for dinner along with a mutual friend from the village who was also his patrilineal kinsman and a small shopkeeper in the same town. Earlier I had met his Jordanian wife and his wife's sister in his university office, and he introduced them to me effusively, and we had a very pleasant conversation. I spent several hours at his home, and I never saw his wife, who prepared the meal in the kitchen and did not join us either during or after dinner. Both Yusuf and his patrilineal kinsman excused themselves after the meal to perform their evening prayers.

Yusuf's pattern of interpersonal and gender relationships in Jordan, then, reflected exactly the same kind of compartmentalization as in England: the university was a space of relatively free interaction between the sexes; the world and the home were not.[12]

Life 'on the border' in Houston, Texas

Zayd arrived in Houston in December 1979 by way of Abu Dhabi where his father, retired from the Jordanian army, was working as a sergeant in Abu Dhabi's army.[13] His original intention was to study civil engineering. After two semesters studying engineering at Blinn College, 90 miles outside Houston, and finding that his high school training had not prepared him for engineering studies and disliking the isolated rural milieu, he transferred to the Aero Academy near Houston airport where in the next year and a half he amassed 150 flying hours with the intention of becoming a civil aviation pilot in Jordan. When he discovered on a month's visit to Jordan in 1983 that the waiting list was two years just to be considered for a position, he switched to data-processing at Houston Community College where he received an associate's degree in 1985.

In the summer of 1986 he returned to Jordan for two months when he pondered the possibility of settling down and working or returning to the United States for further education. (This was the period of my first interview with Zayd.) He returned to Houston Community College in the autumn of 1986 where he took courses, part-time, in government and economics; and subsequently to the University of Houston, where he took a course in business law and management before he dropped out for a semester to work. He returned to Texas Southern University where for two years he took a course overload (18–21 hours), obtaining his bachelor's degree in business administration in 1990.

During this entire restless period of study and work, he was introduced to American society and culture and to the other sub-cultures of Houston through his various jobs, through his girl-friends, through his marriage which ended in divorce after three years, and through his romance and work with the automobile.

Zayd worked almost continually during his eleven-year stay in the United States, at first to supplement the modest scholarship he had from the government of Abu Dhabi and after 1985 to subsist, since he received no substantial aid from his family after 1981. This work-study regime, quite common among students from Kufr al-Ma in the United States, extended their period of study and resulted in a much longer period of exposure to American society and culture than would have occurred otherwise.

Zayd described his first job in Houston in 1980, while he was attending an intensive English-language course, as follows:

> I worked at McDonald's but quit after three days. I wasn't raised to believe I was supposed to do this kind of job. I felt humiliated when someone asked me to pick up the mop and clean the floor. I didn't feel comfortable. The wages were okay, $3.25 an hour.

After he left Blinn College Zayd went to work, part-time, washing dishes at an Italian restaurant for four months, after which he was promoted to cocktail waiter. He said that, again, he felt humiliated the first time he served tea to a customer. 'Then,' he said, 'I got used to the idea, and it was okay.' In 1982 he went to a French restaurant to work as a waiter. Later, he became a bartender and benefited from a percentage of the waiters' tips. For the last several years in Houston in the job that he preferred by far, he worked as a driver for a limousine service during the evening and night, reserving the day for classes and study. On this last job he made $800–$1,000 a month. He said that he never saved money on any of his jobs, making just enough to live on.

He said he lived like his other Jordanian friends who worked hard and studied. He could not lead 'a plain student life' like the other class of students whose fathers were professionals. Early on he had a Syrian room mate whose father was a lawyer; they lived in a nice house and had a nice car in Damascus. He said that during the entire period when he was rooming with this student he acted like this [affluence] was 'no big deal,' though he knew well that life in Kufr al-Ma was entirely different. During his years working in Houston, Zayd absorbed the American work ethic which had initially repelled him. At the end of the long interview with him in 1986, I asked him, 'What do you like best about the United States?' After replying, 'Freedom. Nobody gets in your business. You can do what you want to do,' he said, 'If you want to be lazy, you'll die starving' [in the USA].

In Houston, Zayd dated girls both widely and seriously, although unlike other men from Kufr al-Ma he did not do so compulsively (at one point one young man had the names of 28 girls with accompanying telephone numbers in his address book); nor did he live with women before or after his marriage. Dating was for him, apart from a relished taste of freedom and enjoyment, a further introduction to the multicultural Houston scene. When I asked him about dating in Houston, he said, 'I had many girl friends of different nationalities – Mexican-Americans, British, South Americans and native [born in the USA] Americans.' He took them to dinner, dances and to the park. He had three steady girl friends. The first, whom he met at a disco and whom he described as 'an all-American girl' and a 'good girl', came from a good family (her father was a judge and her mother a teacher), and was seven years older than him. He visited her aunt and uncle in Houston, and when it was time for her to leave Houston, she asked him to join her in a business venture in St. Louis. I asked Zayd whether he ever contemplated marrying her. He replied:

It was inside me that she would not like it here [in Jordan]. I don't want someone who can't speak to my mother; I don't want to do that to my parents.

His second steady girl friend was from Wales. He met her on a blind date arranged by a Qatari friend. Zayd described her as 'young, beautiful and energetic'. He said that he was thinking of marrying her – that Wales and Jordan had some similar tribal customs – but it never got to that point. They broke up over an incident on the dance floor. He took her to a dancing place, and she asked him if he wanted to dance; he replied, 'No,' and went off (presumably with male companions) to another part of the dance hall. When he returned 'she was dancing with another guy'. He said that he got mad out of jealousy and called her off the dance floor, and then she got mad, and they broke up.

His third steady (and current) girl friend, whom he described as 'very nice and educated', was studying to become a certified public accountant. I asked him if he ever thought of marrying her. He replied:

> She isn't an ideal woman for a wife; it is not beauty I want; she is too committed to her work in a bank; she takes her work too seriously, thinking of promotion and the prestige of work.

I asked him then whether he would contemplate marrying a girl from Kufr al-Ma. He replied:

> I can marry someone from here. [I'll have to] sit down and talk with her; I want to know what she gets out of life, and I want to tell her what I want. I don't want to tell her what to do. [I want it to] be a two-way street. I want someone to be able to argue with me and tell me when I'm wrong or right. I want someone who's compatible with me. I don't want to marry someone 17 years old and baby her and have kids every year. I want someone who is educated and intelligent.

It was clear at this point in his life and in his acculturation to the United States (1986) that Zayd had not resolved the clearly different imperatives of Jordanian and American family values or courtship patterns. When I suggested in our interview that he could not 'court' a girl from Kufr al-Ma, i.e., get to know her in a casual relationship over a long period – since courtship was unacceptable in the village – he said:

> I'm starting not to like it [now] about the village. I know [a] different [way of life] now. I don't mind sitting with her family and talking about different things in life. I want to be able to sit down and talk and see how the person feels.

It was clear that Zayd had assimilated the American view of courtship, the American view of marriage as a partnership, and the American 'yuppie' view of educated, intelligent spouses who would construct their own guidelines for their life together. On the other hand, he held a view of the consanguine (pleasing the parents) as opposed to the conjugal (pleasing the wife) family; he repudiated the notion that women's work was as important as men's (though he strongly advocated women's work outside the home); he could not marry a woman who did not understand or appreciate his own culture, e.g., that women should be bound by a code of modesty and honour; and he rejected the view that women should make the basic household decisions. This latter view became clear in his comments about his best Jordanian friend in Houston in 1991. He criticized his friend for allowing his wife to talk him into an early marriage, into buying a house in Houston rather than investing the money in a sound business venture with a future, and, most recently, into contemplating moving from Texas to New Jersey. The logical and unacceptable conclusion of the wife's decision-making was, in his view, that on divorce, 'she takes the kids'.

In 1986 I asked Zayd, 'What are your views of women working outside the house?' He replied:

They should. Now, especially. A man cannot provide enough [in income]. Now fifty-fifty is good. It is good for the woman to go out of the house where there is only preparing food and [being] with kids, so that she can come into contact with society. I find it very disturbing to find an educated man marrying a ninth or twelfth grader. I don't know how they'll relate to one another.

This was clearly a view far removed from the patriarchal views of male dominance and women's segregation within the home. Zayd also expressed the view that marriage should be a partnership, a 'two-way street'. On the other hand, after six years in the United States he retained a patripotestal view of decision-making and accommodation (by the wife):

If I found the right girl there [in the USA] who was willing to learn the language and my beliefs and thoughts, I'd marry her. If she loves me enough to agree to do the things that please me, I can marry her.

In 1991 his basic orientation had not changed. In reply to my question of whether – if he married in Jordan and returned with his Jordanian wife to Houston to work (as he planned) – would his wife be happy there, he replied, 'The Arab woman – her life is her home and her husband.' He said that (in the States) he would teach her and give her the benefit of his experience; he would send her to school.

His determination to maintain his own cultural roots in a hostile environment was extended not only to his prospective wife but also to his future children. He feared bringing up his children in the United States. There were drugs and [pretty soon] 'you can't distinguish them from American kids'. To avoid this result he planned to return to Jordan with his family after working in the United States for five to seven years. 'I want them [his children] to turn out my way,' he said. Earlier one of the few comments he made about his marriage in his early student days was, 'Fortunately, we had no kids'.

In 1986 Zayd's failure to develop a viable way of 'living on the border' was conveyed by his answer to my question, 'Would you go to the United States again?' He replied, 'If I knew I was going to feel this way – frustrated and confused – between my country and the USA, no. My roots are here, but I like the things over there.'

In contrast to his volubility regarding his girl friends before and after marriage, Zayd was very reticent about his marriage. The three-year experience had clearly soured him on certain aspects of American culture and society. He had married, he said, 'to try it out' and to get (American) citizenship. His wife was addicted to drugs. He twice secured steady jobs for her , but she could not hold them. He failed in his attempt, as he said, 'to get her to go straight'. Finally, he paid her ticket to California where her mother lived, and told her he never wanted to see her again.

Zayd's real romance in and with the United States was captured in and with his relations with the automobile. The automobile was, in addition, a comfort, a focus of work and future work, and a testing ground for his entrepreneurship. In his first five years in Houston he bought and sold six automobiles, starting with a 1973 four-door Dodge he bought in 1981 for $550, and ending with a 1975 Toyota Celica he bought for $1,200 in 1985. He said he needed a car because the metropolitan transit system in Houston 'was not great', and that it took an hour to get to school or work using it, whereas the car took 15 minutes; and the petrol went down to 75 cents a gallon. Each time he bought a car he (or his mechanic friend) improved it either in its body or engine, and sold it for more than he bought it. Through his dealings with automobile salesmen and automobile customers he practised bargaining skills and, as he said, 'became Americanized', by always buying on the instalment plan. In his last two years in Houston he very much enjoyed driving the limousine. In the course of doing so he met a variety of people, some of whom he liked very much such as Hakeem Olajuwon, the Houston basketball star, who autographed a picture for him. Others he disliked, such as the clients from the rich neighbourhoods whom he regarded as arrogant and demanding.

But the automobile was also a romance and a comfort, bound into one. Whenever he was feeling bored or depressed he would get in his car and drive around Houston. First he would drive through Allen Parkway to see how the dregs of society lived (and count himself lucky not to be there) and then he would drive through River Oaks to see 'a clear and beautiful area' and imagine living in one of the multi-million dollar homes.

Just as Yusuf had segregated social networks in London and Leeds, so did Zayd in Houston: he met Americans in school and Arabs after work. Though he did go with a few of his American classmates to their homes to work on study projects and occasionally went to lunch with them on or near the campus, apart from his dates, he never socialized with Americans or got to know about their home life, a fact he recognized and regretted.

During his last four years in Houston he participated regularly in a ten-person basketball group made up of, as he said, 'more mature individuals', all Arabs, mainly Jordanians, most over thirty, who had survived the initial period of adjustment and struggle with schooling (many had their degrees) and had 'sown their wild oats'. Zayd referred to the pre-1986 period in Houston as 'a lost period'. He said in our 1991 interview in Houston, 'I want to have friends more than before,' and later in the interview, 'We want to identify with a group. It's [the friendship circle] helping now.' In discussing the character of this circle in Houston, Zayd said that a friend would help him move, lend him money, and invite him to his parties. Once a week friends communicated by telephone to inquire about one another's welfare. The basketball group would meet regularly on Sunday morning to play and, afterwards, go out to a park or a restaurant. That this was not simply a meeting to play basketball but a commitment seriously under-taken was indicated by Zayd's telling me that once he had driven to Galveston late on Saturday, got delayed, and nevertheless started back to Houston at 6 a.m. Sunday morning in order not to miss their 10 a.m. basketball game. The basketball group provided mutual reinforcement for a group of 'sojourners' (rather than immigrants or exiles), that is, foreign students who, after a long period of exploration and struggle, were deter-mined to maintain their cultural identity and were at that stage in their life/career cycle when they had both the time and the strong desire to develop a mechanism to do so.

What is most interesting in Zayd's course of 'antagonistic acculturation' is his close kinsmens' failure to play a part in it. Zayd came to Houston, in particular, in December 1979 because of the presence of his close cousin on his father's side who had arrived a few months before; Zayd roomed with him for a few weeks until the latter left for college in San Antonio. In the ten years that had elapsed since then, Zayd said that he had seen this cousin no more than ten times. Another cousin, brother of the first, came to San Antonio in 1986, and he had seen this cousin no more than five times since then. Both of these cousins subsequently married Americans from Texas and neither invited Zayd to attend the wedding. Zayd said that the weddings were very small affairs held in other cities. The fact that Zayd's support group was composed entirely of friends found in Houston and excluded his close cousins is certainly not a pattern that anthropol-ogists familiar with the strong kinship orientation of Jordanian rural-tribal culture would expect.

Although in the latter part of his eleven-year stay in Houston his basketball circle served as an anchor, in his earlier years in Houston Zayd bobbed about in a multicultural environment. I have already referred to his variegated multi-ethnic dating patterns. In 1986 I asked him, 'What was most difficult about adapting to American life?' He replied:

The pressure. I was living with my family; everything was paid for. For the first time I lived on my own [and] met different nationalities. The way I was treated, I had to get used to it. I had to learn more about them – the Lebanese. Everyone treated me different. I came from Jordan, and we had a strict upbringing. The Lebanese were touched by French culture. And the Saudis – they think they're better than the rest of the Arabs. Sometimes they [the Lebanese] don't call themselves Arabs. Some are ashamed to be Arabs – they think we are no good, and we don't feel that way about them.

I asked, 'Did you suffer discrimination in the States?' Zayd replied:

[Yes], the cowboys, the rednecks from Pasadena, Texas, hate blacks and foreigners. They used to pull up their cars alongside ours, and they tried to shoot at us. [They] called us camel jockeys and sand niggers. The cowboys mistook us for Iranians and said, 'Iranians go home', and we weren't liked. To the American who can understand, I will stop and explain that [we aren't Iranians]. But some are hard [enough] to look at [never mind] talk to.

In 1989 a professor at Texas Southern pointed to the foreign students in the class including Zayd and said, 'You come here to get an education which we taxpayers pay for.' Zayd said, 'My blood was boiling.' He went to the office of the professor and said:

Professor, I need to speak to you. We're not coming to beg. We got a visa. Your government allowed us in. We're doing our share. We're paying our tuition. He replied, 'You know I didn't mean you. Those Nigerians steal books.' Zayd replied, 'As of now I don't respect you.' The professor replied, 'I like your guts.'

After, as Zayd said, 'playing with fire', since this was the only professor who taught a required course in his curriculum, Zayd bought him a book, increased his class participation, and got an A in the course.

This defiant attitude toward offensive remarks made about foreigners within the university contrasts with Zayd's behaviour when the Gulf War broke out in 1991. I asked Zayd, 'Did the Gulf War lead to any changes in your life here in Houston?' He replied:

No, not really. I tried to be less visible as an Arab. I limited my going out. I avoided Middle Eastern nightclubs and belly-dancing places, because I thought 'the crazy Americans' would bomb them. (During that period someone asked him at a petrol station, 'What language are you speaking?' He replied, 'Turkish'.)

In 1991, Zayd brought together his evaluation of Americans and the multicultural environment of Houston in which he lived in a discussion of borrowing money while we were addressing the general question of his social network in Houston. He said, referring to Jordanians:

> They are more reliable; you can count on them. They're there for you. Money? You can borrow $1,000, and he'll give it and trust you [to repay it]. The American won't give you $20. I never asked them [for a loan], but that's my perception of it.

And Zayd said he would not lend an American money. On the other hand, he lent another foreigner, a Nigerian, money, a couple of hundred dollars 'and it worked out okay'. 'I don't know whether it's my pride or not,' he said, 'in not asking [Americans for money] or [the anxiety of] not knowing the answer.'

It is the field of religion and morality that brings most sharply into focus Zayd's rejection of assimilation as a possibility. He was shocked on his first arrival in 1980 on descending from an apartment in Houston to find two young men hugging one another on the street corner (apparently this was a gay neighbourhood). He immediately ran upstairs and told his room mates that they had to move out of the neighbourhood, and they did. Zayd's view of conjugal roles, the gender division of labour, and the proper upbringing of children all related to his underlying feeling that life in Houston was topsy-turvy, spawning a confusion of cultures and categories: 'Pretty soon you can't distinguish them [Jordanian children] from American kids'.

In 1991, Zayd contrasted this situation with his life as a child in the village. He said that his father used to wake him up at about 5 a.m. when he got up to say his prayers, and he would relish the early morning and the birds and take his books out to the fields to study; he memorized things so clearly then that he could recite chapter and verse in the classroom that morning. He said that, when he was young, he used to recite the Qur'an in the village mosque. Since he had mentioned the Qur'an, I interjected, 'Have you heard anything about Salman Rushdie?' Zayd replied that the Qur'an was the 'Hidden Tablet' (*al-lawh al-mahfudth*). 'This is God's,' he said, holding up the small copy of the Qur'an in his hand. 'Nobody can come close to it' [i.e., it is inimitable]. But I noticed that he did not kiss the Qur'an when he picked it up, as the pious Muslims of Kufr al-Ma would have done.

Zayd had clearly been seduced by the superior material culture he found in Houston, Texas. When he returned to the village in the summer of 1986 he criticized everything including the cars, the roads, the lack of hot water, the lack of phones, and the behaviour of the drivers. And he had rejected his father's plea to, 'Hurry up, come back; we want to get you married and get you a car and build you a house'. In 1991 Zayd said:

I don't want that average living. I guess that was one of the bad things that happened to me here [in Houston]. You drive down the street and see all these Mercedes Benz's. But he interrupted the thought/image of Houston's overwhelming material superiority by saying, 'I'm going to go back. . . . At the end of my life I want to be close to God. I'm not practising my religion now, but later . . .' [and his voice trailed off].

If he could not assimilate in 1991, nor yet wholeheartedly embrace the culture and society of Jordan, and while he yet harboured feelings of loneliness, even anomie after finishing his degree, he had definitely moved beyond the dilemma that he had clearly articulated in Jordan in 1986: 'My roots are here, but I like things over there.' Unlike Ali and Yusuf, Zayd finally had come to terms with a 'life on the border'. He had repudiated the view that his life would be focused on having an average living (upon receiving his degree he had in fact rejected a job in Houston paying $20,000 a year with regular expected increments). He would return to Kufr al-Ma, marry and build a house there. But he would return again to the United States, this time with his Jordanian wife, and work. He would raise a young family in Houston. But then he would return again to Jordan when they came of school age so that they could learn the values he prized. However, these values now included freedom, striving, hard work, and marriage as a two-way street as well as honour, modesty, respect for the consanguine family, patripotestiality and the serenity of religion.

CONCEPTS: OLD, REFINED AND NEW

Although the principal goal of this chapter is to document the experience of migrants from a humanistic perspective, a secondary goal is to call attention to concepts that might be refined and made more useful for analysis, e.g., acculturation and assimilation, and to introduce new analytical concepts. In a 1986 study Robinson pointed to the usefulness of the concept of encapsulation to understand the non-assimilation and to a great degree, non-acculturation of South Indians in Britain.[14] Robinson argues that two modes of class analysis ('exclusionary' and 'usurpationary closure') are not sufficient to understand the behaviour or cognition of South Asians in Britain, and he calls attention to the pronounced tendency of South Indians to live in enclaves and to retain 'close-knit social networks designed to minimize cross-ethnic primary group relations . . .'. This 'encapsulatory closure' is tied to a belief in return migration and is 'designed to maintain or strengthen cultural boundaries and faiths'.[15]

What the migrants' cases above have dramatically illustrated is not so much ethnic enclaves, but a process termed, after Singer, 'compartmentalization'.[16] Compartmentalization for Yusuf and Zayd is in part a constrained choice (and to that degree 'exclusionary'), but in part a conscious strategy that ensures the elaboration of a rooted identity. Yusuf's life was compartmentalized in Leeds between university and mosque and in London between cultural centre and student tutoring with limited exposure to the world beyond. His childhood upbringing and education had pre-adapted him to follow a strategy of successful 'controlled antagonistic acculturation' in England. Zayd compartmentalized his life in Houston between university, work, and in the later stages, the basketball network.

It is important to note that the elaboration of Ali's and Zayd's identities were vicarious – they were living out their fathers' ambitions for them – and, in that sense, their identities were rooted in patrifilial succession. Perhaps it is the development of these particular rooted identities that allowed them to successfully complete their higher educations over a very long period in an alien environment.

Mandel has pointed to a quite different aspect of the migrant experience in her concept of the 'constantly shifting centre'. Discussing the experience of Turkish migrants who oscillate (in their bodies and minds) between Germany and Turkey, she says: '. . . migrants are shaping a new emergent identity – one no longer oriented towards a concrete centre, but increasingly towards a necessarily elusive "other place" '. She elaborates by saying that this 'results in a situation in which the centre finds itself wherever the migrant is not . . .'. (Mandel 1990: 154, 167). The Turkish migrant increasingly finds himself or herself uncomfortable in both worlds (Germany and Turkey).

The experience of Zayd demonstrates a process that is similar to that described by Mandel, and yet quite different, and more optimistic, in its implications. In the first five years of his stay in Houston Zayd, (in Robinson's terms) was a marginal man, uncomfortable in both worlds (Jordan and the USA) yet attached to both. But by 1991 he had accommodated to a life in two worlds, both geographically and psychologically, as his future plans attested. Because of this fact, I propose the term, 'living on the border' to suggest an adjustment to living in the postmodern world, rather than a permanent state of alienation within it.

NOTES

1 See Eades (1987) and Kearney (1986) for reviews of the anthropological and social scientific literature on migration.

2 The author has conducted anthropological field research in Kufr al-Ma on eight separate occasions over thirty years, the longest being the initial year of dissertation field research in 1959–60 and the shortest and last of a week's duration in 1989. This chapter is part of a work in progress which focuses on the significance of international migration in the postmodern world and the impact of that migration on the rural society of northern Jordan.

3 The strongest cultural barrier to the prospect of women leaving the community to pursue education was the code of modesty. For a detailed analysis of the modesty code and its behavioural implications see Antoun (1968). One of the

most interesting implications of international migration for Jordan is how it has inspired the reinterpretation (and not the denigration) of traditions, particularly the tradition of modesty and honour.

4 For a detailed definition, description and analysis of the accommodation of tradition see Antoun (1968).

5 Acculturation is the process of borrowing cultural traits without a change in the basic values of the borrowing individual. Assimilation is the process of absorption of cultural traits along with their underlying values, thereby entailing a change of individual identity. 'Living on the border' is the psychological state and socio-cultural process of linking seemingly separate socio-cultural worlds in a conjoint and viable mode of livelihood and style of life. It often (but not necessarily) involves sporadic geographical mobility. The works on which I draw for the development of these concepts are Teske and Nelson (1974) and Rouse (1991). I have also found Fischer and Abedi's discussion of 'the crazy space between exile and migration' useful and provocative (1990: particularly, ch. 5).

6 All three students, then returned, were interviewed in Jordan in 1986. In addition, Zayd was also interviewed in Houston, Texas in 1991.

7 For a portrait of Ali's father see Antoun (1979: 220–1 and table 7, 214–15).

8 I am using the terms modernity and modernization in Nash's sense: 'Modernity is the social, cultural and psychological framework which facilitates the application of tested knowledge to all phases and branches of production. Modernization is the process of transformation toward the establishment and institutionalization of the framework of modernity' (Nash 1977: 21).

9 In the 1980s a movement occurred, mainly inspired by urban intellectuals, to abolish tribal law in Jordan. Tribal law stipulated collective responsibility both on the perpetrator's and the victim's side for individual crimes of honour (like murder, automobile homocide, rape, burglary, elopement and other violations of the modesty code), the appointment of tribal arbitrators (from among the elders of the region), and the imposition of truce periods, banishment and eventual reconciliation (*sulha*). In Jordan the process of tribal law moved in tandem with the prosecution of crimes of honour by civil and criminal courts, and the outcomes of the two processes were intertwined. The system of tribal law was officially abolished by edict in the 1980s, but was soon reinstated by the king after petitions were brought by tribal representatives, particularly from southern Jordan.

10 For a portrait of Yusuf's father see Antoun (1979: 221–3 and Table 7, 214–15).

11 See Teske and Nelson (1974) for a discussion of the concept of antagonistic acculturation.

12 In Jordan, Yusuf also sharply compartmentalized his urban and his village relations. He rarely visited the village; and when he did so, he visited only his parents and in-laws whom he considered enlightened. Villagers took umbrage when he did not invite them to his wedding in town.

13 See Antoun (1979: 217–18) for a portrait of Zayd's father and Antoun (1979: table 7, 214–15) for his leadership attributes.

14 See Robinson (1986, particularly chapters 6, 8, and 9).

15 See Robinson (1986: 113, 124, 176).

16 See Singer (1972) for an application of the concept to modes of cultural change and continuity in India in the late twentieth century.

REFERENCES

Antoun, R. T. (1968) 'On the modesty of women in Arab Muslim villages: a study in the accommodation of traditions', *American Anthropologist* 70 (4):671–97.

—— (1979) *Low-Key Politics: Local-Level Leadership and Change in the Middle East*, Albany: State University of New York Press.

Eades, J. (ed.) (1987) *Migrants, Workers, and the Social Order*, London: Tavistock.

Eickelman, D. F. and Piscatori, J. (eds) (1990) *Muslim Travellers: Pilgrimage, Migration, and the Religious Imagination*, Berkeley: University of California Press.

Fischer, M. J. and Abedi, M. (1990) *Debating Muslims: Cultural Dialogues in Postmodernity and Tradition*, Madison: University of Wisconsin Press.

Gellens, S. I. (1990) 'The search for knowledge in medieval Muslim societies: a comparative approach', in D. F. Eickelman and J. Piscatori (eds) *Muslim Travellers: Pilgrimage, Migration, and the Religious Imagination*, Berkeley: University of California Press.

Kearney, M. (1986) 'From the invisible hand to visible feet: anthropological studies of migration and development', in B. J. Siegel, A. R. Beals, and S. A. Tyler (eds) *Annual Review of Anthropology*, Palo Alto CA: Annual Review Inc.

Mandel, R. (1990) 'Shifting centres and emerging identities: Turkey and Germany in the lives of Turkish *gastarbeiter*', in D. F. Eickelman and J. Piscatori (eds) (1990) *Muslim Travellers: Pilgrimage, Migration, and the Religious Imagination*, Berkeley: University of California Press.

Masud, M. K. (1990) 'The obligation to migrate: the doctrine of *hijra* in Islamic law', in D. F. Eickelman and J. Piscatori (eds) (1990) *Muslim Travellers: Pilgrimage, Migration, and the Religious Imagination*, Berkeley: University of California Press.

Nash, M. (1977) 'Modernization: cultural meanings – the widening gap between the intellectuals and the process', *Economic Development and Cultural Change* 25 (supplement).

Robinson, V. (1986) *Transients, Settlers, and Refugees: Asians in Britain*, Oxford: Oxford University Press.

Rouse, R. (1991) 'Mexican migration and the social space of postmodernism', *Diaspora* 1 (1): 8–23.

Singer, M. (1972) *When a Great Tradition Modernizes: An Anthropological Approach to Indian Civilization*, New York: Praeger.

Teske, R. and Nelson, B. (1974) 'Acculturation and assimilation: a clarification', *American Anthropologist* 1(2): 351–67.

Chapter 10

Two Muslim intellectuals in the postmodern West
Akbar Ahmed and Ziauddin Sardar

Tomas Gerholm

A conspicuous feature of the modern world is the deterritorialization of culture. Whereas cultures used to be more or less firmly anchored in their respective geographical locations, they have now started drifting. Swedish culture, for instance, was confined to a part of the Scandinavian peninsula. Now you find it in small enclaves all over the world. The same goes for religion. Buddhism used to be located in certain parts of Asia. Now you also find it thriving at many Western addresses. Islam is an even better example. Individual Muslims have left *Dar al-Islam* in great numbers to take up residence in what used to be called *Dar al-Harb*, especially Europe. In Western Europe, for instance, the number of immigrant Muslims and their children lies somewhere between six and eight million. In countries like France and England, Islam has become the second most important religion and a similar situation will soon prevail in several other European countries.

This massive culture contact does not occur without creating a spate of special problems, both for the host societies and for the immigrants themselves. In this chapter I want to look at one of the many problematic consequences for Muslims residing in Europe. What happens to the Islamic identity of Muslim intellectuals who live and work in the West under the conditions offered by a Christian or secular host society? I shall attempt to sketch an answer to that question by analysing some texts by a couple of such intellectuals.[1] For this purpose I have chosen Akbar S. Ahmed and Ziauddin Sardar, who both were born in Pakistan but now are active in Great Britain and have been so for a number of years. Neither of them is an official Islamic representative. One could even say that they represent no other than themselves. But their structural positions are representative: one is a Muslim intellectual who is well-established in Western academia, the other is a Muslim intellectual who works ouside the university as a freelance journalist and consequently is not so tightly bound by Western academic conventions. Is this difference between them matched by differences in their versions of Islam?

Let me first indicate what kind of 'consequences' I have in mind. Islam is often presented as an all-encompassing religion which has directives for all aspects of life. Officially, at least, Islam should not be lived in a private religious corner of one's life, hermetically sealed off from a multitude of other activities in which one also engages but which are without religious significance. An authentic Muslim life demands an Islamic infrastructure, i.e. a set of institutions in society like a mosque, a school, a butcher, etc. Such a life also demands a social environment that can at least adjust to the requirements of a practising Muslim, for example leave for prayers and for special Islamic holidays, and perhaps acceptance of the veil at school as well as segregation of the sexes. All this becomes more difficult when Muslims are a minority of the population.

Other and probably more difficult problems arise for those Muslims who enter into spheres of Western life where fundamental Western values predominate. Is Islamic fundamentalism, for instance, fully compatible with a scientific attitude which demands that one refuses to let one's doubt make halt in front of received truths? Such a question could, of course, also be directed to a believing Christian, but the case of Islam is different. Christianity has been secularized and its theology reinterpreted, so that many statements which superficially seem to contradict scientific results are liable to a symbolic interpretation which makes the contradiction evaporate. This has not happened in Islam. It is the only one of the world religions which has survived intact without succumbing to modernist secularization. A closer look at our two Muslim intellectuals working in the secular West will perhaps give an indication of how this problem can be solved.

Akbar Ahmed is a social anthropologist educated in Great Britain at the universities of Birmingham, Cambridge and London. He has been Visiting Professor both at Princeton and Harvard, he has been a member of the faculty of the Islamic Institute of Advanced Study in the USA and the Islamic Academy in England, he has also taught at the University of Washington and the Quaid-e-Azam University of Islamabad. Until recently, he held the position of Allama Iqbal Fellow at Cambridge. This impressive academic record is complemented by his activities as Commissioner of Sibi Division in Baluchistan Province, Pakistan. Akbar Ahmed has a long range of publications behind him, among them several studies on Pakistan, a couple on Islam and one brief attempt to outline what an anthropology of Islam should be like. The text that will occupy me more than the others is his recent *Postmodernism and Islam: Predicament and Promise* (Ahmed 1992). He has been a frequent guest on British television and radio programmes and he has also contributed extensively to the British press. Akbar Ahmed seems to be highly regarded in British media circles: the kind of person one prefers to turn to when one needs an intelligent, knowledgeable and sophisticated Muslim who is well versed in the life of the West.

Ziauddin Sardar was also educated in England where his academic studies dealt with physics and information science. He has been working as a science journalist for British journals and written on Islamic themes for various international publications. His books include studies on science and technology in the Middle East and the Muslim world as well as a couple of books on Islam, among them a discussion of the Rushdie affair written together with Merryl Wyn Davies. Apart from his journalistic and scholarly activities, Sardar has also acted as an 'information consultant' for the Hajj Research Centre at the King Abdulaziz University, Jeddah, and as the director of the Center for Policy and Future Studies at East-West University, Chicago. It is Sardar's discussion in his *The Future of Muslim Civilization* (1987) together with his article on 'The Postmodern Age' (1991) that I have chosen for special scrutiny.[2]

ISLAMIC IDEALS AND MUSLIM REALITIES

Both Akbar Ahmed and Ziauddin Sardar have travelled extensively in the Muslim world and they have also worked there. Although they are now based in the West, especially in England and to some extent also the USA, they remain in close contact with people and events in Muslim countries. This makes their evaluation of actually existing Muslim countries especially worth listening to. Here are a few samples from Ahmed's writings:

> The modern period had led Muslims into a cul-de-sac. Dictators, coups, corruption and nepotism in politics; low education standards; an intellectual paresis; the continuing oppression of women and the under-privileged and grossly unequal distribution of wealth were some of its characteristics. . . . The reality of Muslim life was a far cry from the edifying and noble Islamic ideal . . .
>
> (Ahmed 1992:33)

> The potential of women in Islam is far superior to anything offered by Confucius in China or Aristotle in Greece, or to what Hindu or Christian civilizations offered. Muslim women are central to family affairs from domestic decision-making to rituals. Where their lot is miserable and they have virtually no rights, as in certain tribal areas, it is to be attributed to Muslim male tyranny, not Islamic advice and is in need of urgent redress.
>
> (Ahmed 1992:43)

> The daily newspapers (English and vernacular in Pakistan, for instance) are full of incidents which reveal the situation of women: husbands leaving them penniless for other women or mutilating or killing them on the slightest suspicion, or girls, not yet out of puberty, molested by their religious instructors. Such crimes are dealt with leniently. Both custom

and law take a tolerant view; society does not wish its placidity to be disturbed.

(Ahmed 1988:186)

Those Muslims living in the West and complaining about racism would do well to turn their gaze on their own societies. Pakistanis have been killing Pakistanis, on the basis of race, in the most brutal manners possible for years in Sind province; political messages are carved into the buttocks of ethnic opponents. Kurds have been gassed and bombed in Iraq by fellow Muslims for decades. . . . The concept of *ummah*, the Muslim brotherhood, is an excellent one; but it remains inchoate and needs to be pursued with more vigour than that presently exhibited by Muslims.

(Ahmed 1992:45–6)

Ahmed can be just as critical of Muslim societies as any Western observer; this is obvious. But in the first quotation, the final blame seems to fall on the modernization efforts that followed after colonialism. In the second quotation, one gets the impression that the condition of women may be hard, but that this is above all the case in tribal areas where, presumably, Islam has not really penetrated. This comment leads us on to the main lesson of these quotations: the difference between Islamic ideals and Muslim realities. The former are beyond reproach, the latter are 'in need of urgent redress'.

If we turn to Ziauddin Sardar, the picture is similar. *The Future of Muslim Civilization* is not replete with descriptions of negative aspects of actually existing Muslim societies, but the distinction between ideal and reality is often pointed out and the criticism of the status quo can be very harsh:

Our recent past, and our present, I submit, do little credit to the ideals of Islam; still less do they reflect the civilization that was once the pace-setter of humanity.

(Sardar 1987:xi)

Shariah, as the Islamic way of knowing, doing and being – the core of the world-view of Islam – is not just 'law', it is also ethics and methodology. However, for the last five centuries, *Shariah* as ethics and methodology has been totally ignored. Moreover, *Shariah* as law has now become an ossified, rigid and static closed system of do's and dont's.

(Sardar 1987:x)

The upheaval caused by various 'Islamic' syntheses, and the incompetence of Muslim intellectuals, has led Muslim societies into social disarray. The social order which operates most of the time in Muslim countries is continuously strained, frequently violated, occasionally disrupted. There are always a few individuals who fight against the enforced domination of various 'isms' and for what they consider to be Islamic values and norms. But the majority is uprooted and drifts in the ocean of social change and technological despotism, buffeted by Occidental moral storms, adopting wholesale alien social habits and outlooks, often sinking into crime and corruption, violence and vice. Feudalism and capitalism predominate in many countries, often legitimized by giving them an Islamic colour. The gulf between the least and most wealthy has been allowed to grow; and grow exponentially. . . . It is indeed the politics as practised in the Muslim world of today which are the root cause of the physical, social and economic suffering of the Muslims.

(Sardar 1987:69)

The picture painted by Sardar grows in complexity compared to that of Ahmed. Here it is not only one fatal distinction between ideal and reality, but also an ideal that is difficult to visualize clearly. The past half millennium has been a time of Muslim degeneration. Many are of course aware of this unfortunate development, but are unsure of how it should be remedied or have taken paths that strike Ziauddin Sardar as profoundly mistaken; hence his reference to 'various "Islamic" syntheses'. It is important to try and define the Islamic ideal that Sardar and Ahmed have in mind. Is it the same one? How does it relate to other such visions? Let me start with the anthropologist.

AKBAR AHMED'S ISLAMIC IDEAL

There are several references to Max Weber's concept of 'ideal-type', but Ahmed uses it with certain reservations. His Islamic ideal is not really an ideal-type, for then it would depict 'an average derived over time which reflects combinations, mixtures and modifications' (Ahmed 1988:3). Ahmed's model of Islam has actually more in common with an ordinary ideal, something perfect that one strives to make real or at least to come near to. However, the Islamic ideal is not a pure abstraction. It is based on two things appearing in seventh century Arabia: the Qur'an and the Prophet's *Sunnah*, i.e. his actions and his sayings. 'Together they form the *Shariah*, the "path" for Muslims' (Ahmed 1988: 3). This 'ideal is eternal and consistent; Muslim society is neither' (Ahmed 1988: 3). Such a conception of the Islamic ideal, of what Islam is and how it should be lived, also offers a key to the understanding of the history of Muslim societies and of Muslim movements:

Islamic history offers abundant evidence that there is a dynamic relationship between society and the striving of holy and learned Muslims for the ideal. . . . The vision of the ideal, and aspiration to it, provide Muslim society with its dynamics. . . . Tension, change and challenge are created as people living in an imperfect world strive for it. The ideal allows each individual to possess a charter of action. The interpretation too is individualistic, providing it with a dynamic and volatile nature. . . . Thus the ideal provides an inbuilt mechanism in Muslim society for constant renewal and revival of faith. . . . The phenomenon has been in motion since the seventh century, continually emphasizing the drive to return to the Golden Age, the ideal times of the Prophet.

(Ahmed 1988:3–4)

Of course, the actual contents of the Golden Age are still a matter for interpretation and there may be many individual versions. Ahmed does not delve into these problems, but he singles out a few cardinal Islamic values and also makes an attempt to characterize the straight path that is Islam. Repeatedly, he mentions the 'central Quranic concepts of *adl* and *ahsan*, balance and compassion, of *ilm*, knowledge, and *sabr*, patience' (Ahmed 1992:48). It is the concept of *adl* that serves as the basis for Ahmed's version of the essence of Islam:

Balance is essential to Islam and never more so than in society; and the crucial balance is between *din* (religion), and *dunya* (world); it is a balance, not a separation, between the two. The Muslim lives in the now, in the real world, but within the frame of his religion, with a mind to the future after-life. . . . Islam is essentially the religion of equilibrium and tolerance . . .

(Ahmed 1992:48)

This notion of balance also recurs when Ahmed is dealing with the relation of Islam to other religions and other cultures:

Islam is, above all, the middle way according to the Quran; in its geographical and historical position it became literally so. . . . Islam's intellectual triumphs were recorded when Muslims interacted with Greek, Hindu and Christian thought. From Al Ghazzali to Iqbal the greatest Muslim thinkers have responded to non-Muslim thinking. Traditionally Islam has ideally acted as a bridge between different systems.

(Ahmed 1988:214–15)

Let me now turn from the anthropologist to the freelance journalist.

ZIAUDDIN SARDAR'S ISLAMIC IDEAL

In Sardar's presentation Islam sometimes appears as totally beyond the reach of contemporary man. His discussion of 'Muslim intellectuals' (see note 1) and 'various "Islamic" syntheses' ends on a sombre note:

We do not understand Islam. Our scholars, our religious leaders, our intellectuals, our people do not understand Islam. By understanding Islam we do not mean the capability to explain a *hadith*, or outline the mechanics of certain rituals or recite the verses of the Qur'an. We understand Islam only if we can operationalize its dynamic and vibrant concepts in contemporary society.

(Sardar 1987:72)

Outlining how to operationalize Islam is the daunting task that Sardar has set himself in *The Future of Muslim Civilization*. A first step must be to isolate 'its dynamic and vibrant concepts'. Let us follow him. It seems reasonable to expect to find them within what Sardar calls Islam's 'Absolute Reference Frame', in other words the Qur'an and the Sunnah. The unchangeable and eternal principles of Islam are contained in the Qur'an: 'The Qur'an provides basic guidelines and principles for human transaction and a theoretical framework for the parameters of Muslim civilization' (Sardar 1987:14). The Prophet translated these principles into action, so that the Sunnah may be regarded as 'Islam in action' (Sardar 1987:14). Sardar develops this conception in the following way:

In the operationalization of Qur'anic principles, the Sunnah plays a vital role. The word Sunnah originally meant 'a beaten track', to fashion something, or produce it as a model. The Sunnah of the Prophet is a 'model' of Islam in operation. As such, the study of the Sunnah is essential for the correct understanding of the Qur'an. Situational as many of the revelations of the Qur'an are, their understanding involves the knowledge of the actual life of the Prophet and the environment in which he moved. His teachings and his life are intertwined. The Sunnah therefore is commentary on the Qur'an and its amplification. The two cannot be divorced from one another, for the Sunnah is essentially an implementation of the Divine will.

(Sardar 1987:15–16)

This can of course be said to be the Absolute Reference Frame (ARF). We are still pretty far, however, from a singling out of the 'dynamic and vibrant concepts' that need to be translated into contemporary reality. Instead, Sardar goes into a detailed discussion of what we can actually know of the Prophet's Sunnah as a result of the 'science of *hadith*' which he regards as 'one of the major achievements of Muslim civilization'(Sardar 1987:15–16).[3] This digression is not followed by a handy list of fundamental concepts and values, as in the case of Akbar Ahmed, but it is perhaps possible, nevertheless, to extricate a summary of the ARF.

First of all, it is from the ARF that 'the value system of Islam is derived' (Sardar 1987:18). The defining characteristics of this value system have to do with balance and moderation. 'In Islam,' Sardar says, 'the most significant indicator of man's nobility, besides righteousness, is the use of moderation and balance in his material dealings, reasoned pursuits and spiritual quests' (Sardar 1987:18). Materialism, rationalism and spiritualism are the three basic aspects of civilization and it is the peculiar characteristic of Islam that it achieves a balanced synthesis of them. Sardar tries to describe the three aspects in some detail, beginning with the spiritual dimension: 'Islam places a spiritual cordon around individuals and society' (Sardar 1987:21) by insisting on five spiritual actions: *salah* (prayer), *zakat* (poor due or charity), *sawm* (fasting), *hajj* (pilgrimage) and *taqwa* (God-fearing or God-consciousness) – of which the last-mentioned 'outweighs and excels all other values' (Sardar 1987:22). As for rationalism, 'Islam gives full freedom of rational and intellectual enquiry *within the circumference of its norms and values*' (emphasis added). This modification of intellectual freedom is stressed a little further on: 'Rationality is brought under the reins of norms and values' (Sardar 1987:22). Then the materialist dimension is given its due: Islam 'enjoins Muslims to be self-supporting, to seek certain material benefits, and not to be a liability on someone else, or on the state' (Sardar 1987:23).

If this is a fair summary of the ARF, Sardar would no doubt add, as he does in another context: 'This is the essence of Islam; all else is exegesis and open to reinterpretation' (Sardar 1991:79). In that context – which is a collection of articles dealing with Christian–Muslim relations – Sardar develops the idea of an essence of Islam which is eternal in a slightly more succinct fashion. While trying to distance himself from contemporary attempts to establish an 'Islamic state', he provides another interpretation of the idea that Islam is an integrative, total religion. It is not the case that it has to comprise a state which can lay the foundation of an Islamic social order. No,

> Islam is an integrative worldview: that is to say, it integrates all aspects of reality by providing a moral perspective on every aspect of human endeavour. Islam does not provide ready-made answers to all human problems; it provides a moral perspective within which Muslims must endeavour to find answers to all human problems.
>
> (Sardar 1991:70)

This moral perspective as the essence of Islam becomes even clearer through Sardar's dismissal of the more common ways of presenting Islam as an 'integrative worldview':

> However, Islamic movements have made the fundamental error of perceiving Islam as a totalistic ideology; and the pursuit of this ideology in the form of an Islamic state is supposed to provide solutions to all problems of Muslim societies. Indeed, the pursuit of the Islamic state has itself become an ideology. The Iranian state is clearly based on this

assumption; it also, equally clearly, demonstrates that the realization of the ideological goal does not in fact solve any problems. . . . The reduction of the worldview of Islam into an ideology is, of course, a form of secularization.

(Sardar 1991:70)

Let us leave the discussion of Sardar's Islamic ideal here. Accusing the promoters of the Islamic state of *secularization* may sound like a contradiction in terms, but it leads conveniently to the next part of this chapter: Ahmed's and Sardar's view of the West.

AKBAR AHMED'S CRITICISM OF THE WEST

Postmodernism and Islam contains much material on Western culture and society. In fact, it comes close to belonging to that minute – almost non-existing – genre of anthropological works in which non-Western anthropologists cast an anthropological eye on the West. His analysis of modern mass media especially is well worth reading. But in this context it is his overall evaluation of Western civilization that must be set in focus. Let us start with his definition of what he is evaluating. Under the heading 'The global civilization: the triumph of the West' comes a passage which introduces the 'West':

The West is at present the crucible of what is emerging as a universal culture, one united, quickened and even defined by what we are calling postmodernist developments. We call this 'Western' civilization in that the United States and Western Europe – predominantly white – are at its core, providing the ideas and technological discoveries that fire it. Within this civilization the United Kingdom . . . consciously plays Greece to the Rome of the United States, maintaining a 'special' relationship with it. . . . Geographically, the civilization embraces non-Western nations like Australia and Israel, and even a non-Western people like Japan. After the emergence of Gorbachev, the USSR also looked for its place in this civilization. Other civilizations, even those distinct in their own traditions, like India or South-east Asia, are happily seduced. If non-Western people have serious reservations about some components of the package – domination by American culture, for instance – they would still accept it for the other things it brings, such as democracy, human rights and literacy.

(Ahmed 1992:98)

This 'dominant world civilization' (Ahmed 1992:99) is in itself dominated by the English-speaking nations, the USA, the UK, Canada and Australia, as well as by the English-speaking élites of various other countries. Having delimited the 'West' in this fashion, Ahmed proceeds to his characterization of it:

On the surface this civilization is defined by its consumerism – junk food, clothes, leisure, rock music, television programmes, pop heroes, media celebrities. It also has a *sacred* pilgrimage place. Disneyland is like the Vatican for the Catholics, Makkah for the Muslims and Amritsar for the Sikhs. An *entire civilization is here defined* and many generations, in their millions, visit it.

(Ahmed 1992:99, emphases added)

The adjective 'sacred' seems out of place in this context, especially since we are still reading about the *surface* characteristics of Western civilization (or are the Vatican, Makkah and Amritsar also surface phenomena?). Ahmed sticks to this comparison, however, so apparently 'sacred' should not be dismissed as an occasional slip of the word processor. Further on there is also an astonishing comparison between the mosque in Muslim lands and the shopping mall in Western countries.

In the present postmodernist era the mall for the Americans is the contemporary equivalent of the mosque. It acts as a social focus, and people go to it faithfully, daily, for renewal and companionship. The mall represents an explosion of consumerist images which appeal to the senses. It is the consumerist pleasure-dome and its seductive charms are available round the clock. . . . The mall is the 'total experience', a metaphor for the hyperreality of postmodern life. . . .

In contrast, the mosque brings the believer away from the maelstrom of daily life, suspending it. Calmness and peace characterize it. The believer is encouraged to think of the timelessness of God and the perishability of life on earth. However, like the mall, the mosque has seen a remarkable growth in its numbers in recent years. . . . The mall and the mosque, one a paradise of colour and fun, the other a paradigm of piety, suggest alternative life-styles, opposing philosophies.

(Ahmed 1992:208–9)

One is tempted to conclude that in Western civilization the surface reaches depths that one thought were reserved for other values and activities. But Ahmed moves on, probing deeper into the essence of Western culture, thereby making his own comparison with Muslim culture more complicated – but also more acceptable:

However, *Dallas* and *Dynasty*, Mickey Mouse and ET, Coke and jeans are only superficial symbols of this civilization. Central to it is the belief in capitalism, democracy and, related to it, the equality of women. At its best this civilization engenders a positive attitude to life, trust in science, a determined individualism, the urge always to find solutions, optimism and a respect for law. High standards of living, health and education are presupposed. The intellectual energy is exhilarating and unprecedented. . . .

(Ahmed 1992:99)

These positive findings are not enough, however, to compensate for a fundamental fault with Western civilization, i.e. its ethical vacuum:

The problem with this civilization is the hole where the heart should be . . . ; there is no moral philosophy or set of principles that drives it. What gives it its dynamic energy is individualism, the desire to dominate, the sheer drive to acquire material items, to hoard. . . .

[Western] civilization does not have the answers for the planet; indeed in its arsenal of nuclear weapons, its greedy destruction of the environment, its insatiable devouring of the world's resources, its philosophy of consumerism at all costs, it is set to terminate life on earth in the near future unless it can change its ways fundamentally.

(Ahmed 1992:109)

Ahmed's picture of Western civilization is ambivalent, just as ambivalent as his presentation of Muslim civilization: both have their strong assets, both manifest deplorable qualities. But in the case of Muslim civilization, Ahmed is anxious to point out that the negative sides have nothing to do with Islam. If Muslims were real Muslims, these things would not exist. There is a difference between Muslim realities and Islamic ideals. In the case of Western civilization, I look in vain for an equally consoling differentiation. Of course, there are Western ideals. But in the critical eyes of Akbar Ahmed they do not amount to a 'moral philosophy or set of principles' that could be the answer to the mounting problems of the planet – if they were only implemented. A devastating critique of Muslim societies ends on an optimistic note: 'These are Muslim lapses, a sign of social decay, not Islamic features' (Ahmed 1992:117). His critique of Western societies does not have a similarly happy ending: he does not conclude that 'these are Capitalist (or Socialist or Modernist) lapses, signs of social decay, not expressions of Western ideals.' A possible reason for this difference in his analysis of the two cases could be, of course, that Christianity plays a much smaller role in Western civilization than Islam does in Muslim civilization. If so, Christian ideals could be seen hovering far above Western social reality with little chance of ever affecting it, while Islamic ideals move much closer to Muslim social reality. These circumstances, whatever their factual reality, are worth some further consideration. To clarify the contrast, it would be useful to have an idea of the relevant *Islamic* ideals which, in Ahmed's view, could have a powerful effect on the life on this planet.

On the threshold of the twenty-first century, what can Islamic civilization contribute to the world? The answer is, a great deal. Its notion of a balance between *din*, religion, and *dunya*, the world, is a worthy one. It can provide a corrective and a check to the materialism that characterizes much of contemporary civilization, offering instead compassion, piety and a sense of humility. . . . The qualities mentioned above underline the moral content of human existence, they suggest security and stability in family life, in marriage and in the care for the aged. Recent signs in Western societies indicate that perhaps the time is ripe to re-admit care and compassion into human relations; here, too, post-modernist sensibilities can help.

(Ahmed 1992:117–18)

The Islamic contribution to world civilization would be to fill the ethical vacuum with moral principles. At this point, Ahmed refers to Sufism as an important movement within Islam which has managed to articulate the moral principles of Islam in a particularly pregnant fashion.

In its abjuration of materialism, Sufism provides a balance to the dominant values of Western civilization. . . . Especially in the Sufistic message of *sulh-i-kul* (peace with all), Islam has a positive message of peace and brotherhood to preach.

(Ahmed 1992:118)

At the same time, Ahmed indicates that the West *is* ready to reconsider what he regards as its dominant values, i.e. materialism and consumerism in its various forms. It is not quite clear whether he regards postmodernism as such as a sign of the readiness to 're-admit care and compassion into human relations' or whether he is just referring to the fact that Sufism is a form of Islam that has attracted many Western converts, especially in this century. Before turning to Sardar, I feel it is appropriate to let Ahmed add a few words about Sufism. It seems to me that we are here close to his own position.

An important branch of the traditionalist position, although not encouraged by the more orthodox, is that of Sufism. Sufism is Islam's message of universalism and tolerance. It is therefore appropriate that European Sufis, like Martin Lings and Frithjof Schuon, represent it. Here is one of the most powerful seams of Islamic culture with its widely appealing message. Unfortunately, by its very esoteric nature, Sufism is restricted in its popular appeal to the initiate or the scholar. Its critics claim that the way of the Sufis is no longer a practical one in our world, that Sufism is a form of escapism. Even its admirers believe that its time has gone: [here follows a quote from Arberry 1990]. Sufism is also dismissed by younger radical Muslims (like Parvez Manzoor and Ziauddin Sardar). With it they miss one of the most attractive and endearing sides of Islam, one tracing its origins directly to the Prophet. However, rumours about its demise are premature [here follows a reference to Haeri 1989].

(Ahmed 1992:159)

In my concluding remarks on the form of Islam espoused by Muslim intellectuals in the West, I shall return to the Sufi position.

ZIAUDDIN SARDAR'S CRITICISM OF THE WEST

Sardar's definition of the 'West' is similar to that of Ahmed. He prefers the term 'Occident' which he discusses in several places (e.g. in Sardar 1977). A short treatment is the following:

> I have used the term Occident to designate 'the West' and the Communist bloc. There is little basic difference between the cultural and territorial origins of the capitalist West and the Communist East. This Occident is not restricted to Europe and *outremers* [overseas provinces] but has its *outremers* everywhere. Anything therefore which belongs to Europe – in ideas, modes of thought, behaviour, outlook – whether found in Asia or Africa, is Occidental. Any Muslim who aspires to what is Occidental is thus Occidentalizing or Occidentalized.
>
> (Sardar 1987:11)

A brief characterization of the Occident stresses its self-centredness:

> The Occident has continued to pursue its own goals directed towards economic and technological monopoly and exploitation, choosing to ignore the complaints of the developing nations. It is a civilization based on seeking its own self-actualization, regardless of consequences and side-effects.
>
> (Sardar 1987:3)

The ecological, economical, social and political problems facing the peoples of the Earth – 'the world *problématique*' – are presented as having been produced by the Occident:

> The present predicament of mankind is a natural outcome of a world-view that dominates the globe. Behind that world-view is a history of exploitation, domination and imperialism; and a tradition of Judaeo-Christian heritage on the one hand and rationalism and scientism on the other.
>
> (Sardar 1987:101)

The Occident derives its strength from the Judaeo-Christian tradition and presents a very disenchanted view of man. The instability of the world system is the result of relations of domination which have been instituted on a world level by the Occident. The instability is further aggravated by explosive and destructive over-consumption of the world's resources by the Occident.

(Sardar 1987:106)

Even when the forms of thinking and language of Occidental man ceased to be Christian, he continued to be immersed in the Judaeo-Christian outlook. His daily actions, as Lynn White has pointed out, are dominated by implicit faith in perpetual growth and progress which was unknown either to antiquity or the Orient.

(Sardar 1987:102–3)

In other words, the problems of the world system have been brought about by the Occident which is, in its turn, propelled by the Judaeo-Christian tradition. However, something has happened to Christianity in the process: 'Christianity changed from an enlightened cosmology to a religion of tyranny and vanity' (Sardar 1987:102). Sardar seems to be on the verge of exempting Christianity from the harsh verdict passed on the Occident – Christianity as it was originally, that is. His position remains ambiguous in this book, but it is more clearly spelled out in his article on Christian-Muslim relations in the postmodern age (Sardar 1991). It is difficult to say if this difference is the result of a developing argument or if it is just a matter of a clear difference between the focus of each work. Be this as it may, from the later essay it emerges clearly that *secularism* is the fundamental problem. Secularism has devoured Christianity and actually made Christian preachers and theologians into spokesmen for a secularist oulook. It all started with St Augustine who, according to Sardar, transformed Christianity by introducing a Hellenistic dualism of body and spirit that was not present in the Bible:

Much of Catholic and Protestant church life and polity is based not on the teachings of Jesus but on St Augustine's dualistic neo-platonic worldview. He divided humanity into two groups, living in two cities, created by two kinds of love: 'the earthly city was created by self-love reaching the point of contempt for God, the Heavenly city by love of God carried as far as contempt of self' [the quotation is from St Augustine 1984:593]. St Augustine was concerned only with the loyalty to God, for this loyalty was enough to ensure that all else would fall into place. He thus told Christians to 'love God, and do what you want'. And they did: to the detriment of the rest of humanity.

(Sardar 1991:60)

There is no need to go more deeply into the history of Christian theology, but Sardar's own argument is worth repeating. The Church's attitude to secularism may have been based on St Augustine, but modern secularism has got its special character from more recent happenings:

Contemporary Western secularism is a product of the conflict between science and Christianity that took place in the sixteenth and seventeenth centuries. Secularism dethroned the ruling orthodoxy, the powerful institution of the Church, and gave rise to a vision of society that has captivated the Western mind for the last three hundred years. It was a vision of a [*sic*] society as rationally ordered. This vision produced extraordinary advances in science and technology; but as Stephen Toulmin argues, it has also perpetuated a hidden agenda: the delusion that human nature and society could be fitted into precise and manageable rational categories [Sardar refers to Toulmin 1990]. Contrary to popular belief, secularism did not actually produce a decline in religiosity, it simply transferred religious devotion from the concerns of the Church to the rational concerns of this world. Since the Enlightenment, this religiosity has been expressed in nationalism, communism, fascism, scientism, modernism and has now built its nest in postmodernism.

(Sardar 1991:61–2)

The last two sentences deserve special emphasis in order to bring out the actual meaning of 'secularism' in Sardar's vocabulary. Although it may be difficult to see all the -isms mentioned as expressions of a rationalist attitude, it is easy to recognize a common denominator. They all take man as their starting point believing that he can shape society through his own endeavour, without relying on a transcendental power, and also formulate an ethics of his own.

It is important for Sardar to emphasize that secularism is not inherent in Christianity as a religion – which has been claimed by voices both inside and outside of Western culture – but that it is a consequence of special interpretations, Augustinian and rationalist, of the Scriptures. If this is so, Sardar's project of fighting Western secularism can enlist the support of Christians who have not yet succumbed to the secularist forces. Like Ahmed, Sardar is convinced that the future of world culture is dependent on contributions from several different quarters. To expect Islam to succeed Western secularism as the dominant civilization would be over-optimistic. More realistic is a scenario where Islamic tendencies join forces with similar tendencies within Christianity. It is from this perspective that Sardar tries to find a common foundation for a joint Muslim-Christian ethics. This would be an important step forward, since

Virtually all our contemporary problems are ethical problems: from poverty and redistribution of wealth to nuclear weapons, biomedical redefinition of life, the misuse and abuse of science, alienation engendered by technology, development and underdevelopment, inhuman economic theories; they are amenable only to ethical solutions.

(Sardar 1991:81)

What would the Christian and Muslim contributions to such a joint venture look like? Sardar tries to provide an answer by stripping both faiths down to essentials, dismissing everything else as open to exegesis and reinterpretation. The essentials of Christianity are the following three theses:

1 Belief in the existence of one God, a uniquely perfect transcendent Being.
2 Acceptance of the ethical and religious authority and leadership of the historical personage of Jesus of Nazareth.
3 A commitment to viewing the life of Jesus as a disclosure and human exemplification of the moral excellence of deity such that the imitation of Jesus's behaviour is already a moral action in the believer's life [Sardar refers to Akthar 1990:49] (Sardar 1991:78).

The corresponding reduction of Islam also leads to three theses:

1 Belief in the existence of one God, a uniquely perfect transcendent Being.
2 Recognition of the Qur'an as the Word of God.
3 Acceptance of the Prophet Muhammad as the paradigm of ethical and moral behaviour and his life, the Sunnah, as a commentary on the Qur'an (Sardar 1991:79).

Christians and Muslims who can accept this version of the essential elements of their faith would not, Sardar expects, have any objections to a code of ethics based on elements from both religions. This is his own list of elements which he insists must be treated as interconnected, as forming a system:

> The Bible has furnished us with such theological virtues as faith, love, hope, justice, courage, temperance and prudence. Muslims would have no trouble in accepting these virtues as guides to human behaviour. The worldview of Islam provides us with a number of interconnected value concepts that have a direct bearing on the conduct of human enterprise: *tawheed* (unity of God), *khilafa* (trusteeship of man), *ibadah* (worship), *ilm* (knowledge), *adl* (justice), *ijma* (consensus) and *istislah* (public interest), to mention just a few. Most Christians should have little trouble in accepting these value concepts as the credo on which moral life turns. Combine the two sets of virtues and we have a complicated ethics that is capable of shaping policies and providing distinct alternatives to the secularist options.
>
> (Sardar 1991:83)

As in the case of Akbar Ahmed, we end up with a set of principles that the author presents as the essence of Islam, an essence which if accepted would be a vital contribution to world civilization. It is time to ask how this version of Islam relates to other versions.

ISLAM AS VIEWED BY MUSLIM INTELLECTUALS IN THE WEST

There are differences, of course, between Ahmed's and Sardar's stand-points, but let us begin with the similarities. Both are active in a society where Muslims form a minority and where the state at least formally wears another religious colour. A consequence of these circumstances is that here one will lead a Muslim life in a different way from what would be the case in a Muslim country. Many religions are 'private' in the sense that they can be carried out by isolated individuals. Islam, however, is not such a religion. Ideally it has consequences for all aspects of life. An authentic Muslim life demands an extensive 'infrastructure': mosques, schools, butchers, cemeteries etc. Not all of this is available in a country like England and some of these basic requirements have been won only after hard struggle. Acceptance in the wider society of another religious calendar and its special demands is not automatically provided. These obstacles mean that a 'minority Muslim' wanders the straight path in a different way from a 'majority Muslim'. In many cases, religious consciousness deepens, in others it is flattened out (cf. Schiffauer 1988). Whatever happens, it seems a reasonable hypothesis that Islam – or the way a Muslim life is led – is likely to change a great deal in cases where religion is more or less forced into the private corner of one's life. What effects on one's conception of Islam will this adjustment bring?

In the case of our two Muslim intellectuals, I have no possibility of making a real investigation. Detailed material on their daily lives is missing. I am confined to an examination of the conceptions of Islam they themselves seem to find viable in their own context. A general consequence is the reduction of an all-encompassing religion to a set of essential principles, values and concepts. A non-believer like myself reads the list with interest but without being overwhelmed by the connotations that these principles, values and concepts surely must have for the believer. I am somewhat surprised at the weight my authors seem to give to these ideas. I cannot help doubting that these ideas in themselves will make a deep impact on non-Muslims. At the same time, I realize that Ahmed and Sardar are fully convinced of the power of these Islamic notions. This can be explained by the fact that both of them have seen Islam in action – Islam operationalized, to borrow an expression from Sardar – in Muslim countries. Their awareness of the social weight of Islam is a natural consequence of having lived in circumstances which are heavily impregnated with Islamic conceptions and where everyone shares an Islamic definition of the situation. Islamic reality is socially constructed (Berger and Luckmann 1967), but such a construction is very dependent on the number of construction workers available. This number decreases 'overseas' where – another problem – other realities are also being socially constructed.

The Islam of Muslim intellectuals in the West tends to assume a more ethereal character than it has in really Muslim countries. This is at least my hypothesis. Perhaps it is this paradoxical juxtaposition of ideal Islam, which is all-encompassing, and real Great Britain, where Islam can only be a partial endeavour, that makes Ahmed move towards Sufism. Sufism *can* be a compromise between East and West: it is private enough to fit into the Western social order and it is public enough to remain an echo of the total Islamic order.

Sardar's case is a bit more complicated. In the earlier work he strives to lay the foundation for a *contemporary* version of the 'Medina state', i.e. an Islamic state somehow modelled upon the Prophet's example in Medina. In the later work, however, he dismisses attempts to create an Islamic state and focuses instead upon what could be the Islamic contribution to the global order. Has there occurred a fundamental change, between 1987 and 1991, in his vision of the Islamic future? Or is he – like an old-fashioned Marxist – dealing with two different stages: a 'Bourgeois', united-front stage characterized by the Islamic *contribution* and a later 'Socialist' stage characterized by the revolutionary search for the future Medina *state*?

MUSLIM INTELLECTUALS AS WESTERN INTELLECTUALS

Ahmed's and Sardar's Islam is affected by their life in the West; one begins to wonder if and how their work as intellectuals in the West is affected by their Islam. I shall only venture a couple of tentative observations in this difficult field, which I think would be worth a deeper study.

Akbar Ahmed – 'a friendly and knowledgeable companion through the thickets of both Western and Islamic culture', according to the publisher's presentation of *Postmodernism and Islam* – has taken on a difficult task. If he is to gain attentive listeners in the West, he must convince us of his deep knowledge of both Western and Islamic culture, and perhaps especially the former. It is not enough that he, as an anthropologist, delivers incisive analyses of various Western phenomena, he must also show that he is familiar with things that we, ourselves, consider worth knowing. On the whole, he passes this test with flying colours. If one had expected to come across a staggering statement in connection with discussions of *ilm* (knowledge) or the various attempts at Islamizing academic disciplines, one will be disappointed – or draw a sigh of relief. Ahmed is not prepared to give 'Islamic anthropology', for instance, a really radical interpretation according to which such an anthropology would follow a different epistemology. His answer to the question which is often asked about whether Islamic anthropology would not be a step into a morass of Jewish, Hindu, Buddhist and other anthropologies, is worth quoting:

Western anthropology, it has been argued, is embedded in recent Western colonial history. It is, thus, tainted and its claims to be neutral or fair are weak. Furthermore, it may be argued that there are already existing, fairly well-defined 'schools' in the discipline. Some of these are – albeit loosely – based on nationality such as a Soviet or British anthropology. There are others rooted in ideological ground, notably Marxist anthropology. So why does the concept of an Islamic anthropology raise so many hackles?

(Ahmed 1988:213)

Ahmed may be an Islamic anthropologist, but this identity should hardly send deep epistemological quivers down the spines of his non-Muslim colleagues. Many critical things can be said about his way of comparing Western realities with Islamic ideals, one may question his view that the work of Hasdai Crescas respresents the climax of medieval Jewish philosophy, and so on. But this only shows that Akbar Ahmed is a fully-fledged member of Western academia.

Sardar is a slightly different case. He is remarkably well read within many fields of 'Occidental' knowledge and most of the time I spent reading his texts I had no reason to suspect that shortly, around the next bend, I should have to say farewell, because he is taking off along a path that I cannot follow. The prime example of this is Sardar's treatment of 'Islamic epistemology' and its relation to 'Occidental epistemology'. For me, these terms are merely historical and geographical, but not so for Sardar. For more than two thousand years 'Occidental' philosophers have been trying to clarify what knowledge is and how it can be acquired. Some of these ideas are not accepted by their modern colleagues, but there is a long tradition of such discussions, of a philosophical conversation spanning millennia. It is reasonable to talk of 'Occidental epistemology' in this sense: a tradition of philosophical argument concerning the very basis of what we know and what we can know. It is conceivable, even probable, that future philosophers will discredit much of what we accept today. Through the ages it has been like this. There is no reason to assume that we have reached the end of this development.

For Sardar, the situation is different. For him and for many of his fellow Muslims there is of course a recognition of the changing nature of philosophical arguments. But whatever happens in the future, they can rest assured that a comparison with the unchangeable ARF will decide what can be accepted and what has to be dismissed. 'Islamic epistemology' simply states that we can only have knowledge on the basis of the Qur'an and the Sunnah. This means that 'knowledge' can only be accepted as knowledge if it agrees with the ARF in general and with Islamic values in particular. This reasoning makes Sardar (1987:24) declare that, for Muslims, 'the traditional Occidental epistemologies of Berkeley, Hume,

Russell and others are irrelevant'. He proceeds with the statement that it is 'a corollary of this that a large part of contemporary epistemology is irrelevant also'. For most Western academics, this view of epistemology is unacceptable. They rely on the concept of an absolute truth which is independent of language, religion, culture, etc. Perhaps they are anxious to add that there are many domains where we may never arrive at an absolute truth, and that natural science is the privileged abode of objectivity. The proof of truth in natural science is the many things we have managed to achieve by applying these truths. And the 'many things' amount to radically altered conditions for human life on this planet.

This is the majority standpoint. A vociferous minority take a relativist position claiming that there is no objective truth but that many people act as if they possessed it, and that there is really no reason why one should not let them believe so. I do think Sardar would find the relativist position to be a strange bedfellow, even if it superficially may seem to support his faith in Islamic epistemology.[4] It is time to take a look at postmodernism.

TWO VIEWS OF POSTMODERNISM

Postmodernism is notoriously difficult to define. So long as two persons have not agreed on a common definition, there is no reason to be surprised if they have totally different attitudes to it. This is the case with Ahmed and Sardar. For the former, postmodernism is a positive phenomenon that makes it easier to be a Muslim in the West, and that will also make it easier for the Islamic contribution to be accepted by the dominant global civilization. This position is understandable, if one agrees with Ahmed's main characterization of postmodernism and the postmodernist age:

> To approach an understanding of the postmodernist age is to presuppose a questioning of, a loss of faith in, the project of modernity; a spirit of pluralism; a heightened scepticism of traditional orthodoxies; and finally a rejection of the view of the world as a universal totality, of the expectation of final solutions and complete answers.
>
> (Ahmed 1992:10)

Ahmed's understanding of postmodernism hinges on the loss of faith in 'metanarratives', i.e. orthodoxies, ideologies, complete answers and total explanations, as well as ambitions such as the Modern Project stemming from Enlightenment days. What is left when all this is gone? In Ahmed's view we are left with a spirit of pluralism and a greater tolerance of difference. In such a climate, Islam stands a better chance in the West, and perhaps worldwide.

For Sardar, the situation looks very different. As we could see many pages back, Sardar regards postmodernism only as the latest of the expressions of Western secularism. Secularism has transferred the religious energy to the 'rational concerns of this world' and 'this religiosity . . . has now built its nest in postmodernism' (Sardar 1991:62). Sardar never defines postmodernism properly, but refers to it as the 'most recent panic-ridden offspring' of secularism (Sardar 1991:55) . What has postmodernism to do with secularism? If Sardar at all refers to the same vague phenomenon as Ahmed does, then the answer might be that its strong relativism actually is far from being humble. It is an oblique attack on all fundamentalisms, i.e. on all convictions that there is an absolute truth, whether that truth be founded on Divine revelation or rationalist endeavour. The obliqueness lies in its readiness to tolerate foreign fundamentalisms. By doing that, relativism *de facto* states that there is no absolute truth. And if postmodernists and other relativists do tolerate such extravagant claims when they come from others, it is because they themselves know better. Perhaps Sardar has seen this, perhaps he agrees with Gellner:

> The relativist endorses the absolutism of others, and so his relativism entails an absolutism which also contradicts it. Let us leave him with that problem: there is no way out of it.
>
> (Gellner 1992:74)

Perhaps, also, he would have more sympathy for another absolutism than his own – Gellner's Enlightenment rationalism, for instance – even though he would consider it profoundly mistaken. Two fundamentalisms are at least playing the same game. The irony of the situation, however, is that it is postmodernism with its relativism that makes both Akbar Ahmed and Ziauddin Sardar such successful figures in the modern, secular West.

NOTES

1 It is as well to be clear at the outset about what I mean by 'intellectual'. Ziauddin Sardar has made some incisive remarks on 'Muslim intellectuals' but has also had some very critical things to say about them:

> The mode of thought that characterizes intellectuals is neither science nor theology. It is ideology. An ideology expresses both their world-view and cultural values. The Muslim intelligentsia is that segment of the educated Muslim society where commitment to the ideology of Islam is unquestioned. . . . Their operational knowledge is one of the Occidental sciences – physical, technological and social – acquired either in the Occident or in the Occidental type of educational establishments in their own countries. . . . As Muslims, however, they also have some knowledge of Islam. This is their non-operational knowledge. Islam is either entirely unoperational in their daily life, or Islam's operational forms with which they are familiar are confined to prayers, fasting and other rituals at birth, marriage and death. . . . Yet, as committed Muslims, they feel the need to assert their identity and personality. This the Muslim intellectual tries to do by identifying himself as Muslim and by

asserting the supremacy of Islam. He knows Islam is supreme, but he does not know why. He knows Islam can solve all his individual and collective problems but he does not know how. Islam can certainly solve all problems; but the Muslim intellectuals of today cannot.

(Sardar 1987:66–7)

Let me assure the reader that I am not using the term 'intellectual' in this special Sardarian sense – thus turning Sardar against himself – but in the more general sense of a person dealing with fundamental values and philosophical issues in a 'free' way, constantly ready to turn his or her critical eye on the foundations of what has just been said. The intellectual is a member of the 'culture of critical discourse', to borrow a term from Alvin Gouldner (1979).

2 Before saying more about Ahmed and Sardar, I should perhaps give a brief characterization of myself and the position from which my own perspective derives. I am a Swedish anthropologist with some research experience from what was once North Yemen where I concentrated on the expressions of social inequality in everyday life. I have also dealt with Muslims in the West, especially with converts to Islam, trying to understand their relations both to the community they have entered and the one they have left. As far as religion is concerned, I am an agnostic, tolerant (I hope) of the religious beliefs and practices of others but preferring to see them confined to special sectors of an otherwise secularist social order. And as far as social science theory goes, I have had a Marxist phase to which my Yemeni research put an end. More recently, I have been intrigued by the reflexive mood in anthropology and I have also attempted to spell out a 'postmodernist' view of ritual. To an anthropological reader, it may be informative to say that, today, I vacillate between the positions of Clifford Geertz and Ernest Gellner as regards relativism and rationalism.

3 It is surprising that Sardar does not even mention the critical discussion of the *hadith* that has been carried out by Western scientists. A scholar who seems to be respected by both non-Muslims and Muslims is John Esposito, the editor-in-chief of a forthcoming encyclopaedia of Islam in the modern world from Oxford University Press. In his widely acclaimed *Islam: The Straight Path* he has this to say about the authenticity of the *hadith* literature:

Modern Western scholarship has seriously questioned the historicity and authenticity of the *hadith*, maintaining that the bulk of traditions attributed to the Prophet Muhammad were actually written much later.

(Esposito 1991:81–2)

He does not go so far, however, as Joseph Schacht – 'the most influential modern Western authority on Islamic law' – who regarded all the *hadith* as apocryphal material. Esposito points out that Schacht himself is guilty of questionable science:

Accepting Schacht's conclusion regarding the many traditions he did examine does not warrant its automatic extension to all the traditions. To consider all Prophetic traditions apocryphal until proven otherwise is to reverse the burden of proof. Moreover, even where differences of opinion exist regarding the authenticity of the chain of narrators, they need not detract from the authenticity of a tradition's content and common acceptance of the importance of tradition literature as a record of the early history and development of Islamic belief and practice.

(Esposito 1991:82)

4 The nature of the three main types of epistemology today – religious fundamentalism, relativism and rationalist fundamentalism – and their interrelations have been analysed with admirable clarity by Ernest Gellner, especially in Gellner (1992).

REFERENCES

Ahmed, Akbar S. (1988) *Discovering Islam: Making Sense of Muslim History and Society*, London and New York: Routledge and Kegan Paul.
—— (1992) *Postmodernism and Islam: Predicament and Promise*, London and New York: Routledge.
Akhtar, Shabbir (1990) *The Light in the Enlightenment*, London: Grey Seal.
Arberry, Arthur J. (1990) *Sufism: An Account of the Mystics of Islam*, London: Mandala Unwin Paperbacks.
Asad, Muhammad (1982 [1934]) *Islam at the Crossroads*, Gibraltar: Dar al-Andalus.
St Augustine (1984 [1467]) *City of God*, Harmondsworth: Penguin.
Berger, Peter and Luckmann, Thomas (1967) *The Social Construction of Reality: A Treatise in the Sociology of Knowledge*, New York: Doubleday Anchor Books.
Esposito, John L. (1991) *Islam: The Straight Path*, New York and Oxford: Oxford University Press.
Gellner, Ernest (1992) *Postmodernism, Reason and Religion*, London and New York: Routledge.
Gouldner, A. W. (1979) *The Future of the Intellectuals and the Rise of the New Class*, London: Macmillan.
Haeri, Fadhlalla (1989) *Living Islam: East and West*, Longmead, Dorset: Element Books Ltd/Zahra Trust.
Sardar, Ziauddin (1977) *Science, Technology and Development in the Muslim World*, London: Croom Helm.
—— (1987) *The Future of Muslim Civilization*, London and New York: Mansell Publishing Limited.
—— (1991) 'The Postmodern Age', in Munawar Ahmad Anees, Syed Z. Abedin and Ziauddin Sardar, *Christian-Muslim Relations: Yesterday, Today, Tomorrow*, London: Grey Seal.
Schiffauer, Werner (1988) 'Migration and Religiousness', in *The New Islamic Presence in Western Europe*, Tomas Gerholm and Yngve Georg Lithman (eds), London and New York: Mansell Publishing Limited.
Toulmin, Stephen (1990) *Cosmopolis: The Hidden Agenda of Modernity*, New York: Free Press.

Chapter 11

Diaspora and millennium
British Pakistani global-local fabulations of the Gulf War

Pnina Werbner

INTRODUCTION

The appropriation of the Gulf crisis from a global set of media images, reworked as a locally significant narrative, raises questions about the way in which diasporas fabulate their local experiences in a global idiom. In this chapter I consider the speeches made by British Pakistanis in Manchester in response to the Gulf crisis as an appropriation – and hence localization – of a global fable. Through this fable, I argue, Pakistanis constructed a powerful, ideologically grounded, allegory of their predicament as an enclaved Muslim community in the West, while simultaneously asserting their membership in a global diaspora.

From the start, the Gulf crisis, in pitching Muslim brother against Muslim brother, was the stuff of tragedy. Given also the historical and contemporary political complexity of the events leading to the crisis, and the moral reputations of the protagonists, the construction of villains and heroes in the dispute necessarily involved a process of selection and reworking of phenomenal 'facts'. Saddam Hussein, the ruler of Iraq, the Gulf state kings and princes, George Bush, the American President, could all be constructed in moral terms from different perspectives.

Of course, the television images beamed into British Pakistani homes in Manchester already constituted, for the most part, a moral fable, seen from a Western perspective. The fable cast Saddam as a vicious, tyrannical, insane villain. In Britain, support for the international alliance was very high, one of the highest in the Western world. Against this appropriation, however, Pakistanis created a counter-narrative, a 'resistive reading', an alternative fable, which cast Saddam Hussein in the role of hero. This same fabulation of the events and cast of characters was repeated by different ideological constituencies throughout the Muslim world, from Algeria to Pakistan (see Piscatori 1991). Like its Western counterpart, it was a global fable, globally fabulated.

The Muslim 'street' backed Saddam Hussein, from Karachi to Manchester. As the crisis developed, a global segmentary opposition between popular or radical Islam and the West emerged. In the face of this global narrativizing, how are we to interpret the remaking of this narrative in each locality? If we start from an assumption that global events are necessarily filtered through local experiences, we need to ask why British Pakistanis, a small, socially vulnerable and relatively new ethnic minority, chose to cast Saddam Hussein in a hero's role *against* the overwhelming British interpretive consensus. Since the conflict pitched Muslim against Muslim, while the international alliance included many Muslim regimes, the local Pakistani minority had, theoretically, several choices:

1 It could have accepted the British media's construction of Saddam as a villain.
2 It could have remained neutral.
3 It could have recast Saddam in the role of hero through a local remythologizing.

Either of the first two choices would have served British Pakistanis' *local* interests and indeed, allowed them to express solidarity with their adopted country. That they chose the third alternative necessarily raises questions about the complex nature of the relation between the local and the global.

In order to explain why the appropriation was, in effect, *anti*-local, we need, I believe, to consider two central questions:

1 What purpose do global current affairs, such as the Gulf crisis, serve in the revitalization of communal self-consciousness? And what reflexive images of community did this global raw material enable local leaders to construct?
2 In what respect does the construction or appropriation of myths or fables of current affairs reflect a response to a common global predicament of urban Muslims everywhere, to what extent was it a feature of the spread of a new social movement, and to what extent was it a *tool* of localized agonistic action?

The problem of identity and identification is critically implicated in both questions. It could be argued, for example, that a peripheral Muslim community such as that of Manchester Pakistanis, in fabulating the tragedy of the Gulf crisis from an anti-Western perspective, was merely toeing a 'party line', created and legitimized elsewhere. But even if this was the case, in doing so, leaders were undoubtedly also seeking to assert their identification with this global Islamic movement. And, moreover, the question of *why* this particular global fabulation emerged still remains to be answered.

Many of the commentaries about the Gulf War have stressed the central role of the media and of video technology in its representation (see, for example, Ahmed 1992; Taylor 1992; Norris 1991; Heikal 1992, to mention but a few). Since media coverage in the age of CNN was virtually non-stop, and bombing forays were imaged as video games, both the crisis and war assumed a surrealist, flickering, two-dimensional sense of unreality. Despite accusations of Western 'propaganda', however, Saddam Hussein's achievement in the crisis was to have his own speeches beamed on prime time to a global audience who also witnessed the carnage in Kuwait and Iraq. Given the almost infinite multiplicity of images and information the war generated, it ultimately was left to politicians and viewers to make sense of the unfolding drama.

A narrative construction of reality is not so much a factual distortion (since facts only gain their facticity within narratives) but a perspectival shaping of a morally meaningful 'plot' (on plot see also Becker 1979). According to Aristotle, the plot (Greek *mythos*, *fablos* in Latin) is 'the first essential, the life and soul, so to speak, of Tragedy' (Aristotle 1941: 1461). The plot consists of the action, with the characters being subordinated to it as personified moral agents (on this subordination see the discussion by Rimmon-Kenan 1983: 34–42). Action is '. . . what makes us ascribe certain moral qualities to the agents' (Aristotle 1941: 1460). Hence for Aristotle:

> Tragedy is essentially an imitation not of persons but of action and life, of happiness and misery. . . . Characters [are included] for the sake of the action. So that it is the action in it, i.e. its Fable or Plot, that is the end and purpose of the tragedy . . . the Characters come second.
>
> (Aristotle 1941: 1461)

Although 'plot' is the English translation of the Greek *mythos* and Latin *fablos*, the meanings of 'myth' and 'fable' evoke alternative modes of moral emplotment. If we regard the 'detachment' of a discourse, following Ricoeur, as an essential phase in its construction as a meaningful text (Ricoeur 1982), then the constrast becomes evident: a 'myth' is a narrative of the past which gains its transcendent significance from its detachment in time (it denotes a lost, earlier 'world'); a 'fable' is a narrative about personified creatures, usually animals, which gains its transcendent significance from its detachment in space or domain (the space of nature, the animal world). The legends of the Prophet and his life are myths of origin, shared by a contemporary Islamic global community, a mythic charter of the global 'spread' of Islam; globally significant current affairs have the potentiality to become fables shared in *space* by a contemporary Islamic global community as 'simultaneous consumers' in calendrical time. A global image beamed into millions of individual homes at a particular moment of the day conjures up an 'historically clocked' co-present but spatially dispersed imagined community (see Anderson 1991: 32–4). Through such images, as Anderson argues, the 'imagined world comes to be rooted in everyday life' (1991: 35–6). For the anonymous dispersed individuals who share a simultaneously produced set of global media images to form a 'community', however, they must also share a singular perspective or 'focalization' on these events (see Rimmon-Kenan 1983: ch. 6) transforming themselves thus into an interpretive community.

Contemporary fables of current affairs arguably thus revitalize the great myths of the past and root them in everyday reality, renewing the individual identities of 'consumers' of current affairs through space-time identifications. The particularities of the story told (e.g. the Gulf crisis) achieve their emblematic status through being embedded in some kind of generic tale (Bruner 1991: 7), a fairy tale of good and evil, David and Goliath, Jack and the Beanstalk, a canonical script which through innovative breach, draws a moral lesson anew (Bruner 1991: 11). The power of the fable is thus partly the power of individual identification with the moral hero.

A further important distinction which needs to be set in advance of my main discussion is that between narrative as fable or myth and narrative as allegory. The fable, we have seen, is a transcendent, globalized narrative. To the extent that it makes an oblique ideological critique it can also be regarded as an allegory which comments on a local set of events, values and power relations (for anthropological approaches to allegory as oblique ideological critique see Boddy 1989; Lavie 1990). In this sense the local and global are mutually constitutive. Allegories work by analogy (see Clifford 1974). They move from pretext to text, from the birth of Islam and the persecutions of the Prophet, to the battle of Karbala and the martyrdom of Husain, to the Gulf crisis and the challenge to the West, and finally, to British Muslims' battle to change the British blasphemy law and have *The Satanic Verses* banned, and the battle of black people in Britain against racial violence and discrimination. This reliance on sacred pretexts and intertextuality is a fundamental feature of allegory (see Quilligan 1979: ch. 2).

With these distinctions in mind, it is possible now to turn to an exposition of the British Pakistani Muslim interpretation of the Gulf crisis.

DIALOGICS

I spent the academic year 1989–90 in Washington DC. In September 1990 I returned to Manchester to find Saddam Hussein, the President of Iraq, firmly established as a public hero among Mancunian Pakistanis. The more Western politicians denounced his bestial monstrosity, the more British Pakistanis extolled his courage, his strength and the justice of his cause. 'But,' I asked, 'Don't you care about the Kuwaitis?' 'Not really,' my most moderate friends replied, 'they are Muslims. What difference does it make who their ruler is?' 'But,' I wondered, 'are you not concerned that Saddam might invade Saudi Arabia, take over Mecca Sharif and the Holy Ka'ba?' They merely shrugged their shoulders: 'He won't do it,' they said. 'And anyway,' they implied, 'even if he did, he's still a Muslim.'

Talk of breaking international law and defying the UN charter by gobbling up a member state were regarded with the utmost cynicism. What about Kashmir? And Palestine? Where has UN justice been in relation to those countries?

'But,' I ventured, 'he is a tyrant. There is no democracy in Iraq.' 'Yes,' they conceded, 'democracy is a good thing. There should be democracy. But tell me this,' they added, 'which is the greater evil, America or Saddam Hussein?'

Above all, these Mancunian Pakistanis stressed that the dispute was a private Muslim conflict which should be settled by the Muslim nations without outside interference. They valorized religious identity beyond the national divisions within the Arab world, regarding the latter as superficial and insignificant by comparison to the need to achieve a common front against the outside, Christian and Jewish, world.

What struck me most forcefully, however, even in these early conversations with moderate non-activists, was that once again, as in the Rushdie affair, British Pakistanis seemed to be setting themselves morally apart from British society, denying categorically what their fellow British nationals regarded as axiomatic moral imperatives: 'our boys' were in the Gulf, risking their lives, threatened by chemical warfare, poised to fight the fourth largest army in the world, to defend democratic values against a man who, at the very least, was a ruthless dictator who had invaded and taken over another country.

There were, of course, arguments in the wider society too about the tactical advisability of going to war and the heavy costs this would entail. Many thought sanctions should be given a chance. Many doubted the sincerity of the West and saw the war as having purely economic aims. There was an underlying isolationist tendency: why go to war with possible disastrous environmental consequences and terrible loss of life on a matter not our direct responsibility? The strong if small British peace movement was quite vocal. Had local Pakistanis merely supported this movement (which they passively did), the English would have sympathized with them. As fellow Muslims, their desire to see a peaceful solution to the dispute would have appeared morally commendable.

But British Pakistanis were not simply talking of tactics, environment or the potential loss of life. They expressed no sorrow or concern for 'our boys' in the Gulf, nor did they express horror at Saddam Hussein's tyranny. Instead, they spoke of Christian soldiers desacralizing the holy ground of the Hijaz, of a Western medieval crusader revival, of *jihad*, conspiracy and Western aggression. They thus placed themselves almost entirely outside the broad moral consensus which encompassed both war and peace movements.

This confrontational posture raises difficult sociological questions about the origins of communalism, seen as an ethnic-cum-religious movement.

To what extent is communalism inspired by localized material or political interests, as is sometimes argued? And, if such interests do exist, how are we to interpret and uncover them? What type of interests are they, and what groups precisely do they refer to?

On the face of it, British Pakistanis' political stance struck against their most basic interests as a minority in Britain. Yet what was surprising was their almost naive lack of awareness that this was indeed the case. Later, as murmurs started in the press about British Muslims being a fifth column, as mosques were daubed with graffiti, as racist attacks on Asians (irrespective of whether they were Muslims) increased, some of the more moderate local Pakistani community leaders tried to suppress the most vocal expressions of support for Saddam Hussein. Yet at an all-Muslim conference in Bradford to which the national press were invited, participants almost unanimously voted in support of the Iraqi leader (see Ahmed 1992: 198).

British Pakistanis could have supported the Muslim regimes, including Pakistan, which were members of the international alliance. They could simply have kept their heads down and remained entirely neutral. Both strategies would have suited their interests as a local ethnic-cum-religious group. Instead, those I spoke to chose to take a publicly pro-Iraqi stance. Seen from the outside, even the most liberal members of the wider society could only interpret this stance (as the media and personal acquaintances did) as further evidence of Pakistanis' fundamental irrationality. For the less charitable the stance bordered on treason. It is worth pointing out, however, that there was nothing *illegal* in the British Muslim stand on the Gulf crisis – members of the community were perfectly entitled to hold deviant political views; it was just that these views seemed so out of touch with the social environment in which they were articulated.

To seek the roots of this British Pakistani political dissent, I begin my account with an analysis of some of the rhetoric at a political meeting held in Manchester in October 1990 as part of the *eid-milad-un-nabi* celebrations, a meeting which took place in the shadow of the Gulf crisis.

THE MEETING

The meeting was held to mark the Prophet's Birthday and was followed by a procession from the city centre to the Central *jami'a* Mosque. It took place in the oak-lined and ornately heralded Council Chambers of Manchester City's Town Hall. Around the hall were large banners in English, bearing a series of religious and political messages: ISLAM MEANS PEACE AND SUBMISSION TO THE ALMIGHTY GOD; ALL MAIN RELIGIONS IN THE U.K. SHOULD BE GIVEN LEGAL PROTECTION; THE BLASPHEMY LAW SHOULD BE EXTENDED TO ISLAM AND ALL OTHER MAIN RELIGIONS; OUR MESSAGE IS PEACE AND LOVE FOR EVERYONE; MUSLIMS ARE PEACE-

LOVING AND LAW-ABIDING CITIZENS; WE LOVE ISLAM AND THE PROPHET OF ISLAM; THE HOLY PROPHET IS MERCY FOR ALL WORLDS. The banners thus made implicit references to the Rushdie affair through the demand for a change in the blasphemy laws, while asserting that Islam is a religion of peace, and thus rejecting the association of Muslims with violence which the Rushdie affair had generated in the public mind. This message was particularly significant, since the year before, at *eid-milad-un-nabi*, the same congregation had supported a public call for the death of the author, made in front of MPs, the Bishop of Manchester and the national media.

The first speaker, following the opening prayer and sermon by the *maulvi*, was a local English convert. His speech echoed with the familiar cadences of traditional English dissent. From the start of his speech, the speaker stressed that Islam is a religion of *change*, i.e. of reform. He went on to explain the kind of change he had in mind:

> And this world, Islam says, must be changed to end all oppression. All men and women, Islam says, must be treated with respect and dignity. There must be no inequality, no injustice, no exploitation, no brutality, but all men and women must be brothers and sisters, part of a Muslim nation and part of a Muslim state. Islam is the belief in Allah *subhan-atʿallah* but it is also a belief in a unique type of society. A unique social structure. The Prophet *saʿlat-u-waʿsalaam* was sinless and perfect, he was Allah's instrument to transform mankind [the audience murmurs its approval] and change the world.

Here then is the visionary depiction of an Islamic utopia translated into the everyday language of human rights and social equality. The speaker then went on to praise the Prophet as the object of supreme love, and to reject Western profligate life styles, base materialism, alcoholism and greed which undermined Islamic spirituality, love, purity. Finally, the speaker returns to his central theme: Islam's message is one of liberation.

> We would show the Prophet *saʿlat-u-waʿsalaam* as the liberator above all others, as the friend of the poor and downtrodden everywhere. *Milad-un-nabi* would also be the beginning of economic and political campaigning to rid the world of racism. *Milad-un-nabi* should be a celebration against racism. To rid the world of class oppression. To rid the world of exploitation, to rid the world of maltreatment of women, and all the other evils that the Prophet . . . set out to end.

We see here the fusing of global discourses of liberation, anti-racism and even feminism with a discourse of religious love, much as early Methodism fused love and dissent. And, moreover, just as English radical movements had their demons and demonology (see Thompson 1963: 832), so too Islamic radicalism has its Satans, of which the USA and the West are perceived as the external source of corruption and evil (see Beeman 1983). This demonology was more evident in the second speaker's speech.

The second speaker's brief was to comment on the Gulf crisis, and after stressing the immutability and centrality of an Islamic identity – 'Islam is not like a scarf on the head; it is like the colour of the blood running through all the parts of the body', the supremacy of the Prophet and the importance of parading one's Islamic identity publicly – he finally turned to his subject matter: the distortions perpetrated on the public by the media (on this theme see also Ahmed 1992; Norris 1991), and the need for an independent and objective explanation of the crisis from a Muslim perspective:

> So what I'm going to do is I'll take you along, briefly, through the ideas [surrounding the Gulf crisis] so that our young Muslims in particular, and our Muslim brothers whose mother tongue is English, they and other people may be able to join me and see what the true Muslim perspective is. What is it? [i.e. what is the Gulf crisis?] Why is it? Who created this? How shall it end?
>
> I as a Muslim, Mr. Chairman, believe that the whole thing will be resolved by Allah almighty. The superpowers may do anything [they like], but at the end of the day things in the past have always happened and Allah *subhan-at'allah* ultimately has pulled the strings, and things have happened . . . these people [Bush and the Western powers] are in for a big shock, those who are thinking that they will control the destiny of the Gulf. They look upon the [crisis] as an Arab question, an oil question, a Middle Eastern question – I say to them: No! This is a Muslim question. This is a question of the followers of Allah *subhan-at'allah*, all the world over and the followers of the *sunna*, and it will be *Ahl-e-Sunnat wa jamaat* [the followers of the Sunna, a reference to members of the Barelwi movement which includes the present congregation] who are the greatest overwhelming majority of the [Islamic] world population who ultimately will be expressing their will.

In his speech, the speaker expresses an almost millenarian faith that God will protect His followers from diabolical conspiracies. Implicit in this expressed optimism is, however, a real fear that the West is too powerful, and that only God can help the Muslim world to overcome its Satanic opponents. The speaker himself does not speak from a sense of *personal* failure. Similarly, Mancunian Pakistanis as a community have, on the whole, prospered. But relative economic success has not brought with it political power and here lies a deep source of frustration. By reflecting on global events, the speaker displaces this local sense of political powerlessness onto an international arena.

Next the speaker goes on to condemn the sham and hypocrisy of Western claims to be following 'international law'. Like others at the meeting, he evokes the problems of Kashmir and Palestine. But he also denounces the whole international system, the very structure of the United Nations, which he regards as biased, and based on unjustifiable inequality.

In speaking of Palestine, Kashmir and Afghanistan, the speaker expresses the direct identification of the present congregation with Muslims in different parts of the world. Islam is a universal, transnational ideology, and Muslims are concerned with the affairs of Muslims living beyond the narrow limits of their immediate community. What the Gulf crisis has underlined, according to this speaker, is global injustice. And the reason for this is not hard to seek – sheer economic greed. Thus the speaker continues:

> The real question is not international law – the real question is oil, it is economic considerations, it is the access they want in order to ensure that their own interests are protected – the West wants to protect its own interests.

But worse still, American greed is matched by the greed of the Gulf states' leaders. These Muslim autocratic corrupt regimes created by colonialism have allegedly made a pact with the American President. The external, corrupting evil influence (Beeman 1983) has made a deal with the internally corrupt. The West, however, has failed and is crumbling from within (see also Voll 1987):

> So what I am saying to you today is that international law is a word of the mouth, it does not stand anywhere. The real cause of their going there is because of the corrupt, indecent, immoral, hollow kings – these kings today are just like crowns on the head and inside there is nothing – you touch them and they fall to the ground because they have no character. Ordinary Muslims in the world have great character. I have hope in the ordinary people of the Muslim world but I have no hope whatsoever in any Amirs or upon any sheikhs or any kings whatever name they may take.

Here the configuration of the new populist Islamic radicalism takes shape. The 'ordinary people' are extolled. They form a worldwide community. The corrupt, spineless regimes of the oil rich Gulf states are merely Western creations – Islam accords them no legitimacy. Was the Prophet a king? And if he, the most supreme of all human beings, was not a king, is anyone else entitled to claim kingship? The target of all the speeches is a single target: inequality. Inequality *between* nations and inequality *within* nations. Oddly enough, however, this advocacy of equality goes along with membership in a movement which recognises an essential inequality: just as the Prophet was the most supreme of all prophets, so too among the living and dead there are saints (*awliya*) who are intrinsically superior to run-of-the-mill, 'ordinary' human beings. (Thus for Sufi followers, saintly authority substitutes for scriptural authority. See Gellner 1992.)

To understand this apparent contradiction we need to recognize that at stake is not merely Paine liberalism and the radicalism of the Enlightenment, but an Islamic version of Bunyan's quest as well. Kings are intrinsically inferior to pure men of God. Hence God's message of equality is the supreme message and its carriers, Holy Men, are superior to any Amir or Sheikh, however powerful and wealthy the latter may be. The places of these holy men, the shrines where they are buried, are for the congregation gathered at the meeting – all followers of Muslim saints – places of supreme sanctity. Like the first speaker, this sanctity is combined with a modernist perspective. Hence, the imperial puppets in the Gulf states must

> realize – Muslim civilization, Muslim life style, Muslim economic ideas, rejecting interest [usury], Muslim contribution to medicine, the Muslim view of life, is challenging the Western view of life. The West believes in enlightened self interest – working your way in an enlightened way. They believe in interest, protecting your own interest. We believe in selfless devotion to God, we believe in loving . . .

Why has Saddam Hussein, himself a corrupt, ruthless dictator, escaped the infamy of the Gulf state rulers? Is not Iraq too a Western creation? Partly, the opposition to the Gulf state rulers is a sectarian opposition to the Wahabi movement. But the main reason Saddam is praised is because he dared to challenge the West directly, and to question the old colonial divisions forced upon the Arab world. For the battle is not only a battle about power, oil and money; it is, above all, a cultural confrontation – a battle for cultural supremacy; almost, even, a battle between the idols of Western materialism and the Muslim all-powerful God. It is a battle for the 'control of historicity' (Touraine 1991: 16). Touraine argues that a social movement

> produces an ideology, i.e. a representation of its social relations; it also produces a Utopia, by means of which it becomes identified with the states of the struggle and with historicity itself.
>
> (1991: 98)

Transcendent values and local adversaries are juxtaposed. Thus, the speaker moves from the international scene to the local, British scene:

> Now Western culture feels threatened. Look here, these Muslims in Britain, we thought they would slowly dissolve into British society just as sugar mixes with milk, and then they will all be gone. But look at them – they talk like Muslims, they look like Muslims, they behave like Muslims, they respect their parents, they respect their family, they work

for longer hours, they are not behaving [like others]; they don't taste alcohol, they do not go gambling . . .

Once again we come back to familiar non-conformist, puritanical values: respect for authority, family norms, hard work, abstinence, frugality.

so they find that these Muslims are a strange sort of people – that we [i.e. the English] had been thinking that they would all be mixed up [assimilated]. We [Muslims] will not disrespect our faith, our culture. I work alongside English people. I respect them. But I do not allow them to interfere in those areas which are the areas defined by the Qur'an and by the *sunna* of the Prophet Muhammad *swalla'llahu-e'layhay-wa'sullam*. My daughters, my sons, my wife, my family, my neighbours, my town, all these people I regulate with the light which comes to me from studying the life of Muhammad *Rasul Allah*.

The battle is for cultural equality and autonomy:

We live in a multicultural society [hence] British culture cannot be accepted as superior to Muslim culture. All cultures are equal. We have every right [to practise according to our beliefs], and in the Gulf situation the whole world is watching how all these idols, these images of the cultures of the West are cracking; these *lat* and *manat* and *hubel* [pre-Islamic female idols worshipped in Mecca which are mentioned in *The Satanic Verses*] of the West, the United Nations is coming up.

But historicity and culture are now global landscapes, as are the political and ideological landscapes which shape them (see Appadurai 1990):

We look towards the Ka'ba and *masjid el nabwi* [the mosque where the Prophet is buried in Madina], Mecca *muazma* (the great) and Madina *munarwa* (the light) with respect, the people who rule over those parts should not look towards Washington and New York with the same sort of loyalty. Loyalty ultimately belongs to God, and I say that there should be justice, there should be equality, there should be understanding, there should be humanity, and the Gulf crisis will undergo changes, God always keeps on making changes, we have also to change ourself. [Here the speaker quotes a verse from the Qur'an and translates it into English.] God does not change any nation or people unless that nation changes itself.

This powerful speech shows how closely British Muslims identify their particular cause – the promotion of Islam in Britain in order to preserve an Islamic identity for future generations – with the global cause of Muslims. Similarly, the fight against religious legal discrimination in Britain is seen as an extension of a broader, international fight against Western domination. To overcome this domination and internal decadence the community must first change itself, a central tenet of Islamic modernists (see Ahmad 1967: 262). In this fight the national divisions within the Arab world are regarded as a major weakness exploited by the West. The divisions are artificial, colonial inventions; the rulers of these Arab nations are mere colonial puppets. By implication, the solution would be to create a new, unified Islamic empire which would be powerful enough to meet the West on its own grounds. At the time of the meeting, in October 1990, British Pakistanis were still hoping that Saddam Hussein was the man to achieve this power and unity, with his powerful army and intransigent stance against the West.

The final speaker at the meeting stressed the need for Muslim empowerment through public political action. Speaking, like the previous speaker, in English, he praised Saddam Hussein

> for putting some of the important issues that the Muslim world faces today on the agenda of international debate. I have got today's paper [in front of me] and I will read two lines from it. It says: 'Anyone with a sense of sympathy, a sense of humanity, must sympathize with the Palestinians. Their lands are occupied, they have no political rights and they are daily the victims of a misguided policy which believes that the security of Israel must rest on the closure of schools, illegal settlement and even collective punishment.'
>
> These are not the words of Palestinian leaders. These are not the words of those Muslim leaders who are condemning Saddam Hussein. These are the words of Douglas Hurd, the Foreign Secretary of this country. He did not utter these words for 21 years, for 22 years, for 23 years of the occupation of Palestine. He has uttered these words to justify the Western action in the occupied lands of *hijaz* and *najr*. Today Kuwait is not occupied. Kuwait is in the hands of the Muslims and the Arabs. Maybe the rulers may be disputed. But the occupied lands are the lands of Palestine. The lands of Kashmir. And the lands of Hijaz and Najr which are today called by the name of its family, Saudi Arabia.

Only action, protest and resistance can sway Western regimes and compel them to recognize the value of Islam. And the bearers of the banners of protest are 'ordinary' Muslims, including the Muslims of Britain; they are the true Muslims, pitched against their false leaders. The speaker attacks attempts by the press to describe the internal divisions among British Muslims:

> We are *ahl-e-sunnat-wa-jamaat* – the true faith of Islam. And these Wahabis, Deobandis as well [fundamentalist and reformist Muslims], they are distractions, they are descriptions of small sects who have migrated, who have moved away from the real thing. So when we

describe ourselves, describe yourself not as 'Barelwi' but as 'the true Muslim'.

British Muslims are facing a crisis – a crisis because British Islam to some extent is dependent on the money which is coming from foreign countries [i.e. Iran and Arab oil-rich countries]. To build the mosques here, to pay the wages, to pay the salaries of some of the *imams* [clerics] who occupy the *mimbars* [pulpits].

He calls on these *imams* to resist Saudi political pressure and attacks the collaboration between a religious establishment and the quietist tendencies of certain religious streams. He attacks the media for misrepresenting Muslims because 'the effects of the Crusades, although hundreds of years ago, are still persisting in the Christian psyche [this theme has emerged since the Rushdie affair]', and because 'by and large the media in this country is [*sic*] being controlled by Jewish and Zionist forces'.

Revealed here are some of the fundamental elements characterizing social movements: the raising of consciousness; the struggle for autonomy, for the control of a cultural field; a grass roots oppositional politics; the stress on identity; the imagining, in Castells' words, of 'reactive Utopias' (see Castells 1983). A genuine movement has to transcend a sense of localism and a narrow concern with a single issue (see Hannigan 1985: 449). The speeches reported here reveal this transcendence as well as the application of the wider allegory to local predicaments.

While a social movement transforms a local sense of injustice 'into a wider ideological critique', to be effective it must also transform it 'into a programme for action' (Hannigan 1985: 442). A major criticism of the French new social movement approach has been that it has failed to address adequately the question of how this organization and the process of mobilization is achieved (Hannigan 1985: 446; for an attempt to identify the organizational processes underlying ethnic social movement mobilization see Werbner 1991c). The speaker here evokes his frustrated sense of impotence: if for others rhetorical identification suffices, for him words without action are hollow. What is lacking, the speaker laments, is proper *political organization and mobilization*.

We are one and a half million Muslims in Britain today [official estimates report just under one million British Muslims], perhaps more, but when they [the politicians] issue statements about the Middle East, about Israel, they do not look at the Muslim lobby. Because it does not exist. It is the duty of the leadership of the Muslim community to create that lobby, create that influence, and it is today, this year and last year, which has seen the Islamic, British Muslims going through a crisis [he is referring to the Rushdie affair]. I hope that the positive side of it will be the creation of a strong, a powerful Muslim influence in the affairs of this country. *Inshallah* within ten years we should have fifty members of parliament. Hundreds of councillors up and down the country sitting in the town halls.

This brings us back to the question of fabulation: why do the speakers cast Saddam Hussein, despite his record of tyranny and aggression, as a potential hero and saviour rather than in the role of villain? The answer lies in the subordination of character to action in tragic fables. As a culturally enclaved minority in the West, British Pakistanis are having to come to terms with an experienced, everyday loss of autonomy and cultural self-control which permanent settlement in Britain entails. Hence settlement is associated with a growing fear of an impending 'structural paralysis' (Gearing 1973). The threat of this paralytic malaise is a nightmarish potentiality for the speakers in the meeting, a hidden, buried intelligentsia of local preachers and lay activists. Its implicit danger exceeds even the reality of everyday racism.

Lack of cultural autonomy is particularly evident in the field of education. Hence the speaker goes on to complain that in this field there is 'total discrimination, and open discrimination.' While Church of England, Catholic and Jewish schools have all been granted state-aided status, Muslims are denied this right, 'some phony reason is found by the Minister of Education to deny state-aided status to Muslim schools'. Once again the call is to self-help and activism, and the speaker appeals to wealthy Muslims to contribute towards the building of Muslim schools for several years, 'until we are able to force the British Government to provide state-aided status for that school'. Repeatedly, he returns to the theme of British Muslim powerlessness and inaction:

We are a million Muslims. We are not able to get five thousand people to go to Downing Street to be able to protest about this basic inhuman injustice! Mrs. Thatcher was there, at the United Nations' Conference for Children. There are a number of Muslim children, British born, British children, whose father is not able to join them because of the immigration rules, whose father is being deported, day and night, because of immigration rules. Why are we such dead people who are not able to stand up for our rights and be able to fight? I don't say break windows, but fight, fight for your rights by joining the political process in this country, by joining the demonstrations which are taking place, and by organizing demonstrations up and down the country to ask for your rights, because even when a child doesn't cry, the mother [who] doesn't give the milk [fails]. We are an Asian society and to preserve our rights, to preserve our identity, to preserve our integrity we need to fight, and fight hard. So be prepared from now on to lead that fight. Manchester has started, twelve years ago – the first procession in this country took place in Manchester twelve years ago to celebrate the birthday of the Prophet Muhammad [in fact, previous processions had been held in

Birmingham]. And I say now that on other issues Manchester should give the lead. . . . The Celebration is not just to describe *eid-milad-un-nabi* but it is also about fighting for the rights of our people.

ISLAM, MODERNITY AND THE FIGHT FOR LIBERTY

'Why are we such dead people?' We hear in these words the heartfelt call of the layman, the political activist, who evokes in his populist rhetoric concrete images laced with calls for action. I turn now, therefore, to these forgotten preachers of Islam.

The meeting in Manchester was organized by the local vicegerent (*khalifa*) of a British-based, Sufi Qadri order, and the majority of those attending were members or supporters of the order. Followers of Sufi orders celebrate not only *eid-milad-un-nabi* and its processions, but annual *urs* memorial festivals (see Werbner, forthcoming); and they follow customary ritual practices such as that of addressing the Prophet directly (see Malik 1990). As a political-cum-religious movement these followers are known collectively as 'Barelwi'. In Manchester, it was some of the Barelwi followers focused around the *maulvi* of the Central Mosque who were the most radicalized. In their processions on the Prophet's Birthday this group asserted the legitimacy of the movement in general, while attesting also to the ascendancy of their particular Sufi regional cult in the city (see Werbner 1991b).

Their radicalism could also be explained in terms of felt threats to sectarian beliefs (see Modood 1990; Ahmad 1991). In the Rushdie affair they were enraged by the attack on the Prophet Muhammad, who is the subject of supreme adoration for Barelwis as for all Sufis; in the Gulf crisis, support for Saddam Hussein stemmed from their continuous opposition to the Wahabi movement and its Saudi rulers, regarded as the desecrators of saints' shrines throughout Arabia, including that of the Prophet himself (see Ahmad 1991).

Elsewhere I have discussed the ambivalent, intercalary positioning of *'ulama* of the Barelwi movement, caught between charismatic saints and lay followers (see Werbner n.d.). While saints tend to be pragmatic and quiescent in their political dealings, these learned doctors often articulate a radical Islamic rhetoric of protest. Their 'fundamentalism', however, is not the familiar one of Reform Islam but an ecstatic fundamentalism which defends the faith in saintly spiritual powers, and in the symbolic complex of ritual behaviour around saints' tombs and lodges.

In Britain as in Pakistan, Reform clerics are locked in battle with these saintly clerics. It is a battle conducted on both sides by Sunni, *shariʿat*-trained, learned doctors. As articulated intellectually by the Barelwis, it is a battle between the heart and the mind, love and pedantic scholarship, ecstatic devotion and mere religious observance, mystical symbolism and lifeless literalism. It is, importantly, a *modern, contemporary* battle. In the course of this apparently purely religious dialogue, broader political issues are debated, and it is to these I wish to turn.

The current fusing of politics and religion in Britain is clearly rooted in South Asian discursive formations. Very generally, secular Muslim politics in South Asia have never been quite free of religious involvement. Despite the evident modernist secularism of the Muslim League's leaders (see Alavi 1988), the League's fight for Pakistan was conducted in a religious idiom. Moreover, the League relied on alliances with religious organizations. Hence, in mobilizing support in the Punjab, it appealed to powerful saints who weighed heavily with the electorate (Gilmartin 1979; 1984; 1988). It also made common cause with some of the Indian religious movements (including the Barelwis) which supported the Pakistan movement. Other Reform groups were against the movement, while still being anti-colonial; they chose to support Congress and the unity of India (see Ahmad 1972:258–9; Hardy 1972). Of the latter, some revised their political stance after Partition, as in the well-known case of the Jamaat-i-Islami headed by Maududi, which had taken an anti-nationalist, and particularly anti-Muslim League, stand (see Binder 1961: 70–97).

While secular politicians appealed to religious symbols, then, religious groups became increasingly politicized. In general, as the anti-colonial movement gathered pace, and as Pakistani independence seemed imminent, virtually all the various religious groups, from landed charismatic saints to urban puritanical scholars, supported the cause of liberty against repressive, *external* domination. The problems of civil rights and liberation remained, however, the domain of the League and the Modernists.

After Partition the cause of 'liberty', as far as the learned doctors of all persuasions were concerned, came to be buried in conservative religious politics. Whereas large rural saints engaged in quietist patronage power politics (see Sherani 1991), the *ulama*, many of whom became once more employees of the state, also founded political parties which fought alongside and against each other for greater say and influence in the state apparatus (see Binder 1961; Ahmad 1972; Malik 1989; 1991; Iqbal n.d.).

Irrespective of political affiliation, however, it has always seemed impossible to conduct a purely secular politics in Pakistan. Like the Muslim League, so too the People's Party, which won the elections in West Pakistan on a socialist ticket, nevertheless utilized an Islamic idiom and appeared to have increasingly relied upon saintly patronage to mobilize political support (see Sherani 1991). Nationalism in Pakistan is inextricably intertwined with Islam, the *raison d'être* for the very existence of the state, and it has hitherto proved impossible to separate the two.

On one side, then, are the sober and determined puritanical Reform scholars. Against them are aligned pacifist saints and fiery, populist scholars. The interests of the scholars on *both* sides remain, as before, mainly to increase their political influence in the state or local community; they are not interested in civil liberties, economic equality or democratic rights. These have always been associated in Pakistani politics with secular or 'modernist' groups. But on either side is also a third element which is usually ignored in discussions of Pakistani religious politics – lay preachers, a buried intelligentsia of community leaders involved in mosque politics. It is they who, in the present Islamic revival, articulate grass roots sentiments and help explain the processes which have given rise to the current movement of Islamic radicalism.

MOSQUE, COMMUNITY AND LAY PREACHERS

'Loyalty ultimately belongs to God, and I say there should be justice, there should be equality, there should be understanding, there should be humanity.' So proclaims one of the speakers at the meeting discussed here. The move from God to liberty and equality is not deductive; it is intuitive and emotional. We love God and the Prophet, hence we detest autocratic greedy leaders. Like lay Methodist preachers the men involved in mosque affairs speak for the ordinary man, not necessarily for the religious establishment of their particular brand of Islam (on a parallel feature of Methodism, see Hobsbawm 1957: 126–49; Thompson 1963: 430–40). Indeed, it is my impression that they speak with the *same* political voice whatever Muslim religious movement or sect they happen to be affiliated to.

These lay preachers have introduced a radical change of rhetoric. Not Islamic authoritarianism but Islamic love, equality and individual liberties. Yet the underlying tension between love and authoritarianism *within* the movement itself is also evident (as it was in Methodism). Barelwis do not need to be rich, learned, educated or prominent. All they need in order to qualify as good Muslims is to love the Prophet of Islam and his *awliya* (his chosen 'friends', i.e. Sufi saints). The movement is an essentially egalitarian one. At the same time its leaders – Sufi Shaikhs are highly authoritarian; yet, paradoxically, it is precisely *because* they are spiritually superior, by birth and ascetic practice, to secular, powerful, wealthy monarchs and rulers, that their disciples feel able to challenge the legitimacy of those leaders, and to make demands for equal political and economic rights.

Representations of saints and scholars by Middle Eastern scholars have tended to portray a neat, logical, dualistic alternation model, positing a series of corresponding opposites – saints and scholars, tribe and city, syncretism and reform, kinship and decadence, purity and literacy, pluralism and monism, hierarchical intercession and egalitarianism, tolerance and fundamentalism (see, for example, Gellner 1981: 1–84; Keddie 1972). What this dualistic model misses in the South Asian case, however, is the presence not of two but of *three* independent interacting social categories – saints, scholars and laymen – allied together within a *single* movement. Between them they negotiate the rhetorical narratives of contemporary Islamic religious dissent. The oscillation is an internal one – between quietism or conservatism and radical populism – and it is related, above all, to the interpretations of political events and constellations as these are perceived to impinge on the actors, either as direct participants, or as members of broader Muslim communities, national and transnational. To label these lay preachers 'the Muslim street' is, as Thompson has argued in relation to the English bread 'rioters', to misread the level of organization and moral political rationality of urban Muslims (Thompson 1971).

The speeches at the Town Hall in Manchester combined theology, especially the adoration of the Prophet and his exemplary life, with a stress on the pride of bearing an Islamic identity and the uniqueness of being Muslim. At the same time the radical challenge to the established order was unmistakable. The attack was three-pronged: against the injustice of international law and global decision-making, both of which ignored Muslim *national* interests; against the corrupt illegitimate regimes of the Gulf states, denying the *economic* rights of 'ordinary Muslims'; and against British legal discrimination which denied local Muslims their basic *citizenship* rights. If the latter referred to immediate local interests, speakers clearly felt that their specific complaints could only be addressed in broader, more global and general terms. In formulating their dissent the speakers drew upon what has probably become a global set of political calls for 'justice' (on such a rhetoric see also Ahmed 1992: 195–6). Hence the unmitigated radicalism of participants.

There are other parallels to be drawn with the late eighteenth and early nineteenth century, with work on the 'labour sects' in Britain. The mosque, like the chapel, is the centre of communal affairs, drawing labour migrants into communal activities. It is the base for teaching collective discipline, organization and internal fund-raising, the springboard for regional and national political alliances, a training ground in polemics and adversary politics.

The link between saints and doctors among Barelwis means that the movement is a powerful *urban*, as well as rural, organization. Indeed, it creates organic links between town and village, and its lodges and mosques provide welcoming havens and communal centres for migrant travellers.

Mosques – in the plural, for they have proliferated in British cities – are supported not only by Pakistani factory workers but by small shopkeepers, market traders, petty manufacturers, artisans, professionals and a few larger businessmen (see Werbner 1990: ch. 10). These are all men with a sense of individual pride, a measure of personal autonomy, who hold strong ideas about the rights due to them as citizens and productive workers. They are not people to be pushed around. Yet they lack real political power and influence in Britain and this powerlessness has been underlined in recent years by the Rushdie affair, the general increase in racial harassment, and the Gulf crisis.

Parallels may be drawn to the Iranian revolution in which the urban *bazaaris* played, it is argued, an important role. There too, analysts have shown, Shi'a Islam shifted from a quiescent symbolic interpretation of martyrdom as suffering, to an activist view of martyrdom as personal sacrifice for the sake of a cause (see Hegland 1983; 1987:242–3). The radicalization of urban Iranians arose in response to a sense of direct attack by the state on the clergy and the urban lower middle and working classes who had been relatively autonomous and mobile socially (Beeman 1983).

Mosques are central foci of communal activity for local British Muslim communities. They bring together Muslim religious experts and local community activists, and the dialogue between these two groups, enacted publicly during public ceremonials or religious meetings, has generated greater political awareness, even in groups normally opportunistic and quiescent, such as those of Barelwi followers. Until recently, however, most mosques in Britain, and most religious leaders, remained politically introverted, engaged mainly in internecine religious conflicts and factional rivalries (see Werbner 1991a; 1991b). The publication of *The Satanic Verses* marked a watershed in this state of affairs: it revealed the need for broader organizational frameworks, as well as setting new agendas for common action, required in order to challenge the state and its current laws. The Gulf crisis sharpened this need for political protest and added further complexity to the emergent political philosophy articulated from mosque pulpits and communal podiums.

COMPETING GLOBAL FABLES, AGONISTIC LOCAL ALLEGORIES

The response of Pakistani Muslims in Britain to the Gulf crisis resembled, and was part of, a transnational Muslim response throughout the Muslim world (see Piscatori 1991). In this sense it reflected a global 'ideoscape' (Appadurai 1990) and it was legitimized by leaders of major sectarian divisions and by a Muslim press and media, reporting or reflecting their opinions. The fable was a global fable. But its local production also clearly reflected and embodied local rivalries for hegemony between the extensions of these global Islamic movements in Britain, and between different Sufi orders vying for hegemony in a particular city. To articulate an allegory of resistance and to interpret the allegory in local terms was to stress a commitment to local action. If the pretext was Islamic and global, the text was British.

To move beyond narrative and fully comprehend a social movement we need to go beyond its ideological expressions and discover where structural contradictions and thus agency are to be found. How does political mobilization take place empirically? The fact that calls to action by lay preachers rarely went beyond radical rhetoric was likely to be a source of disillusionment for their audiences in the long run, but as a spontaneous response to current affairs, these fabulations of world current affairs revitalized local Islamic identities and sense of empowerment. They were 'good to think' and 'good to say' or to narrate.

In a critical *tour de force*, Christopher Norris recently attacked Jean Baudrillard's *Guardian* article which appeared two days before the Gulf War broke out. In his article, Baudrillard argued that the war would never happen since it was merely a 'figment of mass-media simulation'; that in a nuclear age 'war had become strictly unthinkable except as a rhetorical phenomenon' (Norris 1991:11). Norris takes the article as an extreme example of postmodernist (neo-pragmatist, deconstructionist) thinking which textualizes reality *ad absurdum*, denying the validity of any distinction between fact and fiction. The consequence of such a tendency, Norris argues, is to deny even the possibility of rational argument over facts between opposed views held by different interpretive communities. Instead, if truth is what is 'good to think' there can be no bridge across the interpretive chasm between language communities.

Against this view, he demonstrates that all narratives, even fictional, are at least partly anchored in experience and thus subject to logical yardsticks of judgement and evaluation. It is obvious, he says, that the fables and narratives of the Gulf War, mostly generated by Western media propaganda, could not disguise the loss of Iraqi life and some of the more blatant atrocities committed by the international alliance. Hence, he disagrees not only with Baudrillard but with Michael Ignatieff who argued in *The Observer*, citing Edgar Morin in *Le Monde*, that all the revelations and developments of the war merely served to confirm for people the moral positions they already held. The war was thus 'an encounter between "blind moralities" ' (Norris 1991: 62).

Although Norris makes a convincing case for the rootedness of narrative in experience, he fails to locate (and hence address theoretically) the reasons for the multiple fabulations of the Gulf crisis. The sheer facts of the crisis were never really in dispute and few startling revelations have emerged since to challenge these facts. All along, the problem has been one of interpretation, a refraction of visions and world views, contrastive political moralities and unlike definitions of what is sacred or profane, permissible or inadmissible, villainous or courageous. At stake in the Gulf crisis were ethical issues of 'historicity': of past, present and future. The facts, viewed differently from different vantage points, led to differing predictions of the course the unfolding drama would take. The reading of motive, intention and character as signposts of future action differed radically. Ultimately it was character, as read on the basis of past action, which was seen to determine the threat of apocalyptic disaster or Islamic utopia. The anticipation of casualties was itself subject to this subtextual reading of character and motive. In addition, the dangers and breaches perceived were also ranked differently – environmental disaster, human life, unsupervised nuclear proliferation, global economic collapse, the threat to national territorial integrity, to the international global order, of Islamic hegemony, of Western desecration – all these were *moral* facts to be configured into a coherent and meaningful plot. To this must be added the problem of real history – the significance attributed to colonial and postcolonial pretexts – and the problem of *disguise*. In matters of ethics and politics, it is often not facts which are disputed or contested, but the ranking of facts in terms of the *hidden* motives they obscure and disguise. The dramatic plot, the fable, is ultimately one of revealed human passion – of greed, cruelty, nobility, humanity, justice, insanity, evil, caring, responsibility.

Any narration of morally grounded facts thus depends on perspective or focalization (Rimmon-Kenan 1983). In explaining a narrative we need to 're-imagine the moral assumptions of another social configuration' (Thompson 1971: 131). This is not to deny the existence of hard realities (images) to be argued over rationally: the Gulf War did take place and human life, the environment, cities and military hardware were destroyed. Palestinians were evicted from Kuwait, Kurds and Shi'ites subjected to genocide, atomic reactors destroyed, missiles dismantled, oil wells lit and capped, sanctions imposed with little effect, and in the upshot, President Bush lost an election while Saddam Hussein survived to tell the tale. All these are facts; none of the fabulators (Muslims, Americans, environmentalists, internationalists, socialists, capitalists) could have predicted them all. They were merely possible scenarios, potentialities to fear or hope for. As Aristotle argues in the *Poetics*:

> the poet's function is to describe, not the thing that has happened, but a kind of thing that might happen . . . Hence poetry is something more philosophic and of graver import than history, since its statements are of the nature rather of universals . . . what convinces is the possible.

Persuasive rhetoric constructs a fable of the possible out of reality's raw material, from the vantage point of a particular political morality. The plot is generic, global and universal. The allegory is local and reflects local predicaments, fears and aspirations. But the fable must tell a remarkable tale worth telling. Once the war was fought and ambiguously lost, there was no point in continuing to narrate this particular fable. Goliath had crushed David – a non-event not worth the candle. The lay preachers who fabulated their hopes of victory turned their imaginations to other global matters – Bosnia, Kashmir, Palestine.

At the height of the crisis preceding the Gulf War, however, there was a moment in which the imagining of a fable of triumph, a fairy tale of heroism, seemed to depict the possible. Under these circumstances it is perhaps not surprising that the clerics and lay preachers of the Barelwi movement in Britain paid little heed to the price they might pay for their dissenting support for Saddam Hussein. Although their statements were only semi-official, and they often retracted the most radical statements when questioned publicly by the media, it seems quite clear that they wanted the wider society to be aware of their disaffection. Theirs was a confrontational posture, as yet not fully worked out, more protest than actual action. The swings between temporary utopian hopes for Islamic dominance, and a sense of communal failure and total powerlessness, were more evident in their speeches than any determination to engage in sustained practical political action. During these swings, what was continually elaborated was a politically constituted religious rhetoric, a rhetoric of dissent which, above all, narrated the particular place of British Pakistani immigrants as 'ordinary Muslims' within Britain and the broader, international Muslim world.

NOTE

A version of this chapter was first presented at a meeting of the Observatoire du Changement Social en Europe Occidentale at Poitiers in 1991. Related versions were later presented at Oxford University's South Asian Studies Centre and at the Pakistan Workshop at Manchester University's field centre at Satterthwaite. I wish to thank the participants in these various conferences for their helpful comments. In revising the chapter for publication I benefited greatly from discussions with Joyce Miller and Don and Leah Handelman. I would also like to acknowledge my indebtedness to David Martin for his notion of a 'buried intelligentsia', and to Hastings Donnan for his very helpful editorial comments. The research on which the chapter is based was supported by a research grant from the Economic and Social Research Council UK, and I am grateful to the Council for its generous support.

REFERENCES

Ahmad, Aziz (1967) *Islamic Modernism in India and Pakistan 1857–1964*, London: Oxford University Press for the Royal Institute of International Affairs.
—— (1972) 'Activism of the Ulama in Pakistan' in Nikki R. Keddie (ed.) *Scholars, Saints and Sufis*, Berkeley: University of California Press.
Ahmad, Mumtaz (1991) 'The Politics of War: Islamic Fundamentalisms in Pakistan' in James Piscatori (ed.) *Islamic Fundamentalisms and the Gulf Crisis*, Chicago: The Fundamentalist Project, American Academy of Arts and Science.
Ahmed, Akbar S. (1992) *Postmodernism and Islam: Predicament and Promise*, London: Routledge.
Alavi, Hamza (1988) 'Pakistan and Islam: Ethnicity and Ideology', in F. Halliday and H. Alavi (eds) *State and Ideology in the Middle East and Pakistan*, London: Macmillan.

Anderson, Benedict (1991) *Imagined Communties*, (revised edition), London: Verso.

Appadurai, Arjun (1990) 'Disjuncture and Difference in the Global Cultural Economy', *Theory, Culture and Society*, 7: 295–310.

Aristotle (1941) *The Basic Works of Aristotle*, Richard McKeon (ed.), New York: Random House.

Becker, A.L. (1979) 'Text-Building, Epistemology, and the Aesthetics of Javanese Shadow Theatre', in A.L. Becker and Aram A. Yengoyen (eds), *The Imagination of Reality: Essays in Southeast Asian Coherence Systems*, Norwood: Ablex.

Beeman, William O. (1983) 'Images of the Great Satan: Representation of the United States in the Iranian Revolution', in Nikki R. Keddie (ed.) *Religion and Politics in Iran*, New Haven: Yale University Press.

Binder, Leonard (1961) *Religion and Politics in Pakistan*, Berkeley: University of California Press.

Boddy, Janice (1989) *Wombs and Alien Spirits*, Wisconsin: University of Wisconsin Press.

Bruner, Jerome (1991) 'The Narrative Construction of Reality', *Critical Inquiry* 18: 1–21.

Castells, Manuel (1983) *The City and the Grassroots: A Cross-Cultural Theory of Urban Social Movements*, London: Edward Arnold.

Clifford, Gay (1974) *The Transformations of Allegory*, London: Routledge and Kegan Paul.

Gearing, F. O. (1973) *The Face of the Fox*, Chicago: Aldine.

Gellner, Ernest (1981) *Muslim Society*, Cambridge: Cambridge University Press.

—— (1992) *Postmodernism, Reason and Religion*, London: Routledge.

Gilmartin, David (1979) 'Religious Leadership and the Pakistan Movement in the Punjab', *Modern Asian Studies* 13(3):485–517.

—— (1984) 'Shrines, Succession and Sources of Moral Authority', in Barbara Daly Metcalf (ed.) *Moral Conduct and Authority*, Berkeley: University of California Press.

—— (1988) *Empire and Islam: Punjab and the Making of Pakistan*, London: Taurus.

Hannigan, John A. (1985) 'Alain Touraine, Manuel Castells and Social Movement Theory: A Critical Appraisal', *The Sociological Quarterly* 26(4): 435–54.

Hardy, P. (1972) *The Muslims of British India*, Cambridge: Cambridge University Press.

Hegland, Mary (1983) 'The Two Images of Husain: Accommodation and Revolution in an Iranian Village' in Nikki R. Keddie (ed.) *Religion and Politics in Iran*, New Haven: Yale University Press.

—— (1987) 'Conclusion: Religious Resurgence in Today's World', in Richard T. Antoun and Mary Elaine Hegland (eds) *Religious Resurgence*, Syracuse: Syracuse University Press.

Heikal, Muhammad (1992) *Illusions of Triumph*.

Hobsbawm, E.J. (1957) *Primitive Rebels*, Manchester: Manchester University Press.

Iqbal, Afzal (n.d.) *Islamisation of Pakistan*, Lahore: Vanguard.

Keddie, Nikki R. (ed.) (1972) *Scholars, Saints and Sufis*, Berkeley: the University of California Press.

Lavie, Smadar (1990) *The Poetics of Military Occupation*, Berkeley: University of California Press.

Malik, Jamal S. (1989) 'Legitimising Islamization – the case of the Council of Islamic Ideology in Pakistan, 1962–1981', *Orient* 30(2): 251–68.

—— (1990) 'The Luminous Nurani: Charisma and Political Mobilisation among the

Barelwis in Pakistan', in Pnina Werbner (ed.) *Person, Myth and Society in South Asian Islam*, special issue of *Social Analysis* 28, University of Adelaide: 38–50.

Modood, Tariq (1990). 'British Asian Muslims and the Rushdie Affair', *The Political Quarterly* 61(2): 143–60.

Norris, Christopher (1991) *Uncritical Theory: Postmodernism, Intellectuals and the Gulf War*, London: Lawrence and Wishart.

Piscatori, James (ed.) (1991) *Islamic Fundamentalisms and the Gulf Crisis*, Chicago: The Fundamentalist Project, the American Academy of Arts and Science.

Quilligan, Maureen (1979) *The Language of Allegory: Defining the Genre*, Ithaca: Cornell University Press.

Ricoeur, Paul (1982) *Hermeneutics and the Human Sciences*, edited and translated by John B. Thompson, Cambridge: Cambridge University Press.

Rimmon-Kenan, S. (1983) *Narrative Fiction, Contemporary Poetics*, London: Methuen.

Sherani, S. Rahman (1991) 'Ulema and Pir in the Politics of Pakistan', in Hastings Donnan and Pnina Werbner (eds) *Economy and Culture in Pakistan*, London: Macmillan.

Taylor, Philip M. (1992) *War and the Media*, Manchester: Manchester University Press.

Thompson, E. P. (1963) *The Making of the English Working Class*, London: Penguin.

—— (1971) The Moral Economy of the English Crowd in the Eighteenth Century', *Past and Present*, 50: 76–136.

Touraine, Alain (1981) *The Voice and the Eye: An Analysis of Social Movements*, Cambridge: Cambridge University Press.

Voll, John O. (1987) 'Islamic Renewal and the "Failure of the West" ', in Richard T. Antoun and Mary E. Hegland (eds) *Religious Resurgence*, Syracuse: Syracuse University Press.

Werbner, Pnina (1990) *The Migration Process: Capital, Gifts and Offerings among British Pakistanis*, Oxford: Berg Publishers.

—— (1991a) 'The Fiction of Unity in Ethnic Politics: Aspects of Representation and the State among British Pakistanis', in Pnina Werbner and Muhammad Anwar (eds) *Black and Ethnic Leaderships in Britain*, London: Routledge.

—— (1991b) 'Factionalism and Violence in British Pakistani Politics', in Hastings Donnan and Pnina Werbner (eds) *Economy and Culture in Pakistan*, London: Macmillan.

—— (1991c) 'Black and Ethnic Leaderships in Britain: a Theoretical Overview', in Pnina Werbner and Muhammad Anwar (eds) *Black and Ethnic Leaderships in Britain*, London: Routledge.

—— (forthcoming) 'Stamping the Earth with the Name of Allah: Zikr and the Sacralising of Space among British Muslims', in Barbara Daly Metcalf (ed.) *Muslims, Identity and Space in the West* (provisional title), Berkeley: University of California Press.

—— (n.d.) 'The Making of Muslim Dissent: Lay Preachers and Radical Rhetoric among British Muslims'.

Index